KILLER AIRBAGS

THE DEADLY SECRET AUTOMAKERS DON'T WANT YOU TO KNOW

Jerry Cox

D0915850

The Forerunner Foundation, Inc.
Washington, D.C.

First Paperback Edition

Cataloging-in-Publication Data Available from the Library of Congress

ISBN 978-1-71602-741-3

Cox, Jerry, author
Killer Airbags: The Deadly Secret Automakers Don't Want You to Know / Jerry Cox

Cover by Crescent Studio Design

www.killerairbags.com

KILLER AIRBAGS

CONTENTS

PROLOGUE
Promise and Betrayal

Acknowledgments

Bibliography

Notes

Index

PROLOGUE

Promise and Betrayal

There's a good chance you or someone you love is driving one of *70 million* cars with a pipe bomb ticking away in their steering wheel. If you are driving a Honda built in the early 2000s or a Ford Ranger from the mid-2000s, your airbag is more likely to kill you than to save you in a crash. Japan's Takata Corporation put defective airbags in one out of every four cars on American roads, including some of the most expensive rides in the world – BMWs, Mercedes, Ferraris and Teslas – but expect no help from your dealership. Sixteen years into this travesty, they will still sell you a car with an airbag inflator stuffed with an explosive they know is unstable. Federal safety regulators were complicit in much of this horror show, so don't count on them to tell you the truth about how this happened. In this case, "Uncle Sam" has been watching out for everybody *but you.*

Takata's airbags have already killed or maimed more than 300 people and likely will blast at least 1,000 more. Tens of millions of Americans have been swept up in more than 100 piecemeal safety recalls, a colossal bankruptcy proceeding and multiple class-action lawsuits. Through it all, carmakers, government officials and the American legal establishment have covered up their roles in an appalling scandal.

In 2016, 13 years after Takata's airbags began to blow, three of the company's U.S.-resident engineers were secretly indicted by a federal grand jury. The company kicked off 2017 by admitting it was a criminal. In 2018, it cashed out its untainted assets and hid behind a bankruptcy declaration. Don't expect any accused criminals to face punishment, however. Takata's plea bargain had almost nothing to do with shattered human lives. Instead, the American criminal justice system guaranteed Takata's biggest customer, Honda Motor Company, hundreds of millions of dollars despite its own enthusiastic adoption of the defective airbags and regulatory violations that left its customers and the government in the dark for an entire decade about the obscenely gruesome things they were doing to unsuspecting motorists.

No one else will tell the whole truth about Takata's "killer airbags," even though that company was responsible for the biggest safety recall of cars or any other consumer product in history. *Killer Airbags* exposes it all. It is an explosive exposé and an infuriating but important case study of how regulators and corporations cynically put a price-tag on all our heads, enriching shareholders at public expense. It's a jarring message, part *Unsafe at Any Speed*, which spurred federal safety regulations for cars in the 1960s, and part *Merchants of Death*, which revealed the tobacco industry's decades of lies about the dangers of smoking. There are lives to be saved and vital lessons to be learned by car owners – the people on the firing line of this safety crisis – and by the unelected bureaucrats who set government policy. *Killer Airbags* provides an intimate, first-person look at the people who decided for each of us what safety equipment we are obligated to buy, then betrayed us all so a greedy auto industry could rack up record sales and profits.

Airbags and other vehicle safety requirements were forged by a decades-long war between safety-minded citizens and car-makers, but vehicle safety today is mostly a myth. The U.S. government's constant yielding to industry demands to limit and delay fixes for built-in safety defects has been disgusting and lethal—just look at the recent, record-breaking surge in traffic deaths nationwide. And this will only get worse under a Trump Administration that gave Takata's lawyer direct control over the automakers' flagging recall campaigns.

Buckle up! *Killer Airbags* tells the sordid tale of how Takata, Honda and other greedy carmakers betrayed public safety and made fools of feckless federal bureaucrats. What you learn from this book could save your life.

PART 1

The Price on Our Heads

Christmas, 2015

South Carolina

Joel Knight's wife told police he got out of bed happy and healthy on the morning of December 22, 2015. He had just one more day of work as a welder before Christmas, so he shaved, got dressed, kissed his wife goodbye, then climbed into his nine-year old Ford Ranger pickup, buckled up and headed out. He stuck to the 45-mile-per-hour speed limit on a straight, open stretch of State Route 522 near his home in rural Lancaster County, South Carolina, but when a cow wandered onto the road, Joel had no time to stop, no way to avoid the collision. He stomped on his brakes and swerved to the left, but not far enough: he plowed into that wayward cow, crumpling the hood and right front fender of his 3,500-pound truck. The good news is that his seat belt worked perfectly; it kept him firmly in place, with his face about 18 inches away from the hub of his steering wheel, so the collision left him without a scratch. But that seat belt also set Joel Knight up to be slaughtered, a perfect bull's-eye for his exploding airbag, which shot a chunk of metal through his throat. The shrapnel severed his spinal column at the neck and nearly decapitated him. He bled out in just a few seconds.

A few weeks later, Ford Motor Company snail-mailed Joel's wife a safety recall notice, informing her of the defect that had killed her husband. Joel Knight had received no such warning about that lethal flaw, but a few privileged people knew by then that an airbag from the same supplier had killed a pregnant woman and her unborn baby a few months earlier. I was one of those people. I knew Takata was aware of four other deaths 18 months before their airbag snuffed out Joel's life. I also knew that Takata airbags had killed a soccer mom in Virginia, a restaurant worker in California and a high school cheerleader in Oklahoma.

Why did I know this? During the first week of 2014, Takata's top American executive decided to hire a strategic communications advisor to help explain to the world why those deaths from "anomalous airbag deployments" were no big deal. The perfect guy to hire, he figured, was a known champion of the U.S. federal mandate that required all cars to be equipped with airbags, someone who helped pass pro-airbag legislation and got the Supreme Court to make the requirement stick. I was that guy.

Takata did not share the most horrific details of those "anomalous deployments" with me, but I eventually did my own research and found a gruesome photo of what one of them did to Joel Knight. He was still held in place by his seat belt, arms at his sides with his almost fully detached head flopped onto his right shoulder. The fountain of blood that showered the cab of his truck had also cascaded down Joel's shirt and jeans. The deflated white airbag hung from his steering wheel, limp, shredded and spattered with Joel's blood. During my many years of work in transportation safety I had been required to look closely at many kinds of human tragedy – bodies burned beyond recognition in highway accidents, a sonogram of a dead airline flight attendant's unborn child, a motorcyclist pancaked by an 18-wheeler. But Joel Knight's beheading clung to me. Night after night, I was jolted awake by panic attacks that grew worse every time a Takata airbag claimed another victim. Seven more people were slaughtered in 2016. Four people were killed by their airbags just days apart in July 2017. Three more died in 2018. Another death was reported in September 2019. Hundreds of other drivers survived Takata airbag explosions but suffered grievous injuries, including lost ears, noses, eyes and teeth.

I told Takata repeatedly that the right thing to do – the only thing to do – was to tell the truth, but its billionaire CEO didn't want to talk about saving lives. His priority was "cost-avoidance," so he could make billions more for himself and his family. Having represented vehicle manufacturers in products liability cases from my first days out of law school, starting with tires that disintegrated at highway speeds and truck tire rims that sprang apart and tore off people's faces, I knew how these cases always ended up. So did Takata's personal injury defense lawyers. The American legal system makes it easy for manufacturers to cover up motor vehicle deaths and crippling injuries caused by their products with out-of-court settlements that compel victims – and their families – to keep silent. For weeks that stretched into months, I lay awake wondering whether Joel Knight would have made it home for Christmas if I had convinced Takata's Japanese owners to start telling the truth.

2014

Tokyo

One afternoon in 2014, Shigehisa Takada, head of the world's second-largest manufacturer of airbags for automobiles, mysteriously disappeared from his office atop a Tokyo skyscraper and was M.I.A. for several hours. When he returned, no one in the company's inner circle had ever seen their normally serene leader look so rattled.

Word quickly spread that Takada's 73-year old mother, Akiko, had summoned the 48-year-old multi-billionaire to an undisclosed location and spanked him. Hard. Takata Corporation's stock price had leveled off after years of record highs, profit margins were shrinking and costs were mounting because of a glitch in their fastest-growing product. Airbags are supposed to inflate instantly and protect occupants in a crash but Takata's miniaturized devices sometimes blew up in people's faces, shredding them with shrapnel. By mid-2014, seven drivers had bled to death with their throats slashed, and more than 100 other people had been grievously wounded. News reporters had treated the airbag explosions as freak occurrences, as if these hapless drivers had been struck by lightning, but investors were getting worried about the hundreds of millions of dollars they had invested with

Takada and his family, which controlled 80 percent of the stock in a company worth $4 billion.

Something had to be done, but insiders knew the young chairman was not up to this challenge. One let slip to a reporter that Shige ("she-gay"), despite his $2 million a year salary, was "paralyzed to make decisions on his own." For years, company officers had belittled him behind his back, calling him "Shige-chan" ("Little Shige"), a puppet for his domineering mother, who was related to Japanese royalty and expected every one of her Takata subjects across the globe to jump at her every command. She had been a perfect match for Shige's father, Juichiro, who willed the company chairmanship to Shige upon his death in 2011. Everybody at Takata Corporation called her "O-Okusan" ("Big Wife") because she dominated every big decision there, even while her husband was alive.

Juichiro's father, Takezo Takada, started winning lucrative seat belt contracts with Detroit in 1972, the year Japanese motorcycle maker Honda started to break into the U.S. auto market. When the American government decreed that seat belts were inadequate and mandated airbags for cars, Honda figured it could underprice Detroit even more deeply by buying components from Japanese companies that specialized in making Western technology, but smaller and cheaper. To beat his competition, Juichiro decided to fuel Takata's inflators with an explosive nobody else was using, ammonium nitrate, which cost one-tenth as much as the propellant used by his competitors in Sweden and Germany. The cheaper air bags sold faster than Takata could produce them. After global production skyrocketed 40 percent in the first four years, Takata made more than 200 million inflators. Suddenly, the billions of dollars in resulting profits were at risk. American law required vehicle manufacturers to report all "safety-related defects" to the federal government, warn car owners and fix any defect for free. For years, though, Takata refused to admit the exploding airbags were defective. Instead, its executives whispered about the "root cause" of "anomalous airbag deployments" and "energetic dis-assemblies."

To handle this threat, Big Wife and Little Shige heeded the old Japanese adage, "If it stinks, put a lid on it!" They had their executive vice president, a North Carolinian named Frank Roe, supervise teams of products liability defense lawyers across the

United States that settled dozens of lawsuits, never once allowing victims' lawyers to pry into company records, documents that would have shown how little Takata had actually done to keep its airbags from exploding. Takata skillfully used a tactic as old as the automobile itself: their lawyers softened victims up by burying them under pre-trial motions and other expensive, time-consuming legal maneuvers. And when Takata finally offered a cash settlement, it required the families of the dead or injured to keep quiet and warn no one else about the defect.

Big Wife's "put a lid on it" strategy worked well until 2014, when Takata airbags killed three people in a single month. Roe, who also served as president of Takata's American subsidiary, TK Holdings, Inc., knew these new deaths would surprise the National Highway Traffic Safety Administration (NHTSA, pronounced "nit-sah"), an agency at the U.S. Department of Transportation, which was supposed to monitor highway fatalities, detect trends and expose safety defects manufacturers had hidden from them. Takata also knew NHTSA could require them to recall many millions of the airbags in cars made by Honda and 18 other automakers. A total recall would mean Takata would have to supply a free replacement for every unit it had sold, although at the time it was barely able to keep up with existing demand for units to be installed in new cars. The cost – $24 billion – would swamp the company. That's why Roe shifted his focus from pliable plaintiffs to timid government regulators. He hired lawyers who had written the American laws and regulations and knew the loopholes. He also knew first-hand how toothless NHTSA could be. While Juichiro was chairman, Takata had failed to initiate a timely recall of several million defective seat belts. Their cheap plastic buckles deteriorated so badly after long-term exposure to sunlight that they popped open mid-crash, letting drivers and their passengers fly face-first into windshields and rib-crushing steering wheels. NHTSA eventually imposed a miniscule $50,000 civil fine, sofa-cushion change compared to the millions of dollars the company had saved on replacement costs by ignoring the law and delaying the recall. By the time Takata mailed its seat belt recall notices to the original purchasers, many of the vehicles had been resold several times, so the current owners did not receive warnings, much less the free fix they were guaranteed under American law.

Big Wife was sure Roe could bury the airbag problem the same way. And if he couldn't, she had a more potent weapon to deploy. One of the most powerful political appointees in the history of federal vehicle safety regulation happened to be the only Japanese-American who'd been a U.S. Secretary of Transportation. Norman Yoshio Mineta became Big Wife's paid consultant on all things American the minute he retired from government service.

By the end of 2013, Roe doubted his teams of litigators and former NHTSA lawyers could hush up the exploding airbag scandal much longer. He met with his lobbyists in Washington at the Patton Boggs law firm and let them in on a dark secret: the company had repeatedly falsified engineering test reports to hide the product's propensity to explode. Roe added that at least one reporter was investigating this story and that personal injury lawyers in major American cities were trolling for clients. The revolving-door lawyers Takata had hired straight out of NHTSA were warning that even their most passive ex-colleagues were losing patience with the company's main excuse, that no additional recalls were needed until they identified a "root cause" of the explosions. With all these lids about to blow off, Roe started searching for someone to develop a strategy for managing the coming avalanche of ugly news. The company would need cover while it took the first steps toward saving lives, but none of its executives were prepared to answer the pointed questions government regulators and the media might soon be asking. Roe hired me, a known champion of the airbag mandate who had worked on the issue in the U.S. Senate and then litigated it in the U.S. Supreme Court. Takata urgently needed a "truth squad," I told them, to accomplish several important objectives. It could keep the U.S. government's focus on the most dangerous airbags the company ever made, the first few million ammonium nitrate-powered units that came off their woefully incompetent assembly lines between 2000 and 2004. It would also buy Takata time to work out financial arrangements with their core customers, the carmakers, to share recall costs and assure a continuing supply of replacement inflators by keeping Takata from going bankrupt.

The head of corporate communications for Roe's American operation, Alby Berman, flew to Tokyo in January 2014 and presented my plan directly to Chairman Takada. His response: "We are not satisfied with our current operating profit margin."

The company, Takada decreed, was governed by a "directed cost-avoidance mode of operation." We nervous Americans were directed to stand down.

Later that year, Roe dusted off my "truth squad" plan and relabeled it a "strategic information management system." That recommendation arrived in Tokyo on October 24, 2014, the same day Shige Takada received a counter-proposal from Norman Mineta. The former U.S. Transportation Secretary offered a simpler scheme. He told Takada all his company really needed to do was to scare off its potential adversaries in the American government by "expanding its network of allies and confidants inside Washington" and give NHTSA a "facelift." It was simply a matter of writing the right-sized checks to the right people, starting with Mineta. The company could acquire "Secretary Mineta's leadership [to] grow new relationships in Washington." Mineta said nothing about letting Americans know how to save them-selves from a bloody, horrific death. Within days, Takata Cor-poration brought in two other former Secretaries of Transpor-tation, Rodney Slater and Samuel Skinner. They joined Mineta in gathering tacit endorsements from almost every former top federal vehicle safety official who was still breathing.

I got the message. Profits mattered to Takata; human lives did not.

2016

Houston, Texas

Huma Hanif, a 17-year old immigrant from Pakistan, was living the American dream. She was just weeks away from high school graduation. To meet expenses and get a jump-start on college tuition, she took an after-school job at a sandwich shop.

On a Spring evening in 2016, Huma's older brother and sister helped her fill out her college applications. The next day, with her head full of dreams about a future career in nursing,

Huma started her 2002 Honda Civic in the student parking lot and headed for work. She had not gone far when a Honda CRV stopped in front of her to make a left turn. Huma was wearing her seat belt. She was not speeding. She was not texting. Nevertheless, she hit the other Honda. The mild impact barely damaged either car, but her airbags activated.

Sensors in Huma's Civic detected the collision and set off an ammonium nitrate propellant. The driver's cushion popped out of the airbag module in the hub of Huma's steering wheel as intended, but something unexpected flew in her direction. The metal canister that was supposed to confine the explosion broke into tiny, jagged fragments. One of the shards, twisted into the shape of an origami bird, punctured the cushion and shot into the right side of Huma's neck. It slashed the two most crucial blood vessels in the human body, her carotid artery and jugular vein. Huma, otherwise uninjured, unfastened her safety belt and stepped out of her car, desperately clutching her throat. Blood spurted onto the ground as fast as her heart could pump it out, so she collapsed within a few seconds and died. Classmates on the bus home from George Ranch High saw her crimson-coated body on the ground, surrounded by Good Samaritans who dashed across the street from a corner barbershop. There was nothing anyone could do.

"Everyone should have walked away from this accident," Ft. Bend, Texas, County Sheriff Troy Nehls said at a press conference the following week. The sheriff made national news when he displayed for television cameras Huma's perforated, blood-soaked airbag and the gnarly metal fragment that shot through the fabric and slashed her throat.

Huma's death was not a complete surprise to Honda. In 2011, they formally declared that the Takata airbag in her car was unsafe. In accordance with minimum legal requirements, Honda mailed an ambiguous safety recall notice covering the already nine-year old car. As another five years passed, none of the previous owners or used car dealers – businesses that had easy access to the safety recall warnings – bothered to do the free fix. The Hanif family insisted they never received notice of the deadly threat.

The Hanifs were shocked to learn that Huma was the second Houstonian killed by a Takata airbag in a 2002 Honda. Just

14 months earlier, in January 2015, in Spring, Texas, Carlos Solis, a 35-year old father of two teenagers was wearing his seat belt when he, too, had a fender-bender. The airbag in his Honda Accord ruptured. Shrapnel the diameter of a hockey puck slashed through his throat and lodged in his spine. He bled out and died. No one told him, when he bought the car a year earlier, that Honda had issued a safety recall notice to replace his defective Takata inflator. Nobody took the Accord to a dealer for a free replacement. Honda's idea of fixing the problem was to send his wife a recall notice two weeks after the airbag they put in his car killed him.

Honda offered the Hanif and Solis families the company's "deepest sympathies." Several months after Huma died, the carmaker wrote the Hanifs a check big enough to show just how sympathetic they were and made the family swear not to reveal to anyone what they agreed Huma's life was worth, in dollars and cents. Media outside of Houston barely mentioned the shocking deaths of two young people who did nothing worse than trust decades of government promises that airbags were essential lifesavers.

2016

Washington

Tragic stories about the rising Takata body count left me, for the first time in my career, with no idea what to do. A life-saving technology that I helped get mandated had become a *life-taker*, and no one was willing to stop the killing. Officials in the U.S. Department of Transportation noticed the problem in 2009, long before Takata hired me, and started an investigation that closed as soon as it opened. In 2015, when people started getting slaughtered by Takata airbags on a monthly basis, NHTSA finally threatened to order wider recalls that could have cost Takata billions of dollars. Instead of demanding action, a half-dozen former NHTSA leaders pocketed hefty consulting fees from Takata for lending their names to a "quality assurance" report that addressed every Takata safety lapse *other than* its killer airbags. Takata's big-name "allies and confidants" nearly buried the scandal.

One former U.S. Department of Justice official personally received $1.2 million to negotiate an arrangement that allowed the company and its regulators to make it look like something was being done to protect the public. Takata agreed to pay NHTSA a $200-million civil fine, but the agency was badly outlawyered and its order was riddled with so many loopholes that the government never collected more than a tenth of that amount. Thanks to heavy pressure from Takata and its auto manufacturer customers, NHTSA officials decreed that Takata could stay in business and keep selling new defective airbags to replace the old defective airbags through 2019. Recall repairs would drag on past 2040.

Pressured by Congress in the waning days of the Obama Administration, the Justice Department started a criminal investigation. Despite hundreds of deaths and horrific injuries, federal prosecutors in Detroit let Takata plead guilty in January 2017, to a single count of financial fraud. The U.S. government required the company to pay $1 billion in fines and restitution, but not to the people killed or maimed by exploding airbags. The new car industry came first. Almost 90 percent of that money went to the carmakers who had eagerly padded their profits by choosing Takata's cheap airbags over safer, but more costly, designs. Only 12 percent of the money was set aside for the hundreds of maimed people and the families of those who had died. In exchange for assurances that Takata would pay all that money to car companies before it went bankrupt, prosecutors indicted none of the company's senior executives and assured that three Japanese engineers charged with falsifying safety test results would never face criminal prosecution. Even after the company got stuck with recall costs and the stigma of being a convicted felon, a federal bankruptcy judge put Takata's corporate customers at the head of the line for additional compensation, while thousands of future personal injury and wrongful death claimants will be lucky to get a pittance for their suffering.

I am haunted every day by those gruesome photos of Joel Knight, the metal shard that killed Huma Hanif and the certainty that as many as 2,000 more people will be maimed or killed by defective airbags. Most of the people who turned these deadly "safety devices" loose on American drivers were essentially declared "too big to jail" as part of the criminal settlement, but we should all know who they are. The revolving-door government safety regulators who got rich by helping Takata executives duck responsibility for this human and economic fiasco also need to be publicly shamed. My overarching goal, however, is to make sure car owners learn how to protect themselves because the government and the automotive industry are still actively working against them.

Federal safety officials will tell you, of course, that they are actually doing a great job. The government assessed almost *seven billion dollars* in penalties against car companies between 2015 and 2017. General Motors never admitted to any criminal conduct, but it agreed to pay Uncle Sam $900 million in connection with an ignition switch defect. Takata faced $200 million in civil fines for safety violations in November 2015 and another one billion dollars to settle criminal proceedings in January 2017. Honda paid the government $70 million for its own decade-long failure to report death and injury data. The reports Honda unlawfully withheld – hiding 1,729 deaths and injuries over 11 years – could have alerted safety regulators to the Takata defect sooner. In January 2017, in the same federal courthouse in Michigan, the day before Takata agreed to plead guilty of wrongdoing that had already killed and maimed hundreds of people, Volkswagen admitted to criminal evasion of air-quality rules that did not kill or injure anyone. Takata got away with a $25 million criminal fine, plus restitution payments of $975 million. The feds hit Volkswagen, by contrast, with $4.3 billion for fibbing about their diesel engine emissions.

Safety defects kill people but criminal fines don't kill automakers. Takata's stock rose 16.5 percent the day it declared itself a criminal. Despite the worst imaginable publicity, Takata's net sales increased almost 20 percent in 2015 and another 30 percent in 2016. Takata's management admitted it was difficult "to quantify how much impact there may be on forward orders" but the company's net sales, operating income and ordinary income "continued to trend upwards" in 2016, even as Takata reported an overall loss of $700 million for the year. Takata was still getting paid handsomely to clean up a mess of its own making, supplying 30 percent of the recall repair parts. Company leaders were determined to ensure "the continuation and growth of the airbag business."

Tokyo had reason to sound optimistic. Four of their car-maker customers were still buying unquestionably defective inflators in 2016 and planting them just inches away from drivers' faces that entire year. Millions of 2016 and 2017 model year Fords, Volkswagens and other makes of vehicles were recalled almost immediately after their proud new owners drove them off the lot.

Recall notices were issued in 2020 for those 2016s and 2017s, but that does not necessarily mean people will be protected. Halfway through 2017, only one out of three recalled Toyotas and Subarus had been "fixed" and Takata's pipe bombs were still ticking in more than four out of five recalled Mazdas and BMWs and almost nine out of ten recalled VWs and Audis. Barely half of American car owners were aware that Takata airbags had been recalled and only one-half of those who were aware of the recalls considered them important. Two out of three had no idea whether their own car was affected. It was no wonder; NHTSA and the car-makers avoided using graphic language or photos or icons to draw people's attention to the severity of the threat and notices were stated in unintelligible, technical language that invited even English-speaking car owners to toss recall letters in the trash.

GM, too, had little to complain about. After recalling 25 million cars for a litany of safety defects – more cars in six months than it produced in the previous ten years, combined – Detroit's biggest car company enjoyed record sales and profits in 2016; in fact, its operating performance in 2016 was the best in its entire 108 years of selling cars. Volkswagen's profits soared in the first quarter of 2017, up more than 44 percent. By instituting "cost-cutting measures," the Germans overcame their infamous emissions-cheating scandal, which put two of their U.S.-based former executives in federal prison.

Honda's profits for 2016 were up 36 percent on record annual sales of five million vehicles. The carmaker's success helped keep Japan's total manufacturing output in third place, be-hind only China and the United States. That same year, Japan enjoyed a $60 billion trade advantage over the United States, with automobiles and auto parts comprising 40 percent of their ship-ments. That is why, for companies the size of Takata and Honda, a billion dollars in government fines for safety violations is chump change.

The Takata airbag fiasco confirms a truth even stranger than the fiction created by Chuck Palahniuk in his novel *Fight Club*. The protagonist in that book, a "product recall specialist" (played by Edward Norton in the movie) holds an important job with a car manufacturer. When a deadly defect surfaces, he calculates how many injury and death claims the carmaker would have to pay before it became more economical to warn people and fix their cars. Forget federal safety laws. Takata proved that your life depends on a mathematical formula: unless the number of defective vehicles on the road ("A"), multiplied by the probable rate of those defects killing people ("B"), multiplied by the dollar amount of the average out-of-court settlement ("C") – A x B x C – is greater than the cost of a recall, there will be no recall. No matter what make or model you drive, that number is the bottom line on your own personal price tag. And even when the math convinces a car manufacturer to issue a recall, an astonishing number of those death-traps remain on American highways, unrepaired. One out of four recalled cars *never* get fixed, and the older a defective car gets, the less attention the owner pays and the less likely it will ever be repaired.

That makes safety defects your problem, not the auto-makers' and not the government's. Numbers tell the story. America endured the sharpest two-year bump in highway fatalities in 53 years and 2015 saw the *largest ever* year-over-year rise in motor vehicle deaths. Industry and the government have allowed the high body count to become the new normal, with roughly 40,000 fatalities each year in 2016, 2017 and 2018 and another 4.5 million serious injuries in 2018 alone. Yet, in recent congressional testimony, the auto industry said, "the overall picture of motor vehicle safety is the best it has ever been." What it really meant is that auto sales were the highest in history. December 2016 brought the strongest monthly sales performance, *ever*. Total new car sales of 17.48 million set a record in 2015, only to be topped by 17.6 million vehicles sold in 2016. Used car sales – 40 million of them – set a record in 2019.

Your government will do almost anything to protect the industry and nothing to protect you. At the start of 2020 – the final year of the first Trump Administration – NHTSA still had no Administrator. Instead, President Trump installed *Takata's lawyer* as general counsel of the Transportation Department in 2017 and as Acting Deputy Secretary in 2019. Unbelievably, the guy who negotiated two sweetheart deals – one in 2015 that allowed Takata to keep selling defective airbags and one in 2017 that shielded Takata executives from criminal prosecution – was put in charge of every government employee responsible for enforcing auto safety laws.

Fight Club audiences laugh when Edward Norton's character lays out his employer's cynical formula. Nobody would consider it funny if they knew it applies to them. Instead of offering dark humor, *Killer Airbags* describes how and why our government lets the auto industry get away with it and lays out the specific steps you can take to protect yourself. Not every giant corporation, in or out of the auto industry, pushes greed to Takata's grim extreme, but every car owner needs to understand that the people who make our wheels have put a price-tag on all our heads. As one hedge fund billionaire put it, "in business there are no problems, there are only expenses. Companies get away with risk/benefit calculations because the government doesn't penalize them enough."

Detroit's cold-blooded calculation shocked Americans in 1966, when Ralph Nader led a revolution in vehicle safety. Be prepared for an even bigger shock if you keep reading. You will learn in PART 2 how the auto manufacturers have forever battled to keep us in the dark about the faults in our cars.

In PART 3 you will see the history of good intentions behind the decision to mandate airbags, despite the inherent dangers of setting off pyrotechnics inside our steering wheels and dash-boards.

PART 4 explains how, out of pure greed, Japanese businesses deliberately hid an airbag defect, even after it had killed or maimed hundreds of people.

PART 5 recounts how Takata enlisted help from former top U.S. government officials to keep the fraud going.

PART 6 reveals how Takata executives avoided criminal prosecution by declaring bankruptcy and what a colossal mess they left behind for tens of millions of vehicle owners and dealers.

If you are less interested in how we got exposed to such danger and more urgently concerned about what specific steps we must take to protect ourselves, skip ahead to PART 7 and share the knowledge and tools presented there with people you love.

PART 2

Killing the Messengers

1962

Detroit

"He's not a queer? Or a commie? Or a dope fiend? And he turned down the hookers?"

The general counsel at General Motors was flummoxed and furious when his spies submitted their final report on Ralph Nader. Aloysius Power had spent serious money on an investigation run by Vincent Gillen, the former FBI agent who had turned up nothing GM could use to silence the young critic of the car company. Nader first made their "watch list" when he was a law student at Harvard in 1958, where he wrote academic papers about the Big Three automakers' vast social and economic clout.

Nader recognized Americans' "love-hate" relationship with the automobile. In those days, "the auto industry" meant Detroit, and "Detroit" meant the "Big Three" – Ford Motor Company, Chrysler Corporation and General Motors Corporation. The "love" part pushed new car sales to an all-time high in 1965; 1966 was almost as good. There were 79 million cars on American roads and 70 percent of families had one. Among workers, 70 percent commuted by car. The manufacture, sale and maintenance of automobiles made up 20 percent of America's gross national product.

The "hate" part was that car accidents were taking a fearsome toll, especially on young male drivers. Car crashes became the leading cause of accidental deaths and injuries in 1929 and, in 1937 alone, the United States lost 40,000 people to motor vehicle accidents. The number of fatalities jumped a shocking eight percent from 1965 to 1966, when more than 53,000 Americans died in car crashes. Among them, young men were perishing in numbers unmatched by the Vietnam War. The rate of deaths and crippling injuries was reliably predicted to increase unchecked.

When Nader finished his studies at Princeton's Woodrow Wilson School of Public and International Affairs and Harvard Law School, his draft deferment ran out. The U.S. Army finally got him and decided the best use for his esoteric Ivy League education would be to put him to work as a cook. When the Army ran out of potatoes for him to peel and returned him to civvies, Nader published a series of commentaries on traffic safety and other consumer-oriented topics in legal journals and general interest publications. The articles caught the attention of Daniel Patrick Moynihan, a young social scientist and aide to New York Governor Averill Harriman (D-NY). Long before he won his own U.S. Senate seat as a Democrat from New York, Moynihan made a mark for himself in 1964 by publishing a review – in relatively plain English – of a technical medical book by a public health physician. Fellow New Yorker Dr. William Haddon, Jr., coined the term "second collision" – "when the car stops and the occupant keeps going."

Moynihan's review piqued the interest of a politician in New York's densely populated neighboring state. U.S. Senator Abraham Ribicoff (D-CT) launched his own career, in part, by demanding more stringent speed limit enforcement. When the peripatetic Moynihan became a Lyndon Johnson appointee at the Labor Department, he hired Nader in 1964 and introduced him to Senator Ribicoff's staff early in 1965. The Connecticut Senator wanted to breathe life into an obscure Governmental Affairs subcommittee he chaired. Nader volunteered to put the square peg of auto safety into the round hole of a Ribicoff subcommittee on executive reorganization. The young staffer cleverly assembled hearings featuring witnesses who wanted the U.S. government to use the "power of the purse" in two novel ways. One was to insist on certain safety features in cars the taxpayers bought. The second idea was to offer the manufacturers federal excise tax breaks to subsidize safety improvements.

In high dudgeon, top executives from Detroit stormed in to testify against such intrusions. It was their sacred corporate prerogative to sell what they wanted to sell instead of what the customer wanted to buy, even when the customer was Uncle Sam. The car executives soon wished they had stayed in Detroit because Nader had armed Committee members with hardball questions. The carmakers' characteristically arrogant, unrepentant answers – based mostly on their insistence that "safety doesn't sell" – were widely reported in the press.

The Big Three bosses did not faze Nader. They just reinforced his belief that carmakers cared deeply about expanding sales and maximizing profits but spent next to nothing on safety. Even before he pitched in for Senator Ribicoff, Nader was hitch-hiking all over the country, comparing notes with plaintiffs' lawyers who had dared to sue for wrongful deaths and personal injuries sustained in car accidents, collecting their files and meticulously building his case. Car owners had filed more than 100 lawsuits against GM arising from several blood-curdling, early 1960s crashes in the Chevy Corvair, the company's hot, new, low-slung sedan with outsized wheels and a bubble top that had on several occasions flipped over and killed passengers. The company marketed it to American moms and dads as an "easy-handling family sedan" but Nader characterized it as a "one-car accident" waiting to happen. He claimed a design flaw made it easy for the rear wheels to tuck under the car, even at low speeds.

The families of the hundreds of people who were killed or injured in Corvairs were able to impose some degree of financial responsibility on GM only if they could find a hungry personal injury attorney willing to bet his contingent fee on out-lawyering one of the world's largest, wealthiest and most powerful corporations. The automaker disclaimed responsibility for the Corvair crashes until courts in some jurisdictions, through a legal process called "civil discovery," started compelling them to reveal what they knew about the defect, when they knew it and why they chose to hide it from the moms and dads who trusted them. GM started writing settlement checks, Nader reported, only when a trial underway in California "threatened to expose ... one of the greatest acts of industrial irresponsibility" of the Twentieth Century.

Chrysler, too, found itself in Nader's crosshairs. He concluded that they sold 30,000 1965 Furies and similar models with bad steering. Chrysler, he wrote, sent a bulletin to its dealers across the country but made "no attempt to get in touch directly with the car buyer or find out how many unmodified cars were never brought back to dealers."

Nader also concluded that GM's 1953 Buick Roadmaster was another "automotive time bomb." Brakes started failing with just a few thousand miles on them. The manufacturer warned dealers but never told customers. Dealers, Nader observed, "do not relish advertising any defects in their cars ... and often were instructed ... only to make the correction if the customer brings his car in on another matter."

The automakers decided customer ignorance was bliss when it came to latent safety defects. From the day the first Model T rolled off of Henry Ford's assembly line, none of the manufacturers, Nader discovered, bothered to find out how many customers ever got warned about defects or kept track of how many dangerous cars got fixed. Killer defects were addressed only in the course of personal injury litigation, usually in state trial courts, so the only available information about stuck accelerators, bad brakes, defective steering and other deadly mistakes lurking in every car of a particular design came out of "settlements or verdicts against carmakers" in individual cases, scattered across the country. The manufacturers started offering bigger – or at least quicker – payments to plaintiffs who *agreed to keep secret* from other potential victims the details of the defect that injured them or killed their loved ones.

1965

Washington

GM had never confronted organized resistance on vehicle safety issues and they were not about to put up with it. They decided to destroy Nader by any means, legal or illegal. That is why the automotive giant paid Vince Gillen to hire a nine-man squad of ex-G-men to figure out, as Gillen put it, "what makes Ralph Nader tick, [his] *real* interest in safety, his politics, his women, boys, etc., drinking, dope, jobs – in fact, all aspects of Nader's life." Gillen's goons weren't subtle; they made sure the nerdy Nader noticed the shady-looking guys in trench coats tailing him every time he left his apartment in Washington's Dupont Circle neighborhood. During his phone conversations, Nader regularly heard clicks that told him his line was being tapped. His phone sometimes rang all night and all Nader usually heard when he picked up was heavy breathing. Nader's mother, Rose, back in Connecticut, got calls around 2 a.m., demanding that she tell her son to back off. Five dozen Nader acquaintances, schoolmates and former teachers were grilled by brawny white guys in white shirts, skinny ties and ill-fitting black suits.

Despite all those intimidation tactics and round-the-clock surveillance, Gillen's spies never turned up any useful dirt on Nader. Nor did they ever learn one of Nader's basic motivations for attacking the Big Three. It was a beheading – the same type of hideous event that motivated me to write *Killer Airbags*. My recurring nightmare featured Joel Knight losing his head in 2015. Nader knew a mom whose daughter died in a 15-mile-per-hour fender-bender. Her 1962 Chevrolet Bel Air was barely damaged but the cheap latch on the glove compartment door gave way, the door popped down to a horizontal position, its thin edge aimed at her daughter in the passenger seat. The car had no seatbelts – in fact, it was designed with no place to anchor a lap belt – so the little girl flew throat-first into the blade-like edge of the door.

Gillen missed the importance of that horror show but his dragnet did turn up some news that infuriated GM. Nader was turning his research on the auto industry into a scathing exposé, one that would be akin to a criminal indictment. In *Unsafe at Any Speed: The Designed-In Dangers of the American Automobile*, Nader was determined to call out specific makes and models of cars, including GM's Chevy Corvair and popular Chryslers and Buicks.[1]

In 1965, Nader clacked out multiple drafts of his 600-page manuscript on a second-hand typewriter. *Unsafe at Any Speed* opens with the grim observation that "for over half a century the automobile has brought death, injury and most inestimable sorrow and deprivation to millions of people." Nader argued that such horrors were deliberately inflicted by car manufacturers to maximize their own profits by shamelessly foisting all the costs of auto accidents onto their customers and society at large.

Nader's fundamental imperative was not so much to force carmakers to cough up money or information as to keep people from getting killed or maimed in the first place. He argued that the best way to save people was to make sure all the costs of car accidents "pinch the proper foot." Nader made *Unsafe at Any Speed* a call to arms for the federal government to step in between auto manufacturers and their customers. It was a radical idea. Nader ruefully pointed out that the first-ever Congressional hearing on traffic safety was convened July 16, 1956. That was 57 years after the first American traffic fatality and after 1.125 million Americans had already dropped into early graves and tens of millions had been injured due to car accidents.

"Traffic safety organizations" of that era, Nader added, were phonies, part of a broader conspiracy devoted "much more [to] a political strategy to defend special interests than an empirical program to save lives and prevent injuries." None of the Big Three spent more than 23 cents a car on the design and evaluation of crash safety improvements, Nader claimed, but they spent a fortune to dampen consumers' safety expectations.

University researchers and some underfunded do-gooder organizations had just begun to challenge the automakers' monopoly on accident and injury data in the early 1960s. Consumers Union, which was funded entirely by subscriptions, decried the Big Three's general "sloppiness in production" and researchers at Cornell University in New York began using Defense Department grants to focus on the deadly effects of the "second collision." Their work, published in a series of reports going back to 1952, showed that the "risk of fatal injury was *increased fivefold* if the occupant was thrown from the car" and led many to start flirting with the radical notion that seat belts should be standard equipment in new cars.

Nader revealed how the automakers, especially GM, had bitterly fought any effort to require lap belts – much less "three-point" shoulder-and-lap belts. With straight faces, they told legislators a driver would be better off "if he has his hands on the wheel and grips the rim sufficiently tight to take advantage of its energy absorption properties." In any case, they shrugged, "there is little interest on the part of the motoring public in actual use of seat belts." The hundreds of thousands of people who were killed for lack of one, it seems, were unavailable to express an opinion.

The real reason to oppose any sort of occupant restraints, according to Nader, was that "the seat belt is an emphatic reminder of the second collision, an item that alerts people to expect more safety in the cars they buy." That is why the Big Three blocked the State of New York from requiring seat belts in 1960 and continued their bitter battle until the state legislature finally enacted a modest requirement, effective with the 1965 model year, that the front seats in all new cars sold in New York must come equipped with lap belts.

A smaller car company, Studebaker, broke ranks with the Big Three and voluntarily installed lap belts, starting with all their 1964 models sold nationwide. They were ostracized by the Big Three, who made it difficult for Studebaker to find any company in America to supply seat belts in sufficient quantities to meet their commitment.

Studebaker also got little credit from Nader, who complained that the groundbreaking state action in New York was too little, too late. "The seat belt should have been introduced in the 1920s and rendered obsolete by the early 1950s .... [M]odern technology could develop and perfect ... a system that ideally would not rely on active participation of the passenger to take effect." Almost in passing, Nader floated a revolutionary idea he picked up from mid-60s aerospace literature. Even without seat belts, "protection like this could be achieved by a kind of *inflatable air bag restraint* which would be actuated to envelop a passenger before a crash."

Detroit chose not to respond to the airbag idea or any of Nader's other wild-eyed notions with anything like substantive details and arguments. GM's CEO ranted in public against "self-styled experts" and such "radical ... proposals ... [as] *federal regulation of vehicle design.*"

Nader argued in *Unsafe* that the federal government could better protect consumers by creating a powerful new federal agency – eventually known as the National Highway Traffic Safety Administration (NHTSA) – to establish and enforce national motor vehicle safety standards. Book publishers were not biting – how could they sell a lengthy exposé about killer defects in cars when people not only trusted Detroit, but lusted after its sexy cars? New York literary agents told Nader his work might be good for a long magazine article, nothing more, so he fed some of his most shocking revelations to a reporter, Princeton schoolmate James Ridgeway, who published them in a high-brow magazine, *The New Republic*. Book publisher Simon and Schuster had passed on Nader's book, but their former vice president, Richard Grossman, who had set up his own publishing house, read the magazine article and was outraged. As Nader closed in on a final manuscript, Grossman sat next to him and edited each page as it came out of the typewriter. On November 30, 1965, Grossman published *Unsafe* because it was an important call for public safety, not because he thought it would be a bestseller.

Grossman was right on both counts: *Unsafe* was important ... and it did not sell, at first. A handful of congressional staffers passed copies around Capitol Hill while car company execs dissected it, line-by-line, looking in vain for errors that would discredit Nader. American consumers kept ogling the rocket-inspired fins, shiny chrome grills and distinctive hood ornaments at their neighborhood car dealerships. That changed in March 1966, when Senator Ribicoff heard about GM's spying campaign against Nader and asked him to testify on car safety legislation. The Connecticut senator subpoenaed GM's CEO, James Roche, who claimed to be "shocked and outraged" that his lawyers had harassed Nader so mercilessly.

Suddenly, millions of Americans got Nader's message, and the media reaction was a frenzy. Nader appeared on all three network evening news programs and made the front page of every major newspaper in America. *Unsafe* instantly became a bestseller. It generated substantial royalties, but those amounts did not compare with the $425,000 Nader won in an invasion-of-privacy suit against GM. Nader devoted the windfall to hiring a whole team of like-minded, "self-styled experts." Before long, the world called them "Nader's Raiders."

1966

Washington

Nader's grand plan for auto safety consisted of three major elements. The first was to build public awareness of the scope and costs of the highway safety crisis. The second was to pass legislation empowering the federal government to address the problem on a nationwide basis. The third was something he called "continuing administration."

Unsafe was a bold stroke toward realizing the first element of Nader's plan. The book struck a nerve with the general public. Almost every American had some personal experience with car crashes but Nader, by shining a spotlight on the carmakers' reprehensible behavior, put the lugubrious toll in an entirely new perspective. People started dredging up ideas that had been laughed off in the mid-1950s. These included an emergency room doctor's prescription that President Eisenhower should set up a national group "to prevent public sale of vehicles that do not meet requirements of safety design." Senator Paul Douglas (D-IL), the kickoff witness at the first congressional hearing, proposed that the federal government should encourage manufacturers to agree on a set of national standards and, if they failed to act voluntarily, to impose legally enforceable safety requirements. Even the National Safety Council, which Nader characterized as a mouthpiece for the vehicle manufacturers, rejected the idea of federal standards because accidents and fatalities were "caused by bad driving." The main response in Detroit was to set up, under cover of an antitrust exemption, a Vehicle Equipment Safety Compact, which did nothing until 1965, when *Unsafe* made the best-seller lists.

The second element of Nader's plan – federal legislation – was more of a bank shot. Nader and his Raiders captured public attention and drew the heaviest fire from the Big Three. That gave a more mainstream, politically powerful, pro-safety lobby a degree of cover. Property-casualty insurance companies and medical professionals began to put their support and their political campaign contributions toward solutions for car crashes and those devastating "second collisions."

Emergency room doctors saw all the disgusting results of car wrecks, up close and personal. Hardened veterans of Korean War MASH units shed tears every time they had to enter "time of death" on a form for yet another pair of young sweethearts who didn't make it home alive from their high school prom.

Insurers took those tragedies less personally, but the constant devastation on the highways required dramatic increases in car insurance premiums that state rate-setting commissions were not always quick to approve. It made economic sense to reduce claims, so Liberty Mutual spent serious money between 1951 and 1961 to prove that even modest design improvements in vehicles would trim insurance payouts. Detroit ignored or derided their efforts.[2] Despite longstanding and vehement opposition to any sort of federal regulation of their own, state-regulated industry, the insurers readily lined up behind President Johnson when he sent Congress the first-ever White House proposal for federal auto safety legislation and a new Department of Transportation to implement it.

The Big Three feared a growing patchwork of conflicting state safety standards even more than a new federal law. Detroit fell into line with the insurers, to some extent. Carmakers sounded cooperative in public hearings on the legislation but did their best to water it down in the "smoke-filled rooms" where the real work of writing new laws has always taken place.

President Johnson's original proposal was weak. It would only *authorize, not require* his new Department of Transportation to impose mandatory safety standards. Detroit floated several ways to tie the new Transportation Department's hands in exercising such authority. Congress revolted. The bills that went to floor votes in both the House and Senate *mandated* DOT to impose *mandatory* standards – and quickly, too.

The Senate Committee on Commerce, Science and Transportation, called "Senate Commerce," for short, had established itself in the 1950s as a hotbed of auto safety advocacy. Senators considered the vehicle safety legislation essential to stop the Big Three's "chronic subordination of safe design" and "inadequate allocation of resources to safety engineering." Safety standards have to be "practicable," they wrote, but in any cost-benefit calculation *safety shall be the overriding consideration.*"

Key committees in both the House and Senate voted to impose criminal penalties on manufacturers for failing to meet the new federal motor vehicle safety standards. When the bills were considered on the floor in each chamber, however, the manufacturers killed those criminal sanctions and substituted a "self-certification" honor system under which anyone caught making a false certification would face only civil penalties and injunctive relief (that is, court orders to do something or stop doing something). When that final compromise was struck, landmark legislation "to reduce traffic accidents and deaths and injuries to persons resulting from traffic accidents" passed Congress without a single "no" vote.

By the time the bill arrived on President Johnson's desk for signature, on September 9, 1966, the National Traffic and Motor Vehicle Safety Act was still a radical departure from previous law. Three of its five major provisions directly addressed cars. The government would do its own safety research and testing instead of remaining at the mercy of the industry for even the most basic data. Car manufacturers would have to notify their customers promptly whenever they learned that a vehicle had a "defect related to motor vehicle safety." Most importantly, Congress instructed the Transportation Department *immediately* to start issuing *mandatory* federal motor vehicle safety standards for new vehicles and to enforce the manufacturers' compliance with those standards.

Nader was unaware that Japanese industrialists were already watching his every success, plotting ways to make any new technology required by his efforts smaller, cheaper and more profitable for themselves.

1967

Washington

The two Americans who invented the first passive restraint for automobile occupants and the first airbag trigger, respectively, in the mid-1950s never made a dime off of their patents. Ford toyed with airbags in 1957; GM took a look in 1960. In 1967, Ford started flinging live baboons into pre-inflated airbags. The results pleased everyone except, presumably, the baboons.

Nobody saw a practical way to make airbags inflate quickly enough – within 40 milliseconds of a crash. Only a mini-explosion could produce high-pressure gas quickly enough to fill a cloth airbag before a driver slammed into the steering wheel. Along came the U.S. military, who invented new ways to trigger bombs raining on Vietnamese jungles and coincidentally solved the airbag inflation speed issue. Ford and a supplier named Eaton, Yale and Towne successfully tested something they called the "Airstop Restraint System." A folded, inflatable bag was stowed behind a car's instrument panel. A state-of-the-art sensor ignited sodium azide, a rocket fuel, inside a metal canister. The resulting thrust pushed high-pressure gas into the cushion. These first airbags dissipated 90 percent of deceleration forces on a vehicle occupant and showed "possible levels of survivability un-approached by any other known restraint system."

Several problems had to be solved before the radical, new system could hit the road. Faster inflation was needed, but the explosions already created noise and pressure that would permanently deafen people inside the vehicle. Eaton said it would take three or four years to work out the bugs; Ford said it would take 10 years. The technology was so promising, three American defense contractors – Rocket Research, Thiokol and Olin Mathieson – got into the act. Human tests on fighter jocks began at Holloman Air Force Base in 1969.

NHTSA recognized immediately that airbags were an essential part of the "technology-forcing" mandate of the Vehicle

Safety Act. Dr. William Haddon, author of the ground-breaking medical book Pat Moynihan made famous, was the first administrator. By 1968, engineers at Eaton were eager to move their airbag invention off the drawing boards and into the dashboards. They convinced Haddon and his special assistant, Joan Claybrook, a Nader protégé, former Capitol Hill staffer and future NHTSA Administrator, to meet with the automakers.

Eaton identified four "show-stoppers" before airbags could become standard equipment. Explosions were still too loud. Some out-of-position vehicle occupants – especially children and women of short stature who might stand or sit too close to the steering wheel or dashboard – surely would be hit and killed by an inflating bag. An inadvertent airbag deployment could make a driver lose control. The optimal speed and strength of airbag deployments could not easily be gauged until scientists could translate impacts on test dummies in mock crashes into real human injuries. Agency leaders in 1968 knew lap belts would still be essential to protect vehicle occupants in cases of rollovers, multiple impacts and other non-head-on crashes.

Congress was adamant that federal motor vehicle safety standards were urgently needed. The Motor Vehicle Safety Act required interim standards to be in place by January 31, 1967, barely four months after the law's enactment. Facing such an immediate deadline, Haddon simply copied federal fleet car specifications. Nader complained that those interim standards – requiring lap belts, padded dashboards, head restraints and collapsible steering columns – were *design* standards instead of *performance* standards, as required by the Act. That made them, in Nader's opinion, too lax. Detroit, of course, complained that they were too tough. Some safety advocates thought lap belts should be required, even though fewer than one of five front seat occupants bothered to buckle them. Others insisted on more expensive three-point "shoulder harnesses." Perfect quickly became the enemy of the good – or, at least, the safer.

1969-74

Washington

Dr. Haddon resigned soon after President Richard Nixon moved into the White House in January 1969. The doctor's government-careerist, acting successor, Robert Brenner, also was impressed with Eaton's airbag work. Brenner made a lasting impression with the pro-safety Senate Commerce Committee when he told them airbags offered the "promise of a major breakthrough in injury prevention" and could reduce the vulnerability of very small cars in crashes with larger cars.

After Nixon appointed John Volpe, the liberal Republican governor of Massachusetts, to lead the new Transportation Department, the nascent auto safety lobby put on the full-court press. Secretary Volpe was skeptical at first, but the technology impressed him. At a conference organized by the politically shape-shifting Nixon White House staffer Pat Moynihan, Volpe's motto was "GET THE BUGS OUT OF THE BAGS!"

Volpe insisted on the appointment of Douglas Toms, the Republican motor vehicle chief in the State of Washington, to be NHTSA administrator. For better and for worse, Toms was a *bona fide* expert on airbags, having studied the technology extensively in the University of Michigan's traffic safety graduate program. By mid-1969, Toms notified the world – including Takata and other Japanese component manufacturers – that NHTSA planned to require automakers to install "inflatable occupant restraint systems" across the front seats of all 1971 model year cars.

Toms turned up the heat in May 1970, when NHTSA requested public comment on a modified rule that was more ambitious, even though it would slide the airbag implementation date back a year. An occupant in any seating position in a 1972 model or later car would have to be protected by *either* "passive restraints" or "three-point" manual belts. None of the insurers filed formal comments. Foreign manufacturers, particularly Volkswagen and Mercedes, declared it couldn't be done.

Domestic carmakers did much public hand wringing about the additional work needed to perfect the systems, but General Motors promised that it would offer "air cushion occupant restraints" in its 1975 models.

"Any delay," Toms argued passionately, "would be unconscionable." A few months later, in September 1970, he created an uproar by publishing modifications to one of the interim standards Haddon put on the books in NHTSA's first days. Starting with 1972 models, instead of requiring lap belts in front seats, the interim standard would make manufacturers choose between "passive restraints" or belts in all seating positions that would enable occupants to experience a 30-mile per hour frontal crash with no serious injuries. NHTSA required audible and visible dashboard warnings when belts were not fastened but the agency explicitly ruled out an "ignition interlock" system that would disable a vehicle until belts were buckled.

Toms naïvely declared that "passive restraints are beyond the controversial point." In November 1970, NHTSA published the first "final" rule explicitly requiring installation of airbags, effective with 1974 models. Seat belts would not be required, but manufacturers had to prove that their airbags would be effective in head-on, 35-mile per hour crashes.

Toms' "Hail Mary" final rule was a strategic and political blunder. For starters, "effectiveness" in meeting NHTSA's new performance standard was to be measured by technical injury criteria that NHTSA failed to explain. Almost as an afterthought, the agency commenced a parallel anthropomorphic crash dummy rulemaking to fill in the "injury assessment" gaps.

Seat belt manufacturers – especially Takata, which by the 1970s enjoyed a growing share of the American market – were apoplectic about any rule that could render their product obsolete. Their Washington, D.C.-based trade group, the American Seat Belt Council, knocked the wind out of airbag advocates, insisting that "airbags *at best* can be … a complement for seat belts." The Council prompted consumers to ask an obvious question: why should they pay for scary, new technology when all they really needed to do was to stop sitting on their existing safety devices? Over vitriolic objections from Nader and his newly formed public interest group, the Center for Auto Safety, Toms felt compelled in March 1971, to issue a second "final" rule that delayed implementation for all seating positions for yet another two years, to the 1975 models.

Toms' tactical retreat left blood in the water. Detroit sneaked in for the "kill." On April 27, 1971, within weeks of Toms' "FINAL" ORDER NUMBER TWO, Henry Ford II and his company president, Lee Iacocca, visited President Nixon in the Oval Office of the White House. Iacocca complained at length about nearly every regulation affecting the auto industry, especially the brand-new airbag mandate. Their conversation was recorded by a "bug" in a potted plant but the public were not allowed to hear the exchange for another decade. GM's chairman, James Roche, visited the Oval Office to make the same plea the following day.

Nixon secretly ordered Secretary Volpe to withdraw the rule, then ordered an aide to solicit campaign money from Ford and the other American carmakers for use by the Committee to Re-elect the President ("CREEP") in the 1972 campaign. Volpe balked. He slipped Nixon a handwritten note and then delivered a more detailed, secret memorandum on April 28, 1971. The Secretary refused to take an action he knew would result in the deaths of tens of thousands of Americans until Nixon gave him the order in person. Nixon forced Volpe's hand and instructed Toms "not to discuss airbags publicly."

The Big Three, who were hit up for donations to CREEP almost the minute they stepped off the White House grounds, expected *something* in return. On August 31, 1971, Volpe told Nixon – once again, in secret – that the Big Three wanted the airbag requirement to "fully disappear" and that the manufacturers' ignition interlock scheme was a ruse. Volpe told Nixon any type of "active" system "will not solve the problem."

Detroit considered the death of airbags the *quid pro quo* for their campaign cash, but Nixon double-crossed them when he allowed Volpe to issue "FINAL" RULE NUMBER THREE on October 1, 1971. It delayed the new safety requirements yet another year, to the 1976 models, because the affected cars would not hit the showrooms until Nixon was scheduled to leave office. The rule threw the carmakers an additional and fateful bone. Instead of requiring them to install airbags, vehicle manufacturers were allowed to experiment on their customers with the "ignition interlock."

After he crushed Senator George McGovern (D-SD), the 1972 Democratic presidential nominee, Nixon purged his cabinet of "non-loyalists." Volpe got a one-way ticket to Rome, where he served as U.S. Ambassador to Italy. Toms remained as NHTSA's bound-and-gagged, lame-duck administrator until March 1973, when Nixon put two oil industry executives in charge of the pesky airbag issue, expecting them to bury it quietly. Claude Brinegar became Secretary of Transportation and James Gregory took charge of NHTSA. They would not ignore the voluminous data showing that airbags could save tens of thousands of lives, so airbags outlived the Nixon Administration.

Nixon was succeeded by a politician who could not have been closer to the Big Three. Michigan congressman and House Republican leader Gerald Ford was elevated to Vice President and then President without being elected to either office because Nixon's Veep, Spiro Agnew, had resigned before Nixon bowed out.

1975-1980

Washington

During the 20 years it took NHTSA to arrive at a "final" final rule, airbag-equipped cars actually hit the road only during the Ford Administration. It was mostly a hangover from earlier battles, when Detroit thought it could delay the looming implementation dates NHTSA set in the first three "final" rules issued by the Nixon Administration. Ford Motor Co. announced it would offer airbags as an option in every car line in 1975. GM undertook the first-ever mass production of airbag-equipped cars. In 1970, it had promised to make a million of them in 1974 and 1975 models and, starting with the 1976 models, to make airbags standard equipment in all of its passenger cars, most light trucks and some multipurpose vehicles. GM reneged a few months into President Ford's administration, so it installed airbags in only 10,000 1974 through

1976 luxury cars. Few people who bought those cars knew airbags were planted in their dashboards.

The carmakers' back-handed marketing convinced all five of the American companies who made airbags – Eaton Corp., Talley Industries, Thiokol, Allied Chemical Corp and Rocket Research – to defer most research and development spending in 1975. By 1978, Talley Industries and Eaton announced that "business considerations" had forced them to halt production altogether.[3] Takata got interested when some of those 10,000 airbag-equipped GM cars crashed and produced the first-ever airbag data involving real people, not crash test dummies. In a half-billion miles of road experience, there were 185 deployments involving 267 front-seat occupants, nearly all of whom survived their crashes.

Nixon's "FINAL" RULE NUMBER THREE had invited car-makers to try to force their customers to wear seat belts. They installed an "ignition interlock" to keep engines from starting until electronic sensors detected that belts were buckled. Takata and other seat belt manufacturers had been touting the idea since 1970 and in 1971 Ford cited it as proof airbags weren't needed. In "interlocked" cars belt usage rates jumped to more than 60 percent. When those cars crashed, drivers experienced a significant reduction in severe injuries.

The ignition interlock proved nearly fatal to federal motor vehicle safety regulation, however. Manufacturers other than Ford warned that the technology was not reliable and consumers would hate it. NHTSA's response, essentially, was that "quality control" was the manufacturers' problem, not the agency's. Federal bureaucrats assumed Detroit's customers would do as they were told. Instead, motorists revolted. Safety was no longer the issue. People hated the idea of taking orders from the federal government about what to do in the privacy of their own cars. Most belt systems were designed without any apparent regard for comfort. Horror stories spread about drivers being stranded by interlock sensors that didn't work. Mechanics did a brisk business, disabling 40 percent of the devices.

Congress stepped in weeks after Gerald Ford became President. Rep. Louis Wyman (R-NH), a congressman from the Live-Free-or-Die State, decided Congress at large was better equipped than the "experts" at NHTSA to reduce highway deaths and injuries. He offered legislation to forbid an interlock or a continuous warning buzzer. It passed the House by a lopsided vote in August 1974. Senator Thomas Eagleton (D-MO) promptly convinced the Senate to tie NHTSA's hands even tighter. Not only were the interlock and continuous buzzer outlawed, NHTSA could not require *any technology other than seatbelts* unless the agency gave both houses of Congress 60 days to veto the rule. President Ford signed the auto safety "two-house veto" into law on October 28, 1974.

The ballyhoo in Congress drowned out the results of NHTSA's first thorough analysis of the costs and benefits of airbags. The agency concluded bags were superior to belts, regardless of whether the vehicle occupants wore them voluntarily or under the coercion of an interlock.

President Ford replaced Secretary Brinegar in February 1975 with a liberal Republican. Corporate lawyer William T. Coleman, Jr., inherited NHTSA Administrator Gregory, who held a series of public hearings in May 1975. The carmakers were determined to sweep airbags into the regulatory trash heap with the ignition interlock. GM announced that its 1976 airbag-equipped models would be their last. Ford said it had no plans to install any form of passive restraint. Mercedes – then a niche player in the U.S. luxury market – said it would redesign their "active" three-point shoulder-and-lap belts with tensioners and load limiters to make them more comfortable and more effective. They mused about installing a driver-side airbag, but only to supplement the seat belt.

Nader, Haddon and other safety advocates vehemently attacked the Big Three for reneging on earlier promises to field more airbag-equipped cars. They threatened legal action against NHTSA to enforce "FINAL" RULE NUMBER THREE, even though Senator Eagleton and others in Congress had cast it into regulatory limbo.

The annual body count was approaching 50,000 and the loss to the American economy from car crashes was pushing $40 billion a year. When Gregory resigned in February 1976, he left behind a memorandum urging both mandatory seat belt use laws and passive restraints, starting no later than the 1980 model year. Dead silence followed for several months.

With President Ford's election campaign looming, Coleman took personal charge of the airbag issue. The new Secretary appointed a "task force" that cut NHTSA out of the loop, then announced more public hearings. The first question presented in Coleman's hearing notice was right out of 1956 – was it appropriate for the federal government to regulate auto safety? The second question was whether safety requirements hurt sales and employment in the auto industry. Coleman appeared to be rolling the clock back, as if Congress never passed the Motor Vehicle Safety Act.

Coleman's advisors urged him to move ahead with "a fully passive restraint standard" and simultaneously promote seat belt use aggressively.[4] Even before the hearings started, Coleman issued "FINAL" RULE NUMBER FOUR, which put off the "passive restraints" compliance deadline to the 1977 models.

After President Ford lost the election, Coleman latched onto a proposal White House economists floated a year earlier. The government could directly subsidize production of half a million airbag cars per year. Considering the financial burdens accidents imposed on the government's employees and social welfare programs, the math favored taxpayers.

The vehicle manufacturers were not interested until Coleman proposed to replace the regulations with a "demonstration program." On December 6, 1976, the Secretary belatedly admitted the obvious, that "airbag technology *does work* and can be produced at a reasonable cost." By his estimate, airbags would save 12,000 people each year.[5] To make it palatable to consumers – particularly to avoid the ugly fate of the ignition interlock – he offered Detroit a deal. If they collectively would market a half-million airbag-equipped cars over two years, starting with the 1979 models, he would use his power to kill the mandate before President-Elect Jimmy Carter's much less corporate-friendly regime took the reins at NHTSA. Coleman insisted that executives from the car companies and their nemesis, the insurance industry, had to drop their holiday plans and convene in Washington on December 20, 1976, to iron out the details.

Less than 48 hours before Carter took office, Coleman announced the deal. Detroit would build a half-million airbag cars. They would pass the costs along to their customers, as usual.

The government would pay nothing, but the insurers would offer discounts on premiums. Nobody dealt the Carter transition team into the deal even though it specifically provided that the plan was automatically null and void if, before August 1983, NHTSA proposed another passive restraint rule.

President Carter appointed Rep. Brock Adams (D-WA) to take over as Secretary of Transportation. Within two weeks, Adams said he found no way to "rationalize" Coleman's 11th-hour demonstration program and tossed it "out the window."[6] In March, 1977, with his distinctive, four-inch high signature on a proposed a new rule, Adams stopped the immediate rollout of 500,000 airbag cars.

Carter nominated Joan Claybrook, Dr. Haddon's former assistant and a House staffer who helped pass the Motor Vehicle Safety Act, to run NHTSA. Detroit vehemently but unsuccessfully fought her appointment. Claybrook wanted to see airbags in new, 1981 model cars, but Adams was planning to run for the Senate in 1980. According to Claybrook, he refused to risk his Senate campaign on airbags, even if it meant people would die.[7] On July 5, 1977, he published "FINAL" RULE NUMBER FIVE, requiring that airbags go "full-frontal" in most 1982 model cars, by which time he would be safely ensconced in the Senate.

The revenge of the Rust Belt started immediately. Rep. Bud Shuster (R-PA) waited seven minutes to introduce a House resolution to veto the rule. Senator Robert Griffin (D-MI) rushed to the Senate floor with his own veto resolution. Shuster's proposal was tabled in committee and Griffin's resolution died acrimoniously on the Senate floor. After a decade of rancorous debate, airbags were gaining the upper hand.

Meanwhile, the Japanese carmakers, who by 1980 were taking the American market by storm, pleaded with Claybrook for more time to comply. Thiokol had perfected airbag systems for subcompacts but the Japanese falsely claimed that the airbag modules Detroit's bona fide rocket scientists had developed would not fit in their tiny cars.[8] The Japanese cop-out gave GM's boss an idea. If manufacturers were going to be stuck with an airbag mandate, why not phase in the requirement to apply first to "small cars" – which at the time was almost synonymous with "Japanese cars"? That would buy Detroit and its big, high-profit-margin cars at least two more years' relief from both the encroaching foreign competition and the regulatory burden.

When Secretary Adams went home to campaign for the Senate in November 1979, Neil Goldschmidt, another rising Democrat and future governor of the neighboring state of Oregon, succeeded him as Transportation Secretary. He liked GM's new approach, especially since it would delay the clash with Detroit until after Carter got re-elected. GM took the idea to Capitol Hill in the summer of 1980. Each manufacturer would voluntarily make airbags *available as an option* in at least one car line (for example, the Chevy Nova) among the 1983, 1984 and 1985 model cars. The airbag mandate would not kick in until the 1983 model year but the Japanese imports would be most severely affected that year. As an additional concession to Detroit, NHTSA would kill State Farm's pet project, a rule requiring manufacturers to design stronger bumpers to reduce repair bills in non-injury-producing fender-benders.

Senator John Warner (R-VA) had no carmakers in his state but he took a special interest in pushing GM's new deal. His new trophy wife, actress Elizabeth Taylor, had become too obese to wear a seat belt without crushing one of her elegant designer dresses. The "Warner Compromise" passed the Senate in September 1980, barely ahead of the presidential election. Just after Election Day, the House defeated it by just three votes.

Even with an unwavering airbag supporter like Claybrook running NHTSA and a supportive, bi-partisan coalition in Congress, President Carter failed to put a single airbag-equipped car on the road. "FINAL" RULE NUMBER FIVE – requiring carmakers to phase in their installation of airbags, starting in the Summer of 1981 for 1982 models with wheelbases greater than 115 inches – remained on the books. Many of the pro-safety messengers thought they had finally won the airbag wars.

PART 3

The Vaccine

1981

Washington

In November 1980, former California Governor Ronald Reagan defeated President Carter by ten percentage points in the popular vote and with an historic 459-49 electoral landslide. Reagan's transition team started plotting the demise of the airbag mandate even before Carter's people finished packing their suitcases in January 1981. Nader was apoplectic. The Motor Vehicle Safety Act — the legislation that made Nader a consumerist icon — was only 15 years old. Despite constant opposition from the auto-makers, several federal safety standards had been imposed or were on the verge of implementation. The Reagan Revolution took Nader back to 1966, to the day President Lyndon Johnson invited him into the Oval Office and handed him a pen he had used to sign the law that created NHTSA. Nader had every reason to be giddy at that signing ceremony, but he was consumed by this sobering thought: *Now the work really starts, to make sure the regulators are not captured by the industry they are supposed to regulate.*

The new Transportation Secretary, Drew Lewis, a former Pennsylvania railroad executive, immediately established a task force to make American automobile manufacturers profitable. Domestic new car sales had swooned in 1980, to 6.6 million from 8.3 million vehicles in 1979. Imports, mostly Japanese, surged in 1979 and Chrysler went bankrupt. Reagan explicitly declared that whatever was good for Detroit was good for America.

The Big Three had a two-part wish list. They wanted to ban imported cars but the Reagan people were ideological "free-traders." Detroit's consolation was Reagan's enthusiastic support for an across-the-board rollback of more than 100 environmental and auto safety regulations.

They had reason to expect help from Congress but the Reagan revolutionaries did not take into account John C. Danforth, an Episcopal-priest-turned-first-term-Republican-Senator from Missouri who was horrified that highway deaths in the U.S. – more than 53,000 that year – were surging at the same time flimsy, lightweight Japanese imports were flooding the American market and threatening to kill thousands more each year. Danforth chaired two Senate subcommittees, one with jurisdiction over auto imports, the other with responsibility for auto safety. The lanky, cerebral heir to the Ralston-Purina animal food fortune supported Reagan's campaign pledge to "make America great again" but he didn't see what was so great about stacking more corpses by the side of road.

On November 4, 1980, Danforth asked me to move to Washington, D.C. to be his new legislative counsel. I was just 25 years old and only a year out of law school, but I had worked my way through Princeton University (*alma mater* to both Danforth and Nader) as a part-time newspaper reporter and as a summer intern for two members of the Missouri congressional delegation. I had returned to the Show-me State after law school at the University of Virginia and worked with an attorney who had been Danforth's chief deputy in the Attorney General's office before Danforth won his Senate seat. I reported for duty in January 1981 and was immediately hurled into the middle of the nasty, protracted war over airbags. On just my second day, Jack – as everyone on Danforth's staff addressed him – instructed me to organize a hearing titled "Government Regulations Affecting the U.S. Automobile Industry."[9] The first time I tried to lay out for him the pros and cons of airbags, Jack signaled a full-stop by flashing both palms at me. "If the airbag rule is cancelled," he intoned in his most serious minister's voice, "people will die." Jack had become friends with another Princeton grad, the conservative newspaper columnist, George Will, who surprised many with a rationale for airbags that Jack found compelling. "There is," Will had written in 1977, "a pitiless abstraction and disrespect for life in such dogmatic respect for the right of consenting adults to behave in ways disastrous to themselves. Besides, too many children are sacrificed on that altar."

Jack's challenge to me was clear: "Your job, Jerry, is to get airbags in cars."

Toyotas, Datsuns and the like tended to be smaller, lighter and more reliable than Detroit's shoddy, clunky gas-guzzlers. Americans were lining up in 1981 to buy them as fast as they could roll off a cargo ship. Crashworthiness was not one of their advantages. The carnage on the highways in 1981 was the numerical equivalent of a small passenger jet crashing in a fireball *every day of the year*, but many people shrugged off traffic fatalities as a necessary part of modern life. Everybody knew the proliferation of smaller cars on American highways necessarily would keep body bag suppliers in business by killing an *additional* 9,000 or so people each year – unless, somehow, *all* cars could be made more crashworthy.

As I struggled to get on top of the facts, I was besieged by dozens of lobbyists, armed with a decade's worth of "point papers," lengthy engineering studies and even film clips shown on briefcase-size "portable" projectors. They queued up outside Danforth's office door in the Russell Senate Office Building to share their materials with me. Through the cacophony and 16-hour workdays, a few uncontested facts emerged. The policy merits weighed heavily for airbags, but there could be serious political repercussions. Thousands of the Missouri voters Danforth needed to win reelection in 1982 worked at a Ford plant near Kansas City and a General Motors factory near St. Louis. Their management told them the airbag rule would cost many of them their jobs.

To prepare for that first hearing, I had to boil down the previous 15 years of legislation and rulemaking into a one-page "point paper" Jack *might* have a moment to digest before the hearing. I typed up facts that were not seriously in dispute:

- More than 150,000 Americans would die in traffic accidents between 1979 and 1981.
- Airbags were proven lifesavers; tens of thousands would have lived and hundreds of thousands would have avoided crippling injuries had the airbag rule gone into effect as proposed during the Nixon Administration.
- The economic losses from traffic fatalities and injuries were catastrophic, especially to the federal government.

- Special-interest pleading at the highest levels of the Nixon, Ford and Carter Administrations, not economic or technical hurdles, kept airbags out of cars.
- Regardless of the airbag's potential impact on safety overall, the explosives that made them work were sure to kill people in certain circumstances.
- Insurers, doctors and consumer advocates opposed rescission of the mandate but some favored a reversal of Carter's implementation schedule to put airbags in small cars first.

When the hearing convened on January 28, 1981, witnesses from the Big Three rehashed all their objections to passive restraints while downplaying earlier promises to offer their customers the option, at least, of buying an airbag-equipped car. Anyone listening to Detroit whine in the jamb-packed Commerce Committee hearing room would never have guessed that GM and Ford, far from needing more "lead-time," had already sold thousands of airbag-equipped vehicles in the mid-1970s.

The hearing left no doubt in Danforth's mind that the tsunami of Japanese imports was the best reason to *keep* the airbag rule, not to dump it. He used his Trade Subcommittee to champion "temporary" quotas to restrict Japanese imports to 1.68 million cars in 1981. That enabled Detroit to jack up the sticker price of their gas-guzzlers by as much as $3,000. They loved Danforth for that. He simultaneously used his Surface Transportation Subcommittee chairmanship to champion the passive restraints mandate. Detroit would need to raise their prices by a couple hundred dollars to cover the cost of the new technology. They hated him for that. They were dismayed at having to work through me – like Nader, an idealistic young lawyer, fairly fresh out of Princeton's Woodrow Wilson School of Public and International Affairs – to influence Danforth's position and divine his next moves. What they *really* hated was their inability to punish Danforth for his pro-airbag stance without jeopardizing his support for import restrictions.

The result was that Danforth got a "pass" from an industry that could easily have forced him to make the same choice Brock Adams made five years earlier – between saving thousands of American lives or winning a Senate campaign. Danforth dared to do both, even though his reelection margin of victory in 1982 was less than one-half of one percent. Jack's grandfather, William H. Danforth, would have been proud. The founder of Ralston Purina and the resulting family fortune, the elder Danforth authored a best-selling book entitled, *I Dare You!*

Donald L. Schaffer, the second-most powerful executive at Allstate Insurance, was a die-hard airbag advocate. Upon Reagan's election, Schaffer led Allstate and its industry trade group, the National Association of Independent Insurers, out of their own trenches. In his testimony and during rough-and-tumble lobbying visits over dinner at expensive, power-broker Washington restaurants, Schaffer struck me like a battle-hardened World War II combat infantryman. Of course, that is exactly what he was. He had heroically survived one bloody fight after another, first in Italy, then in Washington, but he had not yet won the airbag war.

Schaffer, who joined Allstate in 1957, calmly related his 1970s combat stories. He offered hope that the Reagan "regulatory relief" initiative was a temporary setback even though many of his fellow insurers were inclined to fly a white flag. State Farm, the only auto insurer bigger than Allstate, had long been a thorn inside Schaffer's combat boots. When Nixon's NHTSA held public hearings in the 1970s, Schaffer had assigned Allstate's Washington Vice President, Joe Howell, to rally the insurance industry behind airbags. Schaffer was surprised when State Farm's lobbyists brushed him off. At Schaffer's insistence, Howell began trying to coax all the smaller insurance writers onto the airbag bandwagon.

Schaffer and Howell had their work cut out for them. The leadership of both companies were actuaries whose sole mission was to make sure the premiums collected from car owners exceeded the long-term costs of claims. It was a simple matter of math that a death claim would usually cost insurers less than claims for long-term medical care for brain damage and other crippling injuries. For insurers, keeping people alive was not necessarily good business.

In 1981, Schaffer began my education by recounting how he put Allstate in the pro-airbag camp from the get-go. As early as 1972, he argued that "the airbag is not being delayed because the technology isn't ready or because the cost outweighs the benefits. Rather, their installation is resisted for politico-economic and philosophical reasons unrelated to … their ability to save lives and prevent injuries."[10]

Schaffer told me how, in September 1973, he first convinced insurers to take on the Big Three. He notified Nixon's Transportation Secretary Volpe that Allstate would put its money where its mouth was. The insurer would discount certain "coverages" in vehicle owners' premiums for airbag-equipped cars by 30 percent, yet another good reason, Allstate said, for NHTSA to impose an airbag mandate quickly. When GM complained that Allstate's discounts for drivers did not help them afford product liability insurance to cover lawsuits for airbags that inevitably would kill a few people instead of saving them, Allstate promised to cap manufacturers' premiums for such coverage.

One year later, the Nixon White House unwittingly shocked other insurers into joining Schaffer at the ramparts. The federal government froze auto insurance premiums from January to March 1974. The insurers suddenly were facing rapid increases in repair bills and medical costs with no way to outrun them with premium increases. Schaffer positioned airbags as the best way to control claims losses. That whipped virtually all of the car insurers into line behind the new mandate NHTSA proposed on March 19, 1974. A year later, Nationwide and some other insurers stepped up to the plate with discounts of 15 to 30 percent off of premiums for various types of coverage for anyone who would buy a car with airbags. Carmakers, however, made hay of the lack of any correlation between any specific type of passive restraint and the discount a car owner would receive.

Premium discounts were purely theoretical until Detroit sold more airbag-equipped cars. In the mid-1970s, GM produced 1,000 Chevys with airbags and no seat belts. Ford put airbags and manual seat belts in several hundred Mercuries. Allstate not only extolled the virtues of these prototypes in national print media and television spots; they put their own executives and other employees in them. In 1974, Allstate announced a joint venture with Volvo to field the first-ever small cars with airbags. The insurer took a big portion of 75 retrofitted Volvos and 450 large Ford and GM cars. That decision led to an astonishing, providential event that assured Allstate's unwavering support for an airbag mandate and shamed other insurers into showing unequivocal support for a mandatory passive restraint standard.

1976

Langley, Virginia

On a bright Sunday morning in May 1976, 16-year old Chandler Howell was fast on his way to becoming a car accident statistic. His schoolmate, Nora Clarke, was in the front passenger seat, turned clear around so she could share the latest gossip with Chandler's girlfriend, Harriett Sullivan, who was in the back seat. None of them wore a seat belt.[11]

They planned to hang out with other teens in Langley, Virginia, a prosperous Washington, D.C., suburb. Chandler drove past their high school, located next to the headquarters of the Central Intelligence Agency. He was doing 50 miles per hour in a 35 zone on a hilly stretch of Georgetown Pike, a two-lane historic byway, infamous for constant traffic and its lack of turn lanes or shoulders. As Chandler popped over a hill, an older couple in a Cadillac bolted out of a church parking lot, squarely in front of him. When he crammed on the brakes, his wheels locked up. It was the classic "un-survivable" accident – a small, foreign carload of unbelted teens skidding out-of-control, straight into the back of a huge American automobile.

Barely a mile away, Chandler's parents, Joe and Carolyn, were worshipping at the McLean Baptist Church when the sermon was drowned out by sirens screeching from police cars and ambulances converging on the crash site.

"Let's pray those sirens aren't for Chandler," Joe whispered to Carolyn. Being the Washington Vice President for All-state Corporation, the nation's second-largest auto accident insurer, Joe Howell was painfully aware of the skyrocketing highway death toll. Every 15-year old, red-blooded American boy stood a one-in-one-hundred chance of perishing in an automobile accident before his 25th birthday. The death rate was 20 times higher than that produced during the worst days of an earlier generation's polio epidemic. Half of all teens would be involved in a car crash before they graduated high school. Compared to more experienced drivers, teens were three times more likely to crash.

The Howells knew Chandler was out that morning in Joe's brand-new, boxy company car, a dark blue 1976 Volvo 242 sedan, and that he would be picking up friends. They also knew that, for a 16-year old boy behind the wheel, the distraction of having even one young passenger increased the chances of a deadly crash by 44 percent. Surely, the Howells thought, Chandler and his friends had enough sense to wear their seatbelts; they had been told repeatedly that one-half of teens killed in crashes weren't belted.

The emergency responders creating all the racket as they raced down Georgetown Pike expected a grisly scene. Car crashes in their jurisdiction, Fairfax County, Virginia, were piling up, from 13,000 in 1975 to 18,500 by the end of 1976. Crash fatalities also jumped 20 percent, from 53 in 1975 to 64 in 1976; almost three-fourths of the dead were young people.

When they switched off their sirens at the accident scene, the police were baffled. As expected, two totaled vehicles would have to be towed to restore traffic flow. Oddly, however, there were no broken bodies strewn across the highway. An unbelted passenger in the front seat – popularly known as "the death seat" – usually shot through the windshield and face-planted in the middle of the road. Instead, the police saw dazed and confused teenagers standing beside a crumpled foreign car and a mature, well-dressed couple giving a Hollywood-handsome, sandy-haired heathen holy hell as they clutched the backs of their own wrinkled necks and started complaining about whiplash.

The ambulance driver looked for bodies in the front seat of the foreign car. Instead, he found two mysterious objects that looked like empty pillow cases drooping from the dashboard and steering wheel. These first responders were unwitting witnesses to automotive history. Chandler's crash was the first highway accident in the world in which airbags deployed in a compact car.

The airbags had been retrofitted into just 75 regular Volvo production models. Allstate volunteered some of its top executives and sales representatives as guinea pigs. A mechanical autopsy Volvo performed on Chandler's wreckage in Sweden several weeks after the accident confirmed that the airbags in Joe Howell's car functioned exactly as designed. Electro-mechanical sensors developed in Germany immediately detected the sudden deceleration and set off tiny explosions inside metal canisters called "inflators," located in each of the Volvo's airbag modules. A solid rocket propellant called sodium azide ignited and instantly forced nitrogen gas out of each inflator and into two tightly packed cloth bags. The cushions unfolded and inflated in milliseconds – faster than a person can blink.

One shot out of the steering wheel toward Chandler; the other instantly ballooned into the space between Nora and the windshield. The rough cloth skinned Chandler's forearms as his head and slim torso shot forward, but the bag absorbed crash forces that would otherwise have shattered his skull and snapped his ribs. Nora flew sideways into her much larger bag and suffered only a slight cut on her chin. Harriette, in the back seat, was not seriously hurt.

The police refused to believe Chandler was not injured in such a violent crash. They drove him to the closest hospital and left him there, with a speeding ticket crammed into the back pocket of his skin-tight jeans. He was not cited for failing to wear his seatbelt. Virginia law did not require it.

In addition to the airbags, Volvo also built another innovation, a crash sensor, into Joe Howell's company car. Its data and technical analysis of the wreck left no doubt. Without those airbags, both Chandler and Nora surely would have died.

For Joe, Chandler's miraculous survival was God's way of telling him he was right about airbags all along. For him and his employer, the new safety requirement would be a crusade across every branch and level of government, not just another corporate lobbying campaign. Still, Joe knew some airbag opponents were frothing at the mouth.

"Weird things started happening even before I crashed the car," Chandler, who still lives in suburban Washington, D.C., remembered in 2016. In 1976, one airbag-hater started leaving menacing messages on the Howell's answering machine. *"Stop pushing airbags, or we'll take out YOU AND YOUR WHOLE FAMILY."* Joe's other company car – the one Chandler didn't wreck – was an airbag-equipped Oldsmobile Delta 88. The behemoth mysteriously disappeared from the Howell's driveway one night.

"We joked that it was [Ford's then-president] Lee Iacocca who stole the Olds," Chandler laughed.

Joe reported increasingly chilling threats and the Federal Bureau of Investigation stepped in. They bugged the Howell's home phone and assigned an investigator.

"We called the FBI agent 'Hot Shot,'" Chandler added with a grin. "He was so thorough, he would go knock on the doors of girlfriends who called me at two in the morning to make sure they weren't goons in disguise."

The death threats turned out to be nothing more than an annoyance. Chandler, by his own estimation, went on to be "quite famous for about 20 years" because his accident was featured in "drivers ed" videos, television news reports and a film Allstate made. When he landed a summer job at Allstate's headquarters in Northbrook, Illinois, coworkers were impressed that the company's exalted Executive Vice President and General Counsel, Donald Schaffer, threw young Chandler a friendly nod every time their paths crossed.

Schaffer persuaded his company to hire its own automotive engineering director, Jack Martens, to help penetrate the Big Three's constant technical smokescreen. He also got help from former GM President, John DeLorean, to convince the general car-buying public that airbags were a "cool" way to get back to the future. In 1976, when Congress cooked up the "two-house" veto to block airbags and other auto safety initiatives, Schaffer took out full-page ads in the *New York Times* and other national publications. He would have bought television commercials, too, but the manufacturers were the TV networks' mainstay advertisers. They refused to air Allstate's pro-airbag ads.

1981

Washington

In 1981, Schaffer was back on the front lines, with Nationwide, Liberty and other big insurers and industry groups finally behind him. To prepare for the new battles, he and J. Charles Bruse, a dapper young Nebraskan Schaffer hired when Joe Howell retired from Allstate, were fitting me out with combat gear. They stressed how important it was for the historically pro-safety Senate Commerce Committee – especially Senator Danforth and me – to use the ammunition the insurance industry had accumulated; otherwise, vehicle safety would fade from the public consciousness, thousands more people would die needlessly each year, hundreds of thousands would be crippled and a fundamental objective of the 1966 Vehicle Safety Act would be lost forever. Consumers would be back in the 1950s.

Shaffer had good reason to be fearful. Transportation Secretary Drew Lewis, just days into his new job in the Reagan Administration, quickly ordered a one-year delay in the compliance date for Carter's leftover "FINAL" RULE NUMBER FIVE. It required airbags or other "passive restraints" in cars that were about to start rolling off the assembly lines that summer. There was no dispute that Lewis' delay would kill at least 600 Americans and seriously injure 4,300 others.[12] Lewis ignored a cost-benefit analysis prepared by William Nordhaus, a respected Yale economist. It showed costs for the one-year slip outstripping benefits five-to-one.

Raymond A. Peck, Jr., a former coal industry lawyer and functionary in the Nixon and Ford administrations, was nominated to be NHTSA Administrator. As early as April 1981, he started making noises about rescinding the mandate. Peck held public hearings on August 5 and 6, 1981, when Congress began its summer break. Right on cue, the manufacturers showed up with a new story. Airbags were off the table, they swore. Even if the Reagan Administration did not kill the "passive restraint" mandate, Ford and GM suddenly said they would comply only by installing what they called an "automatic seatbelt." The American airbag suppliers declared their great American invention a "dying product."[13]

Volkswagen pioneered "automatic seatbelts" in its smallest American imports, even though it joined Detroit in vehemently opposing any passive restraints mandate. Straps typically ran from the middle of the car doors to spools between two front bucket seats. The straps retracted and locked as the driver or passenger closed the door. Some automatic belts were designed to be easily and completely detached by pinching a buckle, supposedly to allay fears about being trapped in a sinking or burning car. With no ignition interlock, "passive" belts would be so easily "detachable" that usage could end up the same as traditional manual belts – about 15 percent.

While the manufacturers were testifying, Danforth was in Missouri and I was in China on a trip related to my additional responsibility as his national defense advisor. When we returned to Washington, the airbag lobby was downcast. They were particularly disappointed that State Farm seemed to doubt the projected benefits of airbags because they said they would not discount insurance premiums for airbag cars until they could be justified by real-world "claims experience."

Administrator Peck quickly seized upon the carmakers' stated preference for easily "detachable automatic belts." He went on a purported vacation in Colorado, 2,000 miles distant from NHTSA's headquarters in Washington, and wrote a public notice rescinding the Carter Administration's leftover "FINAL" RULE NUMBER FIVE. Peck declared himself "uncertain" how much good detachable automatic belts would do and cited nothing more than his guesswork as the basis to shrug off 15 years' worth of research, negotiations and debate.

Peck returned from his "vacation" on a Saturday and dragged senior NHTSA officials into the office to hear his pronouncement. The agency's head of rulemaking told Peck to his face that his rationale was "stupid." Flanked by his own Reagan-appointed "special counsel" and future Takata lawyer, Erika Z. Jones, Peck announced rescission of the mandate at a news conference on October 23, 1981. Peck promised an expensive new advertising campaign to promote wider use of "active" seat belts without explaining why his campaign would succeed where all prior efforts had failed miserably. After dropping his deadly bombshell in Washington, Peck immediately flew to Europe. He claimed he was putting a "full-court press" on carmakers to install airbags. All of them, of course, trashed their plans for any type of automatic crash protection the minute Peck rescinded the rule and laughed up their sleeves at Peck's charade. Airbag-makers across the western world abandoned the business. Takata, in stark contrast, hedged its bets by dusting off its own, five-year old, rudimentary airbag research and development files.

After Peck's airbag "show trial," Danforth's conversations with Secretary Lewis grew awkward when we were more-or-less busking for federal grants for rail and airport projects in St. Louis. Every time Lewis was generous with the pork, I wondered how much of it was advance penance for stiffing us on airbags. I kept a draft bill to overturn any rescission order in my back pocket most of that Fall. It came in handy when, late on a Friday afternoon, after he unveiled his "stupid" rationale to NHTSA staff, a smug Peck phoned me to say he had killed the rule. Danforth introduced the bill that afternoon and immediately went on national television to denounce Peck's decision. Republicans and Democrats from non-auto manufacturing states cosponsored the legislation. None of us suffered any delusions about resurrecting legislatively either the airbag mandate or the people Peck had killed with the stroke of a pen. Even if the Senate passed our bill, we would still have to beat Rep. John Dingell (D-MI), who chaired the House Energy and Commerce Committee with an iron gavel and did Detroit's dirty work on every issue.

I was flattered when President Reagan felt compelled to announce he would veto our airbag mandate restoration bill if we ever managed to pass it. Danforth, too, was undeterred. He introduced legislation in his other power perch, the Finance Committee, echoing Nader's 1960s tax-incentive proposal. Each airbag car would earn its manufacturer a $300 tax credit; cars without airbags would suffer a $300 excise tax. Insurers supported the new angle in two days of Finance Committee hearings I put together in early 1982. The new Danforth bill sidestepped automatic belts and focused on the true safety innovation, the airbag. Moderates on the tax-writing committee gave Danforth a pat on the distinctive shock of white that ran across the top of his otherwise dark brown hair, but little else.

Peck was busy collecting more enemies. He killed State Farm's pet project, a rule to strengthen bumpers, and cancelled public information programs that were designed to inform consumers about the relative crashworthiness of various cars. NHTSA's investigations into safety defects that might require recalls also ground to a halt and the agency's staff roster began falling by more than a quarter over five years, from 874 to 640 people.

Peck's hatchet job on NHTSA embarrassed even the most strident advocates of "regulatory relief." The vehicle manufacturers' stone wall cracked on March 3, 1982, when a letter from Mercedes Benz landed on my desk. It broke the news to Senator Danforth that all 1984 Mercedes models would be equipped with a driver-side airbag. The Germans stressed that their "face bag" would merely supplement their well-designed three-point seat belt but the decision was a turning point in the war over airbags.

Danforth boiled with frustration, but he was keenly aware of the power of "the bully pulpit." The priest in Danforth decided it was time to rain down some hellfire and damnation. He instructed me to set up a NHTSA oversight hearing on March 31, 1982, and write a powerful opening statement.

"I want *an indictment*," Jack stressed as we sprinted up the Capitol steps for a floor vote a few days before the hearing. "And I mean *an indictment*." Missouri's former "top cop" held both hands up and brought them down in a double-chopping motion. I dodged into a Library of Congress outpost in the Senate Wing of the Capitol that offered a breathtaking westward view of the National Mall. I scratched out a statement that minced no words.

When the big day arrived, I took my place in the center of the tightly U-shaped dais in the Commerce hearing room, within ear-whispering distance of the chairman. It was my first experience on the receiving end of so many clicking/whizzing cameras and blinding klieg lights. I gulped, probably out loud, and stared over Jack's shoulder at Peck, who sat alone at the witness table 20 feet away. Two rows behind Peck, I could see Ralph Nader, waiting gravely for his turn to testify. Directly behind Nader sat my wife, Victoria, who was preparing a report on the hearing for the National Transportation Safety Board, where she was a Reagan staff appointee.

Danforth cracked the gavel and began his opening statement. He recounted NHTSA's history as "an aggressive force for safety," a watchdog against dangerous defects and a driving force in "promoting the advancement of safety technology and in helping American consumers understand the tradeoff between increased fuel economy and safety."[14]

Peck kept a straight face while Jack criticized him for replacing the agency's "can-do" spirit with an "un-do" spirit. He slouched in the witness chair while Danforth accused him of committing mayhem. "No one seriously denies that [Peck's order], which overruled the actions of previous Republican and Democratic Administrations alike, will result in the deaths of over 9,000 Americans a year and the disfigurement of countless others."

Danforth went on to endorse a lawsuit the insurers had filed to invalidate Peck's rescission order. The federal appeals court in Washington, D.C., Danforth said, had received "overwhelming evidence that the rule would have saved thousands of lives and lifted a heavy burden from the shoulders of the taxpayer." As for NHTSA's budget request for the coming fiscal year, Danforth said he saw no reason to appropriate a dime to an agency that was "systematically … terminating one rule after another and … replacing the former approach with nothing." The big question on his mind, he said, was "whether there should be a hearing on the sunsetting [i.e., dissolution] of NHTSA."

When Danforth invited Peck to commence his own testimony, the accused Administrator grinned and replied with a one-liner.

"Aside from that, Mr. Chairman, are we doing OK?"

Every jaw in the crowded hearing room dropped, but no sound echoed off the marble walls. After several seconds, Danforth leaned forward.

"Pardon?" he said.

Peck shifted forward in his seat and doubled down with a "you-heard-me" sneer.

"Aside from that, are we doing OK?"

Danforth paused long enough to summon his deepest minister's voice.

"You – tell – me."

Peck bloviated for several minutes about "management improvements" he intended to make at the agency without directly denying any accusation in Danforth's "indictment." The Republican chairman's Episcopalian version of fire-and-brimstone got major play on every television network news program that night. The word was out across the world. Airbags were not a partisan issue and they were not about to go down quietly. The mandate would be a vaccine against the scourge of auto accidents. But airbag supporters faced a bigger and more immediate need.

How could they inoculate the rule itself against constant attacks by the auto industry?

1983

Washington

The media associated airbags almost exclusively with Ralph Nader and a couple of organizations he founded. Public Citizen, which opened in 1971, was run by former NHTSA Administrator Joan Claybrook in 1981. Another lawyer, Clarence Ditlow, ran a more focused Nader affiliate, the Center for Auto Safety, for decades, until his death in 2017.

Nader, understandably, was apoplectic to see the airbag mandate flat-out killed 15 years after passage of the Motor Vehicle Safety Act, but he had largely worn out his welcome in Republican and Democratic administrations alike. For example, at the 1976 public hearings, Nader called William Coleman, President Ford's Transportation Secretary and the first black man in that job, a coward who was doing for auto safety what the Ku Klux Klan did for civil rights.[15] The attack was a low blow against a man whose mostly white high school disbanded its swimming team rather than allow Coleman – young, athletic and black – in their pool.

During the Carter Administration, Claybrook agreed to a political compromise that would phase airbags in over three years after a four-year delay. Nader called on Claybrook, his strident, hand-picked NHTSA administrator, to resign and then sued to block her decision.

Just months before Danforth "indicted" Peck, Nader had vehemently attacked his wealthy former Princeton schoolmate as "anti-consumer" during a bitter, one-on-one debate that was broadcast live on a St. Louis radio station in October 1980. With debate prep from a 31-year old, Yale-educated legislative counsel named Clarence Thomas, Danforth stood his ground. Just 15 months later, when Nader's turn came to testify before Danforth's subcommittee in Washington, Nader gave Jack no credit for opposing Reagan. Instead, consistent with a prediction future Supreme Court Justice Thomas shared with me the day before the hearing, Nader chided Danforth for floating my ironic suggestion that Congress should de-fund NHTSA to keep Peck from doing any more damage.

In an era when it was considered bad form to shower Cabinet officials in personal insults during a Senate hearing, Nader snidely referred to Secretary Lewis as "the Secretary of Penn Central" who had "duties other than auto safety to fully occupy his limited, one-track managerial abilities." Nader supported radical policy positions, arguing even after Reagan was elected that manufacturers should be required to install airbags that would be effective in 50 mile-per-hour crashes.

Nader had by then shifted his focus to court challenges, a new line of trenches in the airbag war that required little in the way of personal diplomacy. After the Nixon Administration issued "FINAL" RULE NUMBER ONE in 1971, Chrysler asked a federal court in the Midwest to overturn it. It offered the first opportunity for federal judges to interpret the Vehicle Safety Act. Detroit complained that the procedures NHTSA initially established for test dummies were not "objective," as the term was used in the statute, because their necks were inflexible and the agency had not yet established technical criteria for construction of their heads. Two of the three judges on the panel agreed with Chrysler and put the airbag mandate on ice while NHTSA spent another year developing a smarter dummy. Nader's filings in the case prompted the court to issue a crucial dictum.

"The explicit purpose of the [Vehicle Safety] Act, as amplified in the legislative history, is to enable the federal government to impel automobile manufacturers to *develop and apply new technology* to the task," the court emphasized, and to improve "the safety design of the automobile as readily as possible."[16]

When the Carter Administration issued "FINAL" RULE NUMBER FIVE in 1977, a different federal appellate court in Washington, D.C. had to interpret the Vehicle Safety Act.[17] Nader and the Big Three squared off from such completely opposite directions, the court said it confronted "Scylla and Charybdis," the mythological dilemma of being smacked into jagged rocks or sucked down by a whirlpool. The carmakers said the mandate should be overturned because Secretary Adams failed to consider speculation that airbags could be as unpopular as the ignition interlock or the probability that airbags would kill out-of-position children. Nader wanted the opposite result; he expected the judges to reinstate "FINAL" RULE NUMBER FOUR, which applied the mandate to all cars at once instead of allowing a phase-in.

The airbag mandate was still on the books for Reagan to rescind only because the court in Washington, the U.S. Court of Appeals for the D.C. Circuit, unanimously rejected both challenges to the Carter-Claybrook rule. In February 1979, 18 months after NHTSA approved the phase-in, the judges deferred to Secretary Adams' judgment because it was "consistent with the statutory mandate, rational and not arbitrary." The judges added one crucial proviso, however. "[B]ecause the order under review reversed a prior policy, the agency must provide an ... analysis indicating that the standard is being changed and not ignored" and "that it is faithful and *not indifferent to the rule of law*." Secretary Adams' justification for substituting the multi-year phase-in for the "all at once" rule, the court decided, "provided a sufficient explanation why his judgment differed from his predecessor's."

By 1982, Peck's back-of-the-envelope rescission order looked far more vulnerable in court than in Congress. In addition to backing Danforth's bill, Schaffer wanted Allstate to lead a new lawsuit against Peck in the D.C. Circuit. Allstate's Chairman, Archie Boe, complained for years that Schaffer spent too much time and money in Washington on airbags. Schaffer was dismayed when Boe, an ardent Reagan fan, refused to allow Allstate's name on the suit.[18] State Farm, having finally gotten "religion" on the subject, had no such hesitation. The nation's largest writer of car insurance filed its Petition for Review of Peck's order on November 23, 1981. Allstate's trade association, the Independent Insurers, filed its own petition two days later.

By luck of the draw, the *State Farm* case, as it became known to Schaffer's exasperation, was assigned to the three most liberal judges sitting on what is often called "the second highest court in the land." Those three jurists never felt obligated to defer to any executive agency decision that didn't suit their own political tastes. At Danforth's request, I engineered Senate passage of legislation to bar the Transportation Department from litigating the case, so the Motor Vehicle Manufacturers Association took the lead in defending Peck's hatchet job. Three judges heard oral argument on March 1, 1982. I strolled down Constitution Avenue for the occasion and was struck by the divergent presentations by lawyers for State Farm and Allstate's trade association. State Farm rested its case on Peck's failure to modify the rule to alleviate his "uncertainty" about automatic belts by making them more difficult to detach. The Schaffer group insisted that the only solution that fit the statutory purpose was an airbag mandate and Peck had failed to mention, much less consider, the option of imposing one.

Five months later, the judges unanimously issued an aggressive decision reinstating the passive restraint rule, effective with the 1984 models. The U.S. Supreme Court took the case in November 1982. Detroit argued that the Court should review Peck's reversal of prior policy as if it were a decision to issue or not issue a rule in the first place; in other words, the judges could not overturn Peck's rescission order without blatantly substituting their own personal policy preferences for those of the assigned executive branch agency. The insurers argued that courts were not obligated to defer to agency expertise where a substantial record exists, the agency is making a "sharp departure from a settled course" and the action contradicts a statutory purpose.

Based on what I had learned about why Congress unanimously passed the Vehicle Safety Act in 1966, I disagreed with State Farm's approach. The fatal flaw in Peck's rescission order was the absence of any discussion why NHTSA could not set automatic belts aside and flatly require airbags. It was the only true way to advance the state of the art in addressing the "second collision," an essential purpose of the 1966 Act.

During heated discussions about which argument was a more likely winner, State Farm's lawyers scoffed at the "airbag-only" approach almost as derisively as the motor vehicle manufacturers did. They insisted that the only hole in Peck's Death Star was his failure to give rational consideration to making detachable belts non-detachable. Americans had bought almost half a million cars with passive belts between 1975 and 1981 and they had cut the odds of dying in a crash in one of those cars by 50 percent and reduced serious injuries by 65 percent.

Schaffer needed help presenting the legislative history of the 1966 Act to the Supreme Court. He hired me away from my Senate job in January 1983 and put me to work writing that portion of the Allstate group's brief. It was due in just four weeks.

On April 27, 1983, right after Chief Justice Warren Burger swore me in as a member of the Supreme Court Bar, I squirmed in my front-row seat in the Court's hearing room. State Farm was chosen to present oral argument and their lawyer haltingly offered their seat belt argument, not our airbag argument. The Justices grilled State Farm's lawyer but listened politely as U.S. Solicitor General Rex Lee argued the vehicle manufacturers' side.

On June 24, 1983, the Supreme Court unanimously upheld the Court of Appeals' decision to invalidate Peck's rescission order. Justice Byron White wrote for the Court that NHTSA and the manufacturers had it all wrong. Reversal of a well-established policy *was* different from a decision whether to issue a regulation in the first place. Peck was obligated to offer "a reasoned analysis for the change." Justice White, relying heavily on the legislative history I wrote in Schaffer's brief, zeroed in on what he called the "first and most obvious reason" to undo Peck's action. The Court vindicated our argument by repeatedly emphasizing Peck's failure to give any "consideration whatsoever to modifying the standard to require airbag technology to be utilized." The "logical response to the faults of detachable belts," the Court added, "is to require the installation of airbags. At the very least, this alternative ... should have been addressed and adequate reasons given for its abandonment." The legislative history was crucial, Justice White continued, because "under the statute, the agency should not defer to the industry ... [so] it may not revoke a safety standard ... simply because the industry has opted for an ineffective seatbelt design." Then, I was proud to see, the Court endorsed my creed: "The mandatory passive restraint rule *may not be abandoned without any consideration whatsoever of an airbag-only requirement.*"

Schaffer's 9-0 victory over the Reaganauts – and, in a way, over State Farm – was not unvarnished. Instead of reinstating the Court of Appeals' aggressive schedule for implementation of "FINAL" RULE NUMBER FIVE, the Court vacated the lower court's decision and told them to remand (i.e., return) the matter to NHTSA "for further consideration consistent with this [the Supreme Court's] opinion." In other words, President Reagan's political appointees, not a panel of left-wing federal judges, had the ball once again. No one, least of all President Reagan's new Secretary of Transportation, Elizabeth Dole, knew whether to spike it, run with it or pass it like the political time bomb it was.

Even before Secretary Dole set to work, Takata's Washington operatives sent dispatches to Tokyo. Thanks to "the Supremes," a colossal opportunity was about to open up. Detroit had been so certain the Supreme Court would kill the airbag mandate, they had deliberately driven all five of the American suppliers who could compete with Takata out of the airbag business. America's Big Three automakers had lined themselves up like battleships at Pearl Harbor.

1984

Washington

Nothing about Elizabeth Hanford Dole was typical. For starters, she was no standard-issue Senate wife. She had been married to Senator Bob Dole (R-KS) for just eight years when President Reagan appointed her to succeed Drew Lewis as Secretary of Transportation. She had her own, well-established career as a consumer affairs advisor in the Johnson and Nixon Administrations and as a member of the Federal Trade Commission. Nor was she a typical woman of her generation. Female graduates of elite colleges in the late 1950s typically had two career choices, teaching or nursing. Mrs. Dole initially put her political science diploma from Duke University to work as a teacher while she was earning a graduate degree in education, but that was not enough to satisfy the avowed feminist from small-town North Carolina. She was one of 25 women who graduated alongside 525 men in the Harvard Law School Class of 1965.

The "regulatory reformers" in President Reagan's Office of Management and Budget ("OMB") understood the need to strengthen ties with her husband, the new Senate Majority Leader, but were dismayed by Mrs. Dole's appointment as Secretary of Transportation. When the Supremes invalidated the rescission of the passive restraints mandate just six weeks after Secretary Dole took office, OMB panicked. A 9-0 decision against them was inconceivable – until it happened. The White House saw the high court's decision to remand the case to Secretary Dole and not to the Court of Appeals panel that had tried to dictate an early compliance date to NHTSA as a mixed blessing. Secretary Dole, who typically wore a broad smile and spoke with a genteel Southern accent, already was on record that the airbag was "a good safety device" and her husband, in his previous position as chairman of the Senate Finance Committee, had aided but not supported Senator Danforth's pro-airbag initiatives and the quotas on Japanese car imports.

Christopher DeMuth was President Reagan's airbag "hit man." He started college at Harvard when Elizabeth Dole was in the law school, then worked in the Nixon White House for Daniel Patrick Moynihan, the same man who kick-started Ralph Nader's career. Reagan put DeMuth, a respected deep-thinker whose receding hairline made him look more cerebral, in charge of a Regulatory Reform Task Force. A dyed-in-the-wool preppy and University of Chicago Law School graduate who started his career at the vaunted Chicago firm of Sidley & Austin, DeMuth shed no tears when Secretary Dole made Raymond Peck disappear. DeMuth put a like-minded White House staffer, Diane Steed, on the firing line as NHTSA's new Administrator. Steed made sure Erika Jones, who counseled Peck on how to rescind the mandate, was elevated to Chief Counsel, the agency's top legal job.

DeMuth's first order of business was to show Secretary Dole who was boss. The ink was barely dry on the *State Farm* decision when the White House leaked word that DeMuth's Task Force, not Secretary Dole, would decide what proceedings would be "consistent" with the Court's opinion. The most urgent assignment for Steed and Jones was to cook up a winning alternative to the "stupid" rationale Peck offered for rescinding the safety standard.

Danforth felt emboldened by the Supreme Court decision despite his near-political-death experience in the 1982 election. When he became chairman of the full Commerce Committee, Detroit was horrified. Danforth was happy to see the Supreme

Court recognize that airbags, not other sorts of "passive restraints," were the only true advancement in safety technology. He was frustrated, however, by the Supreme Court's refusal to make NHTSA stop spinning its regulatory wheels. Danforth kicked off his Commerce chairmanship by introducing legislation to require airbags in all 1986 model cars. Senators on the committee approved a compromise bill to require every carmaker to offer airbags in at least one of their 1986 models. The bill did not pass the Senate but Danforth pressed Steed to assure his committee that Secretary Dole, not the Task Force, would make the decision on reinstatement of the passive restraints standard. From the White House, DeMuth admitted only that, as an appointee to the President's Cabinet, Secretary Dole's opinion "carried great weight."

GM's chairman, Roger Smith, picked up immediately on DeMuth's cue. He urged Secretary Dole to forget about airbags. Allstate's Don Schaffer also was emboldened by the Supreme Court decision. He urged Dole to ignore Smith, who "cancelled the GM airbag program and caused GM to submit the strategy upon which the rescission of the safety standard was based." Schaffer met personally with Administrator Steed and threatened to haul NHTSA back into court if she did not enforce quickly the already 10-year old "final" passive restraints rule.

Secretary Dole knew a political and legal minefield when she saw one. To buy time, she held yet another round of public hearings. This time, instead of giving lip-service to automatic belts, safety advocates began to say out loud that airbags were the only sensible answer. The manufacturers, foreign and domestic, clung to their 20-year old argument that the best solution would be to persuade or force people to buckle up. Administrator Steed manipulated downward the agency's calculations about the potential benefits of airbags and hinted that NHTSA might, despite the *State Farm* ruling, rescind the safety standard again. NHTSA did nothing in response to the *State Farm* decision until almost two years had passed since Peck's illegal cancellation of the rule.

Sixteen months and thousands of dead motorists later, with DeMuth still trying to "end-run" the Supreme Court decision, Secretary Dole gave the agency just one more month to issue a final rule. The OMB ideologues considered it essential to flip the Supreme Court a middle finger, so Dole went straight to "the

Gipper" himself in June 1984. Anticipating the need for policy triage, Dole kept a neurosurgeon, who also happened to be a buddy of First Lady Nancy Reagan, in her limo, idling on the White House grounds. She did not need to call in the doctor. Reagan personally blessed her solution. Over the following 15 years, airbags prevented 37,000 fatalities in car crashes.[19]

"We saved a lot of people's lives!" Dole proudly remarked to me in 2019.

The "Dole Rule," was published on July 11, 1984, smack in the heat of Reagan's re-election campaign. Her "FINAL" RULE NUMBER 6 was Solomonic; the baby was cut cleanly in half. If the carmakers were so cocksure higher seat belt usage rates would stem the carnage on the highways, she figured, why not give them a chance to prove it? If they could subject two-thirds of the American population to mandatory seat belt use laws before April Fool's Day, 1989 – a date by which Reagan would no longer be in office – Dole decided, "the need for automatic occupant restraints would be obviated."[20] Dole placed a trap door under the passive restraint standard; all Detroit had to do was pull the lever. If the manufacturers failed, however, Dole decided that it would kick in – *six years* after the *State Farm* decision.

As a matter of law and policy, of course, the Dole Rule looked ridiculous. Seat belts – whether manual or passive – and airbags were never mutually exclusive, given NHTSA's consistent estimate that a driver protected by *both* devices had a 15 percent better chance of surviving a crash. Nor was the Dole Rule in any fashion "consistent" with the Supreme Court mandate. If the agency was prohibited from deferring to industry's choice of an ineffective seat belt technology, how could Secretary Dole get away with a rule that depended on industry's success in persuading state legislatures to enact unquestionably less effective manual seat belt use laws? NHTSA's docket was bursting with proof that drivers could not be forced to buckle up. If Peck was irrational not to consider requiring airbags, how could Dole give no consideration to a rule promoting both airbags *and* a state buckle-up initiative?

On the other hand, the rule Secretary Dole imposed turned out to be a masterpiece of practical politics. For 20 years, Detroit had embroiled every level of the Executive Branch, nearly every member of Congress and every level of the federal judiciary in the motor vehicle safety war. Now the Dole Rule invited them to recruit to their cause every governor, every state supreme court justice and every state legislator. Dole also promised Detroit a $20 million matching grant for their "Traffic Safety Now," "click-it-or-ticket" campaign, but the carmakers fell flat on their collective face.

Instead of waiting for the manufacturers to blow their last chance to kill the passive restraints rule, safety advocates went back to court. State Farm's lawyers offered a cogent oral argument why the Dole Rule was inconsistent with the Supreme Court's dictates. Victory was in sight until one member of the three-judge panel, the likely deciding vote in their favor, suddenly died. He was replaced by then-Judge, later Supreme Court Justice Antonin Scalia, who concluded that the 17-year old legal potboiler was not "ripe" for decision, even three-and-a-half years after *State Farm* was decided. Then-Judge, later "Monica-gate" Special Prosecutor, Kenneth Starr agreed with Scalia that Secretary Dole's "buckle-up" challenge to the manufacturers should be allowed to run its course.

The Dole Rule drove some safety advocates insane. The National Safety Council lobbied state governments to water down their seat belt use laws to make them too weak for Dole to count them toward dropping the trap door. Less-effective state laws meant more deaths and injuries, not fewer. State Farm took an even nuttier approach. Their state lobbyists wrote "poison pills" into laws that passed in 16 states. If Dole counted them as "wins" for the carmakers, the mandatory seatbelt use requirements automatically would be repealed.

By the time Secretary Dole left office in 1987, the handwriting was on the wall, writ plenty large for people in Japan to see it. The car manufacturers' click-it-or-ticket campaign was faltering. Chairman Danforth grilled Mrs. Dole's successor, James Burnley, until he agreed at his confirmation hearing that "the passive restraints rule is going to be implemented." The carmakers still insisted that this meant almost half of the 1989 models would have automatic belts, not airbags. During the phase-in, however, Secretary Dole threw Senator Danforth a bone. The Reagan Administration officially conceded that "airbags work well in non-catastrophic frontal collisions," with 100% usage instead of the 12.5% usage rate with manual belts. Americans would suffer far fewer brain and facial injuries.

The new rule involved some complicated math, but Dole arranged for manufacturers who chose to install more airbags in place of automatic belts to get "extra credit" and still meet their phase-in quotas. Suddenly, the manufacturers who swore in 1982 they would install zero airbags were searching desperately for airbag suppliers. Mercedes, the first car maker to break ranks by installing "face bags" in their 1984 models, bought their systems from a German company, Petri AG. Takata immediately bought Petri. By the 1986 model year, Takata's German-designed driver airbags were standard equipment in every new Mercedes.

Ford Motor Company shocked the automotive world by putting driver-side airbags in two of its "plain Jane" models, the 1985 Tempo and the 1986 Topaz. There was a catch, however. Ford expected relief from the passive restraint requirement on the passenger side, where it continued to harbor deep concerns about the risk of airbags killing children. It wanted permission to install only manual lap belts in those models. Joan Claybrook and other Naderites, having been repeatedly burned by manufacturers' unfulfilled promises to install airbags, saw Ford's proposal as a Trojan Horse and opposed it bitterly. For once, Danforth bucked the Nader forces, but only after extracting from Ford a solemn promise to make airbags standard in one million cars, starting with their 1989 Lincoln Continental and expanding across 11 more car lines in 1990.

Chairman Danforth was sympathetic with Ford in part because no other carmaker had been so relentlessly "snake-bit" when it came to vehicle safety. Its 1956 marketing campaign featured safety equipment, including optional seat belts. Ford was unable, however, to find a supplier who could make enough of them, so thousands of safety-minded moms and dads left Ford showrooms disappointed. Even worse, GM's Chevrolet brand beat the daylights out of Ford's sales that year. The lesson became industry Scripture: "safety doesn't sell." In the Summer of 1969, when Ford was Detroit's biggest proponent of airbags, the company geared up for a "boffo" media event. Television cameras were ready to roll when Stuart Frey, the company's chief body engineer, demonstrated the deployment of an airbag in a front seat mockup. Frey hit the trigger and millions of TV viewers saw … *nothing happen*! Yes, people thought, Ford really does stand for

"Fix Or Repair Daily." Another Ford engineer compounded the damage when he quipped that the best way to reduce traffic fatalities would be to install a Claymore mine (a type of bomb) under every driver's seat and wire it to explode if his vehicle got into an accident. Everyone, he estimated, would drive more safely. The ignition interlock, the most reviled safety device since the chastity belt, was also Ford's idea.

Chrysler, too, jumped on the bandwagon with its late-80s models. Lee Iacocca, who almost single-handedly spiked the Nixon Administration's airbag requirement in 1971, had a Road to Damascus moment on his way to the presidency of Chrysler. To everyone's amazement, Iacocca spent a fortune on a pro-airbag ad campaign. His slogan: "Who says you can't teach an old dog new tricks?" Airbags were standard equipment for drivers and front-seat passengers in the company's 1988 models.

On March 12, 1990, two airbag-equipped Chrysler Le-Barons crashed into each other, head on, in Culpeper, Virginia. One driver wore a seatbelt; the other did not. Both men walked away from the accident without serious injury. The media went crazy for survivor stories and Iacocca was deluged with fan mail.

Volvo was another early airbag adopter. In 1987, years ahead of Secretary Dole's deadline for passive restraints, all of its cars had airbags. In 1988, after State Farm finally joined Allstate and other insurers in discounting premiums for airbag-equipped cars, the number of new airbag vehicles jumped from 480,000 of the 1989 models to 3.3 million of the 1990 models. By 1990, opinion polls revealed a tectonic shift in car buyers' attitudes. The slogan "safety doesn't sell" finally was discredited. To the contrary, crash protection had become the customer's most important factor in choosing a new car.

Fully 35 years after Nader floated the airbag idea in *Unsafe at Any Speed*, 30 years after NHTSA proposed a passive restraints requirement and seven years after the Supreme Court slapped down the Reagan Administration's cancellation of the safety standard, airbag supporters won the war. Japan watched – and mobilized. By the 1994 model year, full-frontal airbags were in only 50 percent of GM's new cars but 100 percent of new Hondas. Takata struggled to meet wave after wave of Honda orders for airbags.

1990s

Washington

One of the facts I presented to Senator Danforth in preparation for his first auto safety hearing in 1981 was both incontestable and horrifying. There was no doubt – properly functioning airbags would kill some people.

Detroit's lobbyists harped on that point. They pestered me constantly to watch films they made early in the 1970s showing front seat occupants – youngsters, mostly – being smashed to death during the "punch-out" phase of an airbag deployment. The stars of those disgusting videos were live baboons, not humans, but the point came across like an inflating airbag – the equivalent of a 2,000-pound anvil hitting your face at 210 miles per hour. The videos tracked known, human behaviors. Lots of petite women hugged their steering wheels. Kids who were not belted had plenty of room in enormous American cars to stand up on seats and floorboards. Even in low-speed collisions, their heads and chests would be in exactly the same space where an airbag was being inflated by rocket fuel exhaust. GM released a report in 1974 to document the fractured ribs, fatal brain and neck trauma and punctured aortas people would suffer, especially in a 10- or 15-mile per hour collision that otherwise would not produce any serious injuries.

Lobbyists for the few American companies that were still in the airbag business in 1981 told Danforth not to worry about what those poor baby baboons were telling us. The defense-contractors-cum-airbag makers were developing, among other solutions, new gas-generation systems that would move people out of the way of the "hard" inflation that was necessary to protect an unbelted adult in the milliseconds following a crash. On-board computers could use mathematical formulas called "algorithms" to gauge the severity of a crash, detect the presence and weight of a passenger and adjust the force and timing of the explosion accordingly. Even small cars would not be a problem, they said.

Senator Danforth recognized the downside of airbags. The technology was a type of vaccine, he concluded. The overall societal benefits would outstrip the devastation a few people would suffer. The auto safety vaccine-makers would, with some encouragement from government, minimize the number of people who ended up "taking one for the team."

Even in 1981, the solutions for "punch-out" deaths were not entirely theoretical. One simple idea was to design the airbag to inflate more like a flat pillow and less like a basketball. After tests in some 1972 Impalas, GM fielded its "Air Cushion Restraint System" in 1,000 vehicles. It was the world's first "smart airbag." If the vehicle was travelling at a low speed and hit different types of barriers, or if it was travelling faster and crashed in certain circumstances, the airbag would deploy in two separate stages, with a gentler pushback ahead of the forceful punch-out. It worked well in Oldsmobiles, Buicks and Cadillacs made from 1974 through 1976.

By the time President Reagan was inaugurated, GM had gone full circle. They and other masters of Detroit's universe decided the best way to avoid the passive restraints mandate was to force the five American companies who made airbags out of the business. By 1990, domestic airbag makers were essentially non-existent.

Airbags imported from Japan and Europe started killing people in 1990, the year they first became available. By 1993, they had killed 26 infants and little children in otherwise survivable accidents – the same death count as the 26 people killed by Takata airbag explosions through 2019.[21] At first, passenger airbags were a much bigger problem than driver-side bags. For several years, they killed more children than they saved. Airbag deaths among children under age 10 were one-third higher than what Detroit warned Congress about in 1982. The airbag death toll in "very low-speed" accidents reached 175 in 1999 and 239 by 2002. Detroit's baby baboon snuff films *understated* the risk; they did not predict that airbags would kill a child every week of the year, but that's what happened. The dead children included a seven-year old who was killed in a ten-mile per hour collision, an infant in a car seat who died in a minor parking lot accident and a one-year old whose severed head was blasted out of a car window in 1996.

Juries in wrongful death suits almost never blamed the car manufacturer for death-by-airbag.

Children weren't the only people "taking one for the team." The *Detroit Free Press* reported in 1997 that "one-third of motorists involved in airbag deployments are hurt by the bag ... [including] some broken bones – and even a few deaths." No worries, though; the paper reminded readers that "some people get polio from the polio vaccine."[22]

Chairman Danforth stuck with the vaccine theory. In the months before he retired from the Senate at the end of 1994, he aimed for a new "passive restraint" rule that would treat SUVs and light trucks just like passenger cars. He forced NHTSA to convert the rule into the first-ever airbag-only safety standard and to hasten its implementation.

After feasting on stories casting airbags as a panacea, the media finally started noticing airbag deaths. By 1998, airbags had killed 40 drivers – three-fourths of whom were women – and 65 passengers, almost all of them infants or little children. By 2004, the total number of driver deaths had doubled and adult passengers were more frequently meeting the same grotesque fate as so many little children.

Soon after Danforth retired, the Senate Commerce Committee asked NHTSA to explain why airbags were killing so many people. As it did with the ignition interlock years earlier, the agency passed the problem off as a mere "quality control" issue. For example, NHTSA left it to the manufacturers to decide whether airbags should actuate in a 10 mile-per-hour crash or in an 18 mile-per-hour collision. The manufacturers, however, blamed NHTSA. The technical standards were based entirely on keeping an average-sized, unbelted man – five feet, nine inches tall, 167 pounds – alive if his car were to hit a concrete barrier at 30 miles-per-hour. With that technical criterion, there was no way to avoid a "hard" inflation. Nader's Center for Auto Safety argued that such an inflexible standard achieved the greatest social good, even if it meant "the deaths of a significant number of children."[23] NHTSA's initial solution was to modify the test to "pass" a car in which the average man lives after a 25 (not 30) mile-per-hour crash. NHTSA also invited car owners, for the first time, to apply for permission to deactivate their airbags. The associated red tape meant almost no one took a deactivation permission slip to their dealer who, out of liability concerns, typically would refuse the job.

Instead of saying "we told you so," the vehicle manufacturers doubled down in favor of airbags. The benefit of "depowering" the test standard to 25 miles-per-hour showed up in 1998, when "only" 48 Americans "took one for the team." Two dozen died from hard punch-outs in 1999, 18 in 2000, nine in 2001 and six in 2002. Foreign airbag manufacturers re-engineered the "smart" airbag systems that GM installed in thousands of cars in the 1970s. Picking up where American rocket scientists left off, the Japanese and Europeans led NHTSA toward standards and test protocols for sensors that recognized circumstances where the punch-out needed to be stepped down. These "smart" systems, resurrected from 1970s designs, were required in all new cars by model year 2007.

Japanese carmakers, especially Honda, were keenly interested. After years hating airbags with almost as much passion as his competitors in Detroit, Soichiro Honda had a brainstorm: Honda could do with airbags what other Japanese had already done with cars, radios and a host of other popular consumer goods. They would set someone up to make them smaller, cheaper and more fuel-efficient. Takata was right next door.

PART 4

Empire of the Son

1933

Shiga Prefecture (Near Kyoto), Japan

Takezo Takada was in the right place at the right time. The entrepreneurial weaver, whose surname translates to "high rice paddy," started his woven fabrics company in 1933, in the southwest corner of Honshu, Japan's main island, just before the Imperial Japanese Army set out to conquer the world. The parachute was one of his product lines. He made sure the fabric was folded right and tight and would inflate as soon as the user pulled the ripcord, which he also manufactured. Takada developed a reputation for making extremely reliable products. The Empire of the Sun bought millions of them, so Takezo Takada became extremely wealthy.

Like many businesses that enabled the Axis powers of World War II, Takata Corporation scrubbed its company history of insight into its dealings with the Imperial Japanese Army. Its website always implied that not much happened between 1933 and 1952. In 1945, when Japan capitulated unconditionally to Allied forces, Tokyo's demand for parachutes disappeared. The company desperately needed a peacetime, woven fabric product line and Takada knew just where to find one. He flew to the United States in the early 1950s, where a post-war baby boom helped drive an even bigger boom in auto manufacturing. By 1952, Detroit commanded the largest car market on Earth. More than six million new cars and trucks hit American roads that year while the entire, densely populated nation of Japan produced fewer than 40,000.

Nobody ever heard of an airbag in the early 1950s. The whole subject of crash protection was taboo. Detroit so abhorred the idea of installing seat belts, they went out of their way to include no structure for anchoring them. Takezo Takada foresaw big changes. He was convinced his parachute-weaving technology could be adapted to seat belts, if American carmakers could ever be convinced to install them. He waited and watched as Cornell and other universities in America published research showing how many young Americans were dying or spending the rest of their lives in wheelchairs after their cars stopped and their own fragile bodies did not.

In November 1956 Takezo Takada established Takata Kojo Corporation. Four years later, he started making the world's first "two-point" lap belts for automobiles. Takata Kojo and the Japanese government started touting the benefits and quality of Takata seat belts in 1962. Takata wowed the global media and a growing cadre of American auto-safety researchers in 1963, when it started rolling cars down roller-coaster tracks and crashing them at a test facility in Takada's hometown, Hikoni, Japan. Toyota, a car company three years younger than Takata, was not interested. Mass production of seat belts for automobiles began with orders from Honda, a five-year old motorcycle maker that started manu-facturing cars that year. In 1965, when American carmakers were just starting to yield to state legislators' demands for seat belts as optional equipment, Takata focused worldwide attention on its ground-breaking use of crash-test dummies. Unlike American teenage boys, the Japanese dummies did not get ejected when their car hit a barrier.

Takezo Takada was not the only Japanese businessman who kept his finger on the pulse of the American car market. Saburo Koboyashi, a square-faced engineer who earned a graduate degree from the University of California-Berkeley after the war, held increasingly powerful positions at Honda for 34 years and devised the strategic plan that transformed the backwater motor-bike manufacturer into the world's biggest automaker. Koboyashi did for Japan's reconstruction what Ferry Porsche, the engineer and son of Beetle inventor Ferdinand Porsche, did to make Volks-wagen a major driver in Germany's post-war resurgence.

From his first days as General Manager of Honda's Cor-porate Planning Division until his retirement in 2005, Koboyashi focused on the pot of gold awaiting Honda on the other side of the Pacific Ocean. The American market was so huge, American drivers had to be conquered by any means necessary. Koboyashi watched patiently, noting not just technological developments in automotive engineering but also the uniquely American changes in the regulatory environment, especially related to safety requirements. From half a world away, he closely observed the doings of a few guys from New York and Connecticut – most prominently, author and lawyer Ralph Nader; policy wonk, all-around political gadfly and future U.S. Senator Daniel Patrick Moynihan (D-NY); U.S. Senator Abraham Ribicoff (D-CT); and an emergency room physician named Dr. William Haddon, Jr. Their work convinced the U.S. Congress to do something no government ever considered – to regulate motor vehicle safety design on a national scale. Those four Americans set out to force Detroit, which made a big show of pooh-poohing the implications of Takata's seat belt crash tests, to develop and install new safety technology.

When Congress unanimously passed the Motor Vehicle Safety Act in 1966, the new law excited people all over the world. Americans saw new hope for public health and safety. Japanese industrialists, however, saw it as a wide-open invitation to challenge Detroit's hegemony over the American car market. Japan's miraculous recovery from wartime devastation resulted mostly from taking aim at American manufacturers of almost every product American consumers desired, then beating them at their own game. Japan gave Yankees transistor radios and other gadgets that were smaller and cheaper than American products.

The moment American legislators required the installation of seat belts and began talking about airbags, Koboyashi recognized an opening for Honda, especially if he could recruit other Japanese companies to supply necessary components on the cheap. His foresight – particularly his recognition that woven fabrics would play a key role – changed the world, especially for the Japanese company that supplied Honda's seat belts. The opportunity to sell two manual lap belts for the front seat of every new American car was pure gold. Within a few years, Takata made the only seat belts that could pass a 32 mile-per-hour crash test.

In December 1983, barely six months after an historic U.S. Supreme Court decision assured the eventual implementation of a mandate to install airbags in American cars, Takezo Takada formed Takata Corporation. Within just six years, the company started making driver airbag modules in Japan, then opened a seat belt factory in Michigan. In 1989, it opened TK Holdings, Inc., a beachhead for the Japanese invasion of the American airbag market. Takata's Automotive Systems Laboratory, Inc., a Michigan facility for developing airbag inflators and "modules" (complete airbag systems, ready to wire into steering wheels and dash panels) got started right away. Takata and European companies quickly put the few remaining American airbag manufacturers out of business. Before the end of 1991, Takata was making airbag inflators at a remote Rocket Research Corporation plant in Moses Lake, Washington. By 2012, Takata had bought out six competetors in the United States and Germany. At the company's zenith in 2015, more than 80 percent of its sales were outside of Japan. Takata Corporation employed more than 36,000 employees at 58 plants in 21 nations, realized more than 40 percent of its global sales from airbags and supplied one out of every five airbags installed in new cars in the United States and around the globe.

Other investors – mostly Japanese – got in on the action when Takezo's son, heir, and corporate successor, Juichiro, started selling stock to the public in 2006. When Juichiro died of cancer in 2011, his wife, Akiko Yamada, and son, Shige (pronounced "she-gay") controlled two-thirds of the voting shares. The family's grip on the company minimized the influence of its biggest financiers, Sumitomo Bank and Honda Motor Company, which was at once Takata's biggest customer and a major investor. By 2014, when the company faced a safety crisis of titanic proportions, the grandson-chairman-president officially called all the shots.

The result was what Ferdinand Piech, the grandson of Volkswagen founder Ferdinand Porshe, laid bare in a German television interview in 2012. "The first generation builds. The second generation maintains. My generation is the third. We normally destroy."[24]

On June 25, 2017, Takata Corporation completed the generational arc, from an auto safety empire to a burned-out wreck. Takezo's grandson, who was derided inside and outside the company as "Little Shige," drove Takata Corporation into bankruptcy.

1985

Tokyo

Nobody welcomed the Supreme Court's unanimous *State Farm* decision and the convoluted Dole Rule more than Saburo Koboyashi, Honda's chief strategist. A new American marketing phenomenon – vehicle crash ratings – put Koboyashi over the top. The Insurance Institute for Highway Safety ("IIHS"), a non-profit research group funded by American property/casualty insurers, published results of crash tests they conducted independently. Surveys in the mid-1980s showed sophisticated American car-buyers taking IIHS ratings seriously. Hondas scored poorly, especially compared with some GM models that weighed more than twice as much as a Civic. With the airbag mandate finally secured in 1983, Koboyashi decided Takata Corporation would supply Honda's airbags. But first, he had to convince Takezo's son and heir.

Juichiro Takada, whose employees called him "emperor" without a hint of irony, introduced himself as "Jim" and always wore impeccably tailored Western business suits. His wardrobe reflected his focus on the American market. For years, even as he considered airbags unwelcome competition for his company's seat belts, Jim also worried that safety concerns about smaller cars were eroding the competitive edge enjoyed by Honda, his biggest customer.

When Detroit's Big Three finally went scrambling for airbag suppliers, it dawned on them that the pop-in airbag "modules" they installed in test fleets in the 1970's were too big for their new, smaller cars, much less cars as small and light as Hondas, Datsuns or Toyotas. Koboyashi begged Takada not to pass up a billion dollars.

Whether the potential payoff was in billions or trillions, Jim Takada initially wanted no part of the airbag business. At Honda's New Year's Eve party in 1985, he lowered his wire-rimmed spectacles and announced to the assembled guests that Takata Corporation was not about to go there.

"If anything happens to the airbag," Jim Takada said with eerie prescience, "Takata will go bankrupt. *We cannot cross a bridge as dangerous as this.*"

Koboyashi refused to take "dangerous bridge" for an answer, especially after Honda's new president, Tadashi Kume, decided in 1986 that they would beat Detroit on safety as well as quality by installing full-frontal airbags ahead of the deadline established by the Dole Rule. Takata's expertise in woven fabrics made it the only company in Japan with four competencies crucial to making airbag cushions: weaving, coating, sewing and folding. Takata's lead engineer secretly started making samples. Honda was thrilled with the prototypes. Koboyashi filled Jim Takada with dreams of ever-expanding riches. Takada relented, grudgingly. Initially, Takata Corporation made only the cushions, which unfolded much like parachutes. That was their first, fateful step onto the "dangerous bridge" their "emperor" warned against.

With its purchase of the Fabrics Division of Burlington Industries in 1988, Takata set up an American subsidiary, TK Holdings, Inc., in North Carolina. None of the corporate leadership had any experience with explosives, so Takata started manufacturing airbag inflators in the late 1980s through joint ventures. They teamed up with Bayern Chemie, a German firm, to make driver-side inflators in LaGrange, Georgia, and made a 50-50 deal with America's Rocket Research Corporation to make passenger-side units in Moses Lake, Washington. After they extracted from the German and American rocket scientists all they thought they needed to know about sodium azide, the traditional rocket fuel propellant, Takata bought their partners out by 1991.

The Japanese invested hundreds of millions of dollars in the Moses Lake plant, according to Mark Lillie, a Takata propellant engineer from 1994 to 1999. "We were moving so fast, it was terrifying but exciting," Lillie later testified.[25]

Honda and Takata "were in lockstep to conquer the world," Scott D. Upham, Takata's marketing boss from 1994 to 1996, observed. By the 1992 model year, the Honda Accord scored better in the IIHS crash tests than Ford's massive Lincoln Town Car.

1990s-2010s

Detroit

Takata Corporation was remarkably ignorant about explosives despite its former role as an important cog in the Imperial Japanese war machine. By 2000, however, after 40 years of selling seat belts to carmakers, it knew exactly how to thrive as a vehicle component supplier. In fact, "the emperor" played every car manufacturer in the world like a *kugo*. The launch customer for the new airbag inflator, Honda, gave the new product a lucrative start. General Motors Corporation was the real prize in the American market because it typically spent more than $75 billion a year on airbags, seat belts, bearings, bushings and a host of other vehicle components. GM was notorious, however, for squeezing all of its 27,000 suppliers – 400 of whom got 90 percent of the automaker's business. The component manufacturers considered GM their customer from Hell and consistently ranked them next-to-least popular among the top six automakers. GM's strategy was to calculate each supplier's profit margin to the penny, then play them against one another. They would give the winners near-impossible production goals and tell them "hey, it's your contract – you go figure out how to make good on it!"

When market conditions eventually allowed GM to charge its consumers higher prices, the company eased up on suppliers in a way that spoke volumes about their attitude toward product safety. Instead of paying their suppliers more, GM relieved them of an unwanted obligation in its supplier contract: component manufacturers no longer had to promise that their airbags or other parts would "not at any time ... pose an unreasonable risk to consumer or vehicle safety." [26] In other words, GM told its suppliers they would work for the same money and on the same breakneck schedule, but their products' compliance with the Motor Vehicle Safety Act henceforth would be between them and NHTSA, a bureaucracy that had developed nearly zero expertise in vehicle components.

Takata slyly turned GM's tactics to its own favor. They chose an explosive in their airbag inflator, ammonium nitrate, that cost a tenth as much as the industry's then-standard propellant, guanidine nitrate. With such a price advantage in the "active ingredient," profit margins on airbag modules were easy to achieve. All Takata had to do was tightly control the costs of cushions, actuators and other components. Robert Fisher, the President of Takata's American subsidiary and a leader of the GM Supplier Council, publicly applauded GM's decision to strike the safety assurance clause from the standard supplier contract. He also vowed to help GM on another cost-savings front – "logistics changes" that would relocate safety equipment manufacturing plants beyond the reach of American safety regulators.

Takata led a global race to the bottom – to pay the workers who produce airbags and other vehicle components the lowest possible wages – by "exporting" most of its airbag manufacturing operations to Mexico. To assuage Senate International Relations Subcommittee Chairman Jack Danforth and other American politicians from big autoworker states and to avoid import restrictions, Honda, Toyota and other Japanese carmakers scouted out hardscrabble pockets of the American labor market where people would gladly work for 30 percent less than their unionized countrymen in Michigan. As the Asian auto industry exported its careless attitudes about safety to America, ribbons got cut at huge new vehicle assembly plants across Dixie. Honda and Toyota arrived first, followed by Korean automakers. Cut-rate Asian parts suppliers, who functioned as if they were wholly owned subsidiaries of their country's vehicle manufacturers, were hard on their heels.

With GM and other carmakers holding them to such minuscule profit margins, the transplanted component suppliers could survive only by setting impossible production quotas and shamelessly disregarding the safety of their workers. Korean companies, for example, recently operated a quarter of the auto parts manufacturing plants in Alabama but committed more than a third of the safety infractions. They paid more than half the fines assessed between 2012 and 2016.

Japanese transplants, like Toyota's bearing supplier, Nakajima Manufacturing, are only marginally better. Nakajima has paid more than $100,000 in fines to OSHA for willful violations

of federal employee safety laws. Another Japanese parts manufacturer, Matsu Manufacturing, Inc., notoriously failed to provide
its employees with hands-on safety training. This approach left at
least one employee, quite literally, with no hands. In 2013, a temp
agency in Alabama sent 35-year old Reco Allen to push a broom
on a graveyard shift at the plant for nine dollars an hour. His training consisted of being shown to the broom closet. Six weeks into
the job, when Matsu was producing only 60 percent of the parts it
had promised Honda, a plant supervisor ordered Allen to work
the rest of his shift operating a metal stamping press. Within minutes, both of Allen's arms got trapped inside the machine. *Business
Week* reported that "he stood there for an hour, his flesh burning
inside." When an emergency crew finally freed him, both hands
were essentially gone and his right forearm had to be amputated.

Allen was luckier than Regina Elsea, a 20-year old
Alabama woman who earned $8.75 an hour to work 12-hour shifts,
seven days a week, at Ajin USA, a Hyundai parts supplier. In June
2016 she got impaled by two robotic welding tips. Her human coworkers had no clue what to do. They grabbed a supervisor, but
he spoke no English, only Korean. He fled. Eventually, an emergency crew arrived and took Elsea to a hospital, where she died
the next day.

Asian parts manufacturers had ample reason to think in
purely financial terms. Honda could fine Matsu $20,000 for *every
minute* a parts production shortfall held up a Honda vehicle assembly line. The $103,000 Labor Department fine for incinerating
Allen's hands was no worse than the penalty Honda could have
imposed for causing a five-minute delay moving Civics down a
production line. Elsea's death cost Ajin a stiffer, $2.5 million fine
– plus the cost of the single, artificial flower the company sent to
her funeral.

2000

Tokyo

The new vehicle market was driven by two imperatives during the 1990s. American regulators were pressing carmakers to increase vehicle fuel efficiency ratings at the same time airbags were becoming universal in new cars and light trucks. This one-two policy punch played into the Japanese strengths, so Detroit had to find some way – *any* way – to strip weight out of their overall designs. There was also a pressing need to stop airbags from making such a nasty mess when they deployed. From the airbag's earliest days, manufacturers used a rocket fuel called sodium azide as the propellant. It inflated cushions instantly but also spewed a baby powder-like dust into vehicle occupants' faces and lungs. For example, Chandler Howell, the teenager whose 1976 crash caused airbags to deploy in a compact car for the first time, was sure his car was on fire because all he could see afterward was "smoke." The gas that filled the bags also was toxic.

Airbag manufacturers gradually dropped sodium azide in favor of another explosive called guanidine nitrate ("GuaNi," for short). It shot less "effluent" (dust and toxic gases) into the cabin but did not help miniaturize the size or price of an airbag module. Takata took a cue from an earlier generation of Japanese reverse-engineers who brought pocket transistor radios within financial reach of American teenagers by selling them for one-third the price of an American radio and calling them "toys" to finagle lower import tariffs. In keeping with the corporate mantra of thinking big by thinking small, Takata's Automotive Systems Lab in Michigan "looked at every chemical compound known to man," Scott Upham, Takata's former marketing chief, noted.[27] A different pyrotechnic, ammonium nitrate (nicknamed "AN"), was used mostly to create huge explosions, for example, in mining operations. It was also useful to the terrorist who blew the federal building in Oklahoma City off the map in 1995.

Takata executives knew AN was safer to handle at the factory because sodium azide had a nasty habit of exploding when it was exposed to light, air or jostling. AN released gas that was non-toxic; it spewed far less smoke and particulates. Most importantly, it was more "fuel efficient" in two respects. First, AN's "gas-efficiency rating" – the percentage of solid propellant that turned into a gas – was 92 percent, a third again better than sodium azide. The propellant occupied less space so it would fit in smaller, lighter canisters. Second, Takata claimed that its inflators would allow automakers to produce cars that got better fuel-efficiency ratings and had relatively more dash-panel space available for stereos, navigation systems, cup holders and various other vehicular doo-dads Americans couldn't live without.

Takata started moving away from sodium azide in 1994. From 1995 to 2000, its inflators contained a chemical mix consisting mostly of strontium nitrate and tetrazole. To keep their "secret sauce" proprietary, they code-named it the "3110 propellant." It was not much of an improvement because it was less gas-efficient than GuaNi.

Honda was thrilled, however, when Takata started experimenting with AN. Kevin Fitzgerald, the chief ballistics engineer at the LaGrange plant, needed to calculate AN's likely range of explosive effects. In late 1999, Fitzgerald assigned John Keller, the company's newest mechanical engineer, to conduct a series of tests. Keller showed that the passenger inflators were so overloaded with explosive, bags would inflate too aggressively. Anyone who happened to be close to the dashboard would hit something more like an anvil than a pillow. Even worse, Takata's lab in Armada, Michigan, seemed hell-bent on switching to a cheap propellant that was wildly unpredictable, capable of exploding violently enough to rupture the metal canister that was supposed to release nothing more than gas. Keller told Fitzgerald the AN fractured like china an instant before it ignited, thereby increasing the surface area and, accordingly, the force of the explosion. According to Keller, Fitzgerald discussed the frightening results with more senior Takata executives, then handed the report back to him with these simple instructions: "This has to go away." When Takata announced closure of the LaGrange plant, Keller found employment elsewhere.

Honda decided in February 2000 that Takata's ammonium nitrate-powered inflators would debut in some of their most popular 2001 models for the American market. They gave Takata only until June 2000, when those cars would start rolling off the Japanese assembly line, to perfect the new design.

Takata eventually made 16 different types of ammonium nitrate-powered frontal inflators. They were customized for multiple carmakers but had certain design features in common. A crash sensor sent an electrical impulse to one end of a metal chamber. An igniter inside that chamber instantly burned into another chamber and set off the propellant. The resulting gas escaped the canister through small, lightly covered holes and instantly inflated the cushion.

Over many years, airbag engineers debated which combination of chemicals made the best and most reliable igniters and propellants. Takata's engineers experimented with various recipes until they arrived at a certain secret mix of ammonium nitrate, potassium nitrate, strontium nitrate, BHT and clay. The explosive, code-named "2004 propellant," pressed into certain shapes and sizes, worked in airbag modules for both driver- and passenger-side systems. They kept tetrazole, but only as the igniter.

Takata had two favorite shapes for their little bombs. Some were called "shark fins" because they looked like the menacing part of a great white that broke the water on its way to unsuspecting swimmers in the movie *Jaws*. The other wafers were called "batwings" because they resembled the sign Gotham would project into the night sky to summon the Caped Crusader. The batwings consisted of a torso-shaped lump of explosives in the middle, flanked by two tapered wings. Takata ran a test on a Honda crash simulator in February 2000, using an airbag module with an inflator powered by a shark fin. It failed. Honda dictated a "fix": from that point on, they directed Takata to use only batwings. Takata told Honda they had "concerns about the potential for wafer density variations ... and thus the potential for variability in ballistic performance." [28] In other words, Takata expressly warned Honda in 2000, before any ammonium nitrate inflators were installed in cars, that batwings could explode in unpredictable ways.

Ordinarily, engineers would iron out concerns about the predictability of a new product in the course of two sets of test protocols known in industry jargon as "design validation" and "process validation." For process validation, the exemplars are by definition supposed to come straight off a production line. Honda stubbornly insisted on the batwing design even though it knew Takata had no production assets to make it and had used only shark fins in the design validation tests.[29] Takata's batwing wafers initially were made on an antiquated "non-production press" called the Stokes 340, yet Honda ordered hundreds of thousands of batwing inflators in June, 2000, before any manufacturing process existed.

Takata's first gigantic sale of AN-powered inflators sprang from a single document, a final process validation test report dated June 23, 2000. Paresh Khandhadia, a chemical engineer with a degree from the Institute of Technology in Mumbai, India, who ran Takata's lab in Armada, Michigan, supplied exemplars to Takata's manufacturing facility in LaGrange, Georgia. Japanese engineers who had taken up residence there took charge. Hideo Nakajima and Shinichi Tanaka did not report to LaGrange's engineering director, Bob Schubert. Instead, they worked on Tokyo time – the middle of the night in Georgia – for Tsuneo Chikaraishi, who was based in Echigawa, Japan. Chikaraishi, in turn, reported to Takashi Furosawa, who worked directly for Takata's "emperor," Jim Takada. Khandhadia and the Japanese handed Honda a "perfect" validation test report. It showed the new AN propellant igniting and pushing gas into airbag cushions with predictable force. The Japanese engineers, including Furosawa, along with Khandhadia and Harry Trimble, an American engineer at LaGrange, signed the report.

Kevin Fitzgerald was shocked to hear that Takata was ready to start mass production of Khandhadia's new AN inflators. Loud booms shook the building during the Japanese test runs and Fitzgerald recognized them as inflator ruptures. Fitzgerald became suspicious after his boss, Schubert, was mysteriously transferred from LaGrange to Michigan and Tanaka developed the habit of standing on chairs and screaming at Fitzgerald's junior staff engineers. Working after hours, Fitzgerald got one of his engineers, Tom Sheridan, to sneak him a copy of the June 23, 2000, report that went to Honda. Fitzgerald and Sheridan were appalled to discover that the perfect curves in crucial charts in the report did not match the underlying raw data, some of which showed clear signatures of inflator ruptures.

After Sheridan took an even deeper dive into the test data and compared notes with Trimble, Fitzgerald asked Sheridan to produce an honest report. It gave the new AN inflator a failing grade because its explosive force was too unpredictable. Fitzgerald sent Sheridan's version to everyone who signed the earlier, phony report, asked each of them to sign the corrected version and made a record that Takata executives in Japan received a copy. Fitzgerald confronted Khandhadia, who peered at the corrected version through the small, round lenses of his eyeglasses but refused to sign it. Honda claims it did not audit Takata's fake or real test results.

Instead of calling off production of the explosion-prone inflators, Takata shifted production to a new, purpose-built facility in Monclova, Mexico. Fitzgerald quit in 2000, then was recruited back into Takata's headquarters in Auburn Hills, Michigan, five years later. When Fitzgerald was back on board, Schubert admitted that he had been transferred out of LaGrange because "the Japanese asked me to misrepresent data and I refused." Fitzgerald also learned that Sheridan had quit Takata in 2002 and another propellant engineer, Mark Lillie, had also left Takata's Moses Lake, Washington, plant after Japan issued him instructions to "torture" certain data "until it confesses." Despite the jarring return to his former employer, Fitzgerald had a growing family to consider. He stayed put and took charge of inflator production in Moses Lake and the new plant in Mexico.

Takata had huge financial incentives to "deep six" the Sheridan report. Honda's global vehicle production rose 37 percent between 2000 and 2005, so Takata's biggest customer was buying airbags faster than Takata could make them. Sales and market share skyrocketed. When GM and Ford both ditched other airbag suppliers, Takata suddenly commanded ten percent of the American market and became the second-largest supplier of airbag systems in the world. The old-school woven fabrics maker struggled to digest a gigantic surge in demand, like a python that swallowed a hippopotamus.

The price for raw ammonium nitrate was one-tenth as much as tetrazole. Despite this mathematical fact, Takata's executives always insisted that the carmakers' collective switch to AN-powered airbags "was not driven by cost considerations." [30] Honda documents make it clear, however that the inflator redesign was all about the "Benjamins" (or perhaps the "Yukichis," the Japanese guy on the front of a 10,000-yen bank note). Lawyers for injured drivers say Honda picked Takata due to "inexpensiveness," pure and simple.[31] Nissan saved four dollars on the cost of every inflator. Ford overruled its own inflator expert to choose Takata's AN-powered inflators. The company felt it "had a gun to its head" because no other supplier claimed it could make the number of inflators Ford needed. Companies that made small cars liked the lower cost, too, but the smaller size and lighter weight made Takata's airbags irresistible.

GM was not shy about saving money on airbags. They challenged their legacy supplier, Sweden-based Autoliv, Inc., to match Takata's price for an airbag module, which was 30 percent cheaper, or lose all of GM's business.[32] Autoliv refused GM's ultimatum and took a painful sales hit. To get a better sense of what they were competing against, the Swedes examined the new Takata inflator and recognized the risk of it spewing shrapnel. Still, Autoliv customers continued to "defect" to Takata.

Lax government regulation and industry standards also fueled Takata's sudden growth. Nothing in the Honda specifications or in a separate set of specs established by their American competitors explicitly required Takata to test a propellant's maximum safe service life. For all the decades and effort NHTSA spent to impose the airbag mandate, the agency never established an explicit requirement that airbag modules must be shown capable of lasting as long as a car. Instead, the regulators took the same approach to airbags that they applied to the ignition interlock 25 years earlier. Quality control – even over basic design decisions about safety equipment – was the vehicle manufacturers' exclusive domain.

Takata claimed to offer an important safety benefit. Smaller inflators supposedly freed up enough room inside an airbag module to introduce new, multi-stage devices that would push a person away before the hard punch-out occurred. This would make airbags a safer "vaccine" by reducing the instances of driver airbags killing petite women and passenger airbags decapitating out-of-position children.

Nevertheless, there was plenty of reason to doubt the safety of Khandhadia's new propellant. Even before Takata faked its crucial test report, Lillie feared AN-powered inflators would produce catastrophic failures. According to Lillie, "I literally said that if we go forward with this, somebody will be killed." Lillie's comment made little impression on his Japanese superiors, who told him "the decision has already been made" and that the company was doing the design review not to assure safety but "just to check off the box."[33]

Khandhadia, by contrast, apparently remained proud of his brainchild. On LinkedIn, a social network for professionals, he was still claiming credit in 2017, after Takata filed for bankruptcy, for "mistake-proofing ... Takata's Mexican [inflator manufacturing] plants" and making Takata "one of the top technology leaders in ... automotive safety." He boasted of his "proven record in conceptualization to commercialization ... under severe budgetary and schedule constraints." In FBI interviews and court proceedings arising from the hundreds of deaths and injuries caused by Takata's airbags, Khandhadia was more circumspect. He pleaded his Fifth Amendment right not to incriminate himself.

In the late 1990s, Takata had solved a technical issue called "phase-stabilization," but it knew AN was far more sensitive to moisture than traditional airbag propellants. Still, they based validation of their new inflator on nothing more than a *single run* of a 'high humidity cycle exposure test.'"[34] After years of insisting that their AN propellant was stable and ready for lifetime use, Takata eventually tried to excuse its failure to recognize the potential for degradation, over-powered explosions and inflator ruptures. Such awful results, they said, were not "comprehended within the industry's inflator validation practice when the inflators were originally made."[35] Takata's competitors, however, fully "comprehended" the obvious risk of phase-stabilized ammonium nitrate ("PSAN") deteriorating over time from exposure to moisture. For example, just as sales of Takata's inflators took off, Germany's ZF TRW also figured out a reliable way to keep AN from changing "phases" and density. However, the German engineers quickly realized that phase stabilization was only the *first* technological hump. Daily temperature swings in the presence of moisture would make even PSAN unstable. Miniscule flows of water cut channels into the surface of PSAN tablets, thereby increasing the amount of surface area feeding an explosion. The Germans foresaw the grave risk of inflator ruptures. To ameliorate that risk, TRW figured it would have to keep its ammonium nitrate supplies freeze-dried, the canisters would need a pressure relief valve and various parts of the inflator casing would have to be welded airtight. So many precautions would make their inflators more, not less, expensive, so TRW abandoned ammonium nitrate in 2006 in favor of propellants containing guanidine nitrate.

An American "think tank" put its finger on exactly the same problem. The U.S. Council on Automotive Research ("USCAR") said in 2004 – four years before Honda filed the first Takata airbag recall – that airbag inflators powered by PSAN still must "undergo *added* stability evaluation" to assure "resistance to temperature aging in an environment of high humidity."[36] That was *exactly* the type of safety evaluation Honda *never* asked Takata to perform.

Takata never established a clear process for identifying potential safety defects. As Honda or NHTSA could easily have seen at the time, not a single front-line employee in the entire company had "safety assurance" in his job description. Under the Motor Vehicle Safety Act, it is the responsibility of the carmaker who wants to sell in the United States, not its component suppliers, who must certify compliance with federal safety standards. For years after it cajoled Takata into the airbag business, Honda was still following the first rule of *Fight Club's* Project Mayhem: "you do not ask questions."

Five years into Takata's production of AN-powered inflators, as the three Japanese engineers tinkered with the raw materials that went into the propellant, they "routinely discussed the fabrication of unfavorable testing data and the manipulation of test information" to show success instead of failure.[37] They felt their company gave them "no choice" but to "XX" (delete) the bad test results. All three of the engineers who faked the reports ultimately agreed they were ready to "cross the bridge together."

Takata started testing possible replacements for the wafer recipe in December 2005. A handful of little, round tablets could make

Takata's inflators even lighter and smaller. The redesign also created an opportunity to circle back to the problem they suspected was behind the test ruptures they had covered up five years earlier. The new "secret sauce" included some synthetic graphite and a dash of silica to act as a desiccant – a substance that would, presumably, draw environmental moisture quicker than ammonium nitrate could absorb it. They code-named the presumably crisper propellant "2004L." Process validation tests began in September 2007. Just like the original "2004" explosive, however, the new "2004L" pellets were not subjected to "high-humidity combined with thermal cycling." Despite warnings from USCAR, Takata did nothing to consider "the effect of external moisture intrusion on the '2004L'" as ambient temperatures and humidity levels rose and fell every day a car would be on the road.[38]

An engineer at the LaGrange plant testified that results of tests to measure the airtightness of the canisters also were falsified.[39] Takata additionally failed to make sure tape covering the holes through which the gas would flow into the airbag cushion would reduce humidity inside the canisters. Fluids that were used to clean the metal during the manufacturing process turned out to be incompatible with the tape adhesive.

When the "2004L" explosive also started failing tests, the engineers chalked it up to "elevated ballistic results following environmental aging."[40] Their solution – to adjust the level of moisture that would be permitted *at the point of manufacturing* – was hailed inside the company as a nice, cheap fix, but it totally missed the mark. Instead of protecting the explosive from degradation, the new manufacturing specifications merely increased the amount of time it would take Takata's inflators to turn into pipe bombs and shred people alive.

Takata never punished or reprimanded the Japanese engineers who faked the validation reports and handed them to Honda. To the contrary, those individuals either maintained their positions or were promoted. The engineers knew their bosses were directly in touch with "the emperor," so they kept "XXing." Takata made no public mention of the phony test reports until November 2015 and continued to insist for months that its "data integrity problems" were unrelated to the "root cause" of explosions that were killing people. Even when the company pled guilty to criminal conduct in 2017, the worst it would say about its indicted engineers was that their actions were "deeply inappropriate," as if they got caught eating sushi with a fork.[41]

2000s

Armada, Michigan and Monclova, Mexico

"It's the way we do business in Japan," Bob Schubert told Kevin Fitzgerald and his other American colleagues in 2005. Schubert had been "repeatedly exposed to the Japanese practice of altering data presented to the customer," but no one at Takata took him seriously, even when he put in writing that their employer's habit of falsifying test data "has gone beyond all reasonable bounds and now most likely constitutes fraud."[42] Within a year, according to news stories, he was urging writers of reports on various kinds of tests to change colors of lines in a graphic "to divert attention" from certain negative results and "try to dress it up." He sarcastically wished them "happy manipulating!"[43]

It was – and still is – the way Japan does business. For example, Kobe Steel, Ltd., sold tens of thousands of tons of out-of-specification metal to 500 companies, including Honda, Toyota, GM, Ford and other vehicle manufacturers from 2007 to 2017. Company engineers falsified quality control paperwork to cover up flaws in doors and hoods that could impair two of the most important vehicle safety design features. While airbags keep people from hitting the inside of their cars in a crash, "crumple zones" keep engines and other vehicle front components from intruding into passenger compartments and crushing or impaling occupants. Also, the death rate increases five-fold when occupants are ejected, which can more easily happen if doors pop open on impact. "Out-of-spec" Japanese metal could compromise crumple zones and the crashworthiness of vehicle doors.

For eight years, starting in 2008, Toray Industries, Inc., did the same thing with textiles that are supposed to strengthen car tires. The company's quality managers faked test results because they "felt they had no choice because they needed to keep production moving." Toray kept the fraud secret for an entire decade, until November 2017 – after it reported record profits – because Toray president Akihiro Nikkaku decided it should concern only their tire-maker customers, not motorists whose lives were riding on their products.

Nissan Motor Company made headlines in September 2017, when Japan's Transport Ministry blew the whistle on fake safety certifications. The company recalled every car it sold in Japan between 2014 and 2017. A month later, even in the midst of the public outcry, Nissan technicians were still issuing fake certifications. "They had done it for a long time and … thought it ought to be OK," Nissan CEO Hiroto Saikawa explained when he temporarily shut the company's Japanese assembly lines down in October 2017. A few months later, Nissan was forced to admit it falsified its emissions data and the fuel economy of its cars for five years, from 2013 to 2018. Management blamed factory workers for cutting corners to meet production targets, then hiding the evidence.

Subaru Corporation, 60 percent of whose sales are in the American market, admitted in 2017 that it, too, allowed unqualified workers to perform quality checks. "We are distressed that our company is responsible for something that could cast doubt on the quality of Japanese manufacturing," Subaru CEO Yasuyuki Yoshinaga said. He said nothing about a different Subaru scandal – fake fuel economy data – until December 2017, when someone leaked it to Japanese media.

Mitsubishi Motors Corporation, the world's fastest growing nonluxury auto brand, and Suzuki Motor Company proved in 2016 that Japanese companies are willing to lie about almost anything to maximize their profits and stock price. They confessed to deliberately exaggerating their vehicles' fuel economy ratings. The multimillion dollar fines they paid were not enough to faze executives at the Mitsubishi subsidiary that supplies rubber gaskets and other nuts-and-bolts-level car parts. Mitsubishi Materials Corporation discovered fake quality reports in February 2017 but hid them for nine months. In late November 2017 – *after* they announced their earnings to investors – they confessed that "taking on impossible business caused many products to fail to meet standards."

Japanese trickery with test results enabled the design of Takata's mini inflators but the process of mass-producing them created an additional source of culture clash. American workers resented merciless Japanese production quotas and protested what they considered lapses in worker safety. "It was always push, push, push the envelope," reported Michael Britton, a propellant engineer who left Takata in 2000.[44]

The Japanese had a solution for those pesky American workplace safety regulations. They moved the bulk of their inflator production to Monclova, Mexico, 300 miles southwest of San Antonio, Texas, where Takata typically employed more than 10 times more people than at Moses Lake, Washington. In the first four years alone, the move saved Takata $70 million in labor costs and shaved 20 percent off the price carmakers paid for each inflator. Company managers, for their part, were astonished to see how sloppy their Mexican workers could be. Forklift operators were caught on surveillance cameras spilling crates of brand-new, explosive inflators on loading docks, then sending them along to vehicle assembly lines, unexamined. Even if they had been sacks of potatoes instead of sensitive safety equipment, they should never have been shipped wet, in trucks with leaky roofs. Disgruntled workers also spit wads of spent chewing gum into the canisters, altering the ballistic performance of the explosive wafers.

Fitzgerald was convinced the Monclova operation was "never serious about becoming proficient" and that he had been banished to "the island of misfit inflators." Workers who tested a sampling of inflators as they came off the line had an easy solution when one of them failed. They just kept grabbing another unit until they found an inflator that passed. Fitzgerald decided that the Japanese engineer who took charge at Monclova, Hiroshi Shimizu, brought even less integrity to the process in his "drive to make shipments at any cost."

Starting in 1991, Takata's plant at Moses Lake, Washington, turned out driver-side, sodium azide-powered inflators at a spritely pace – until the whole plant blew up in 1997. For months, the company had to buy inflators from competing manufacturers. That expensive misadventure helped prompt the switch to ammonium nitrate as a propellant. The Monclova plant also blew sky-high, shattering almost every window in the city, within a year after Takata finished moving production of its passenger-side inflators there from LaGrange, Georgia in 2005. Videos of the conflagration went "viral" on YouTube and were still getting plenty of views in 2020.

Days after the catastrophe, Takata resumed production of inflators in the blown-out shell of the Monclova plant, without walls or a roof, exposing its ammonium nitrate supplies to relative humidity as high as 60 percent. After the factory was rebuilt, a supervisor caught workers trying to fix defective inflators on the production line instead of kicking them back. "Rework on the assembly line is PROHIBITED!!!" plant manager Guillermo Apud declared. "This is why we have defect after defect."[45]

Moses Lake bore the brunt of the frenetic effort to meet Honda's unquenchable demand for the new, AN-powered, driver-side inflators. "Takata made promises to customers for volumes that could not be supported by the existing pipeline for the raw materials," according to Mark Lillie. "The culture was, we are making a commitment to the customer and then we will work like the dickens to make it happen – somehow."

Even after Takata abandoned its batwing wafers, mass production was not easy to achieve because its factories had to stamp out three other wafer sizes plus four different sizes of tablets. The correct sizes and combinations had to be loaded into each inflator canister. Takata initially had only one machine to transform the raw explosive mix into wafers and tablets. Known as the Gladiator, the press they set up in May 2000, could produce 300 wafers per minute, not nearly enough to satisfy Honda's voracious demand. As a stopgap, Takata transplanted to Moses Lake the vintage "single-shot press" that produced the original, experimental batwings in Michigan. Although it was considered "non-production" equipment with only manual controls, it kept stamping batwings almost to the end of 2001, by which point two additional Gladiators were in service.

Despite constant warnings that Honda and Toyota would fine the company tens of thousands of dollars for every minute of lost productivity on their vehicle assembly lines, none of Takata's operators or machines were up to the task. The "single-shot" press had no "auto reject" feature, so operators got no warning when they failed to apply proper pressure. Random quality control inspections for density and moisture spotted potentially deadly wafers mostly by chance. Meanwhile, the Gladiators created a false sense of security about the quality of their output. Those machines had an "auto reject" feature that was worthless if the operator figured out how much easier it was to meet his production quotas by switching it off. Wafer quality was no more assured than what came out of the ancient, single-shot press. That meant the press operators – who were working to "keep 'em coming" as frantically as Lucy Ricardo and Ethel Mertz at the candy factory in Lucille Ball's television comedy series – for a full year enjoyed the unsupervised option to churn out potentially deadly wafers. Bad wafers were tough to catch because the density of the batwings – Honda's chosen configuration for the explosive – could only be measured by pinching the bat torso with metal tongs; the gauge would shatter the wings.

Another machine cranked out 3,000 AN tablets per minute. All Takata had to do was to pop the correct number of finished tablets into each canister. The loading equipment also malfunctioned, dropping too many or too few tablets inside a canister. With so many manufacturing glitches affecting driver-side inflators at Moses Lake in 2000 and 2001 and compromising passenger-side inflators in LaGrange in 2001 and 2002, some Takata employees suggested the possibility of asking Honda to initiate a recall. As it was, the company could not keep up with demand for units needed to avoid being fined by car manufacturers for stalling their vehicle assembly lines. From a strictly economic point of view, the last thing Takata needed at that moment was the additional burden of making replacement inflators that would yield no revenue. Nobody at Takata dared to suggest a recall to Honda at that time.

When Fitzgerald discovered that the tablets inside brand-new inflators being assembled in Monclova for Ford and Nissan were already degraded, Takata tried to cover up the problem by peppering the propellant with calcium sulfate, a "desiccant" or drying agent. Tests showed that the inflators still kept exploding, Fitzgerald found, so he tried to get Rob Fisher, the president of Takata's American subsidiary not to send them to the carmakers.

Fisher released them anyway, according to Fitzgerald, brushing off his concerns by saying, "please, Kevin, I don't want to hear about the past. This is coming directly from Japan."[46] Takata eventually admitted that calcium sulfate did not work and recalled those inflators in 2017.

Fitzgerald also reported that Monclova's workers were mishandling loaded inflators and shattering the propellant tablets inside them. Tests confirmed that mishaps were turning those tablets into little bombs, so Khandhadia came up with a solution: he changed the test protocol to cushion the drop surface to make it less like what was actually happening when finished inflators hit the factory floor. The Japanese engineers ordered that production proceed, regardless.[47]

When Takata's American engineers learned of the first inflator rupture, in a BMW in Switzerland, on May 1, 2003, 45 different manufacturing screw-ups were fresh in their minds. They dismissed the rupture as the result of a presumed "propellant overload" and told BMW it was a "one-off." They claimed to have improved the production equipment to assure inclusion of the correct number of tablets in each canister. Whether the explosion in Switzerland killed or injured anyone is one of the many secrets Takata took to its grave when the company liquidated in 2018.

A second rupture occurred in a 2001 Honda Accord in Alabama on May 2, 2004. Honda knew its customer was badly injured by shrapnel but the carmaker did not initiate a recall. Quite the contrary; Honda did not mention the incident to Takata for more than a year. Honda's quarterly Early Warning Report to NHTSA included, among 246 death and injury notes, a vague reference to an airbag injury in May of that year. It could have been a garden-variety skinned elbow, for all NHTSA could tell from the report. There was no indication that the driver got blasted in the face with shredded metal. In fact, there was no place on NHTSA's electronic reporting form to enter such information. Following Detroit's playbook from the 1950s, Honda quickly settled the resulting personal injury suit out of court, presumably paying the victim or his survivors extra to keep quiet. To this day, the name of Takata's first American victim remains a secret.

When Takata's American engineers finally heard in 2005 about the "field rupture" in Alabama, they developed a lengthy list of possible causes. In the end, as with the Swiss explosion, the engineers dismissed the event as another mere "anomaly." It required no action because the physical evidence mysteriously had been destroyed instead of being "returned for analysis."[48] Honda and Takata maintained blissful ignorance about what their products were doing to people. U.S. Government regulators knew even less.

PART 5

Open Kimono

2008

United States

During the financial crisis of 2008, Wall Street titan Jamie Dimon said his company, JP Morgan Chase, could be trusted to comply with banking laws because it was "open kimono" to federal regulators. The reference originated during the American military occupation of Japan, when the traditional, erudite sex worker known as a *geisha* ("arts person") got pushed aside by common whores. A real *geisha* might advertise her wares to wealthy Japanese johns by reciting poetry and performing the Shallow River Dance, in which her kimono gets lifted higher until the *geisha*'s pink *nagajuban* were showing.

When Honda showed up at NHTSA with its first Takata airbag recall in 2008, the carmaker was anything but "open kimono." Their *obi* was cinched as tight as a *taiko*, and for good reason. Both Honda and Takata had been selling their products in the American market for more than a generation. Honda pushed Detroit off center stage in part thanks to the belated implementation of the airbag mandate in the early 1990s. Their American lawyers knew the key statutory and regulatory requirements backwards and forwards because Takata hired the lawyers who wrote them as soon as they left government service.

The black-letter safety recall rules on what carmakers must disclose and when they must disclose it are clear and consistent.

RULE NUMBER ONE: motor vehicle manufacturers and component suppliers are separately obligated to report the existence of a "defect related to motor vehicle safety" within five working days after they discover it – or should have discovered it.

RULE NUMBER TWO: every Defect Information Report must include three crucial details, including a "*chronology* of … events … including a summary of all … field reports;" a "*description* of the basis for the determination *of the recall population*, including how those … differ from … vehicles … the manufacturer excluded from the recall;" and a "detailed description of the … *nature* … of the *defect* …."

RULE NUMBER THREE: vehicle manufacturers must submit to NHTSA a "description of the *plan* to *remedy* the defect" at no cost and to alert vehicle owners within 60 days. Recall notices must go in regular mail but only one mailing is generally required.

"Defect" is defined, circularly, as "a *defect in* … a component … of a motor vehicle …." "Motor vehicle safety" is defined as "performance of a motor vehicle … in a way that protects the public against *unreasonable risk of accidents* occurring because of the design, construction or performance of a motor vehicle …."

In the mid-1960s, when the vehicle safety law was enacted, a new legal specialty called "products liability" was just starting to take shape, in different ways in different states. As Nader revealed in *Unsafe at Any Speed* in 1965, state consumer protection laws typically distinguished between two different types of defects. A "manufacturing (or construction) defect" occurs, for example, when something goes wrong on an assembly line. A worker forgets to stick Widget A into Slot B as a vehicle reaches her on the assembly line. By contrast, a "design defect" becomes apparent when people discover that the designer's chosen combination of Widget A, made out of plastic, and Slot B, made out of metal, isn't going to work over time. Manufacturing and design defects are all the same to a driver whose brakes fail, but it can make an enormous difference in the cost of a vehicle manufacturer's recall campaign. Production records can show which days the problem employee was on the line and physical inspections can distinguish vehicles that got Widget A from those that did not. If it keeps meticulous records, a vehicle manufacturer can easily explain the difference between cars that were affected and must be recalled and cars that are safe. It can be a great relief for a manufacturer to know that cars it assembled on Tuesday are defective and cars that were completed on Wednesday are not.

A "design defect" is a whole other kettle of fish. If Widget A is likely to crumble after a certain duration in contact with Slot B, causing the brakes to fail, then every car designed with the mismatched Widget A in Slot B is defective, regardless of what day it came off the line or how long it will take before the defective part crumbles. A manufacturing defect is a financial tornado; a design defect can be an economic hurricane.

In 2005, three years before Honda filed its first Takata recall and two years after the BMW rupture in Switzerland, Takata's American executives learned about the airbag inflator that had ruptured in a Honda in Alabama in 2004. Takata engineers figured it *had* to be a manufacturing defect. They assumed a safety recall was coming, so they started to devise a more reliable way to press ammonium nitrate into wafers. When they got ready to commence validation tests on inflators with the denser wafers, the Americans were overridden by Japanese executives. They "shut the whole thing down" and ordered "XX-ing" (total obliteration) of the new test data.[49] Perhaps taking a page out of Chuck Palahniuk's novel, *Fight Club*, someone in Tokyo apparently calculated it would be much less expensive to settle with the maimed driver. A kicker in the settlement check was the time-honored way to keep the whole deal secret from the government and, just as important, to keep other car owners in the dark about the risk. We may never know the truth about the 2004 rupture because it remains hidden behind Honda's settlement agreement and attorney-client privilege.

In 2007, three American Honda drivers suffered what Takata euphemistically described as "the unfortunate occurrence of field ruptures." We know nothing about how much those three individuals suffered. Honda swept the bomb debris under the *tatami* mat, just like the 2004 explosion, presumably by writing checks big enough to gag the victims.

As it did with the 2004 rupture, Honda waited an entire year to notify Takata about the three ruptures in 2007. They did not ask their airbag supplier to prepare for a recall. Honda requested something much less expensive: a type of engineering study called a "failure mode analysis." With 45 separate manufacturing screw-ups to choose from, Takata had no trouble identifying one they could claim had already been fixed. They told Honda their Mexican workers had left some of the moisture-sensitive ammonium nitrate tablets out on the humid factory floor during their siestas instead of returning them to dry storage. The "siesta problem" affected an easily identifiable handful of Monclova's inflators, Takata said. In any case, the Mexicans were persuaded by November 2002 that moisture was *prohibido*.

Honda took in stride the news that the airbags in thousands of their popular 2001 Civics were potential hand grenades. For months, they left them out there, inches away from their customers' faces, while they secretly looked for the cheapest fix. Starting in late 2007, Honda sneaked more than 100 airbag modules out of junk cars and test-fired their inflators. The junkyard operation produced an ugly surprise. Takata's new "2004L" propellant – the first in a series of formulas for explosives that contained a drying agent – had the same propensity as the earlier "secret sauce" to spew shrapnel at vehicle occupants.

The subject nobody in the company dared to address in 2008 was whether ammonium nitrate, the propellant in every one of their new inflators, could be both safe and inherently prone to "elevated ballistic results following environmental aging." By that point, Takata had already produced more than 100 million AN-powered inflators that were installed in tens of millions of vehicles, most of them Hondas. Takata engineer Kevin Fitzgerald knew the Japanese "singular focus on production issues was just a way to avoid the unthinkable – that [the choice of ammonium nitrate] was the very issue."[50]

Despite the chilling results of "Operation Junkyard," Honda stuck with its story that all the problems were traceable to just two of Takata's manufacturing errors – the "siesta problem" and non-use of the auto-reject feature on the wafer presses. Takata's American engineers told their Japanese overseers that "the data and records show both are demonstrably false." The Americans made sure Takata's corporate leadership also knew several lots of inflators were shipped to carmakers with unquestionably bad welds.

In November 2008 – more than a year after it learned about the three 2007 ruptures – Honda finally informed NHTSA there were "safety-related defects" in a tiny fraction of Takata airbags. In RECALL NUMBER 1, Honda told NHTSA they had complied with the statutory requirement to identify all "possible vehicles that could potentially experience the problem." They assured the Government that a mere 4,000 Civics, all from the 2001 model year, were built with inflators that "could produce excessive internal pressure."[51] Despite the statutory requirement to provide a "summary of field reports," Honda did not reveal that four people had already come face-to-bomb with inflator ruptures. As with any new recall, NHTSA took no action; it opened a file for Honda's report and the six quarterly follow-ups required under the agency's regulations.

Six months into the penny-ante, 4,000-Civic recall, two young women discovered, the hard way, what Honda meant by "excessive internal pressure." A 26-year old, Jennifer Griffin, suffered a two-inch gash in her neck. The inflator in her steering wheel ruptured when her 2001 Civic was involved in a minor collision in Orlando, Florida. Griffin miraculously survived the dissection of her carotid artery. Exactly one month later, in May 2009, 18-year old Ashley Parham of Midwest City, Oklahoma, was less fortunate. The Takata airbag in the 2001 Accord she was driving – and which had never been recalled – slashed her throat. Her younger brother, who had climbed into the back seat when she picked him up from football practice, was unable to keep Ashley from choking on her own blood. Honda mentioned Parham's death in a quarterly Early Warning Report but it was buried among hundreds of other notes about run-of-the-mill vehicle malfunctions. Despite the statutory requirement to describe the "nature" of the defect leading to a recall, Honda chose not to tell NHTSA the Takata inflator ruptured, much less *why* it ruptured.

2009

Torrance, California

Nobody at NHTSA requested any details about the Parham tragedy but the champion cheerleader's violent death jangled Honda's nerves. Takata's Chairman, Shigehisa Takada, had for months studiously avoided face-to-face meetings with Honda and other automakers who bought millions of his company's airbags. On July 22, 2009, Hidenobu Iwata, the head of Honda's North American operations, caught up with Takada on a visit to California. Iwata did not want to hear any more about errors on the factory floor.

"Why does the propellant deteriorate with age?" Iwata demanded. "Why does it explode? I want to know the truth!"

Takada looked on impassively as his underlings explained that the company was still investigating the "root cause." Honda did not dare let the problem slide much longer. Five days after the Iwata-Takada confrontation in California, Honda filed RECALL NUMBER TWO. It expanded the scale of the Takata airbag recall *130-fold*, from 4,000 to 510,000 vehicles. Civics and Accords from the 2002 model year were added to the "recall population." Half a million cars still constituted only a fraction of the Hondas and other vehicle makes equipped with the AN-powered inflators Iwata asked Chairman Takada about. Takata kept a lid on the "population" of affected vehicles by taking into account only *some* of the flaws in the explosive wafer press operations from 2000 to 2002, even though Fitzgerald pointed to company records showing the claim to be "demonstrably false." It was just a ploy to divert attention from the underlying design of the inflator. Honda gave NHTSA no hint that Griffin had been maimed or that a Takata airbag had sent 18-year old Parham to her grave. As far as Honda and Takata were concerned, each young woman had experienced nothing more than an "unusual driver airbag deployment." As time went by, however, such catastrophic failures became increasingly less "unusual."

Someone at NHTSA eventually became curious why RECALL NUMBER ONE in 2008 did not also cover the 510,000 vehicles that were swept into RECALL NUMBER TWO in 2009. Five-and-a-half months after the second recall started, on November 2, 2009, NHTSA's bureaucratic wheels turned out an obsequious request for information about the glaring discrepancy.

Gurgit Rathore, a 33-year old mom from Richmond, Virginia, could have benefited from a timely Honda response to NHTSA's questions. She died seven weeks after NHTSA started its investigation, on Christmas Eve, 2009. Her 2001 Accord hit a mail truck near her home and the driver-side inflator ruptured. A chunk of shrapnel lodged in her throat, but the deflating airbag cushion caught on the metal shard and yanked it out of her neck, leaving a gaping wound. Her three young children watched her bleed to death behind the wheel. The $3 million settlement Honda reportedly paid the family was the only consolation they got for their nightmare before Christmas.

The head of Takata's North American operations decided to take action. Frank Roe angrily confronted Paresh Khandhadia, the godfather of Takata's ammonium nitrate inflators, and decided to put Kevin Fitzgerald in charge of inflator R&D in Armada. Japan quickly countermanded Roe's order and put Khandhadia in charge of a new corporate function: "Recurrence Prevention." As Fitzgerald understood it, Khandhadia's new job was not to prevent more inflator ruptures – it was to avoid the recurrence of recalls.[52]

Rathore's death motivated Takata executives in Echigawa to direct the American engineers to create a way to "fail-safe" the defective inflators. The Japanese insisted Monclova could change the manufacturing process to deliberately weaken the side of the canister that pointed away from the driver. Inflators would keep exploding but at least most of the debris would shoot into the steering column instead of driver's faces and necks. Fitzgerald was flabbergasted. He knew the only way to fail-safe Takata's inflators would be to abandon AN and use guanidine nitrate or another propellant that would either burn as intended or "dud" itself out.

The Japanese overlords in Echigawa ignored Fitzgerald's objections and commanded the Americans to demonstrate the

Japanese "fail-safe." A Honda representative watched them deploy one of the modified airbags in an Accord. As Fitzgerald expected, the inflator did not spill its own guts inside the steering column. The whole inflator canister shot into the cabin like a cannonball and decapitated the absent driver's headrest, just as Fitzgerald predicted. Fitzgerald recorded the Honda representative's reaction: "This never happened. No videos. No emails."

Echigawa's fake fix didn't seem to bother Takata's Chairman, Shige Takada. Al Bernat, the top engineer in Takata's headquarters in Auburn Hills, arranged for Fitzgerald to explain the situation in person. Fitzgerald told Takada that the essential problem was the company's fateful choice of ammonium nitrate as the propellant. Shige nodded as Fitzgerald explained why there could be no "fail-safe" with that propellant. After Fitzgerald laid it out, Takada stared at him blankly and uttered just five words.

"Honda wants. Honda must have."

When one of Shige Takada's top lieutenants instructed Fitzgerald not to tell Honda that the "fail-safe" was a lie, Fitzgerald reportedly terminated the conversation and told the Japanese executive, "I am not going to jail for you or Takata." Another Japanese executive pushed Fitzgerald to the limit after manufacturing records showed that inflators with potentially deadly manufacturing defects were delivered to Nissan and Toyota. In the middle of a presentation about the slip-up, an executive the Americans called "Yoshimura-san" shouted, "Stop! We will not recall any of Nissan's or Toyota's product. Takata cannot stomach another recall." Yoshimura gagged Fitzgerald: "you are not to say anything to" Shige Takada. Fitzgerald complained to Rob Fisher, who said he would phone Japan, but Fisher then "abruptly ended all further discussion."

Fitzgerald saw only one way to keep new Takata inflators from killing people. When he convinced Takata to stop using AN wafers and switched to tablets, one of his engineers suggested nestling beads of a desiccant called Zeolite among the tablets as a way to slow their deterioration. Acronyms for inflators with the new drying agent were designated with a new suffix, "13X."

Roe wanted to believe "13X" would solve the problem, going forward, but he needed to understand how much trouble the company faced from the multiple millions of inflators Takata had already made without adding that desiccant. He dispatched D. Ross Hamilton, a "corporate governance" lawyer in a respected Greensboro, North Carolina firm, to Michigan to audit the entire X-series development process. Hamilton, a former prep school lacrosse player with degrees from Duke and Wake Forest, met Fitzgerald at the Marriott in Auburn Hills, then turned a conference room in Armada into a "war room." Hamilton spent weeks in Michigan, conducting what Takata's American executives code-named the "Oriental Project." Fitzgerald said he met Hamilton and another lawyer at length, described the fraudulent test reports Shinichi Tanaka gave Honda in 2000 and gave the lawyers copies of the corrected version, which documented the inherent propensity of Takata's inflators to turn into pipe bombs.

Rathore was new in her grave when, on February 9, 2010, Honda started Recall Number Three. It swept up another half-million cars. Despite a legal requirement to provide a "chronology of all principal events" leading to the manufacturer's decision to initiate a recall, the report gave no hint that people had been killed in the weeks and months before it was filed. It did tell NHTSA, indirectly, that the scope of the Takata problems went far beyond the relatively tiny number of Hondas covered by the first two recalls. Honda calmly slipped two gigantic admissions into its defect information reports: model year 2003 also was involved and the problem was not limited to Civics and Accords. The airbags in popular family vehicles Honda sold under the names CRV, Odyssey and Acura also could kill people.

Honda faced another problem. The more recent ruptures didn't jibe with Takata's stereotypes about lazy Mexican workers and harried American machine operators. To cap the number of vehicles subject to the new recall, Takata dipped into its list of 45 manufacturing screw-ups. NHTSA was told these newly identified defects resulted from "isolated manufacturing issues" at Takata plants, each of which was fixed by a certain date. When Takata's factory records showed that those "isolated" failures weren't actually resolved until much later than the date given in Honda's Defect Information Report, Honda started to plan for another grudging recall.

A couple weeks after RECALL NUMBER THREE began, on April 2, 2010, Kristy Williams of Morrow, Georgia, suffered a slash across her carotid artery without even being in a collision. Her 2001 Civic was stopped at a traffic light when her airbag suddenly exploded. She survived, but only after profuse bleeding, strokes and seizures. The resulting brain damage left her with a severe speech disorder.

The third defect report and Williams' brush with death should have made NHTSA wonder whether Takata and Honda were complying with the statutory requirement to describe "the basis for the determination of the recall population [and] how those vehicles differed from similar vehicles the manufacturer excluded from the recall." How did Honda get from 4,000 to half a million and on to a million recalled vehicles over the course of just two years? Instead of asking that simple question, NHTSA accepted RECALL NUMBER THREE at face value.

All sorts of ugly secrets were sticking out of Honda's kimono by 2010. NHTSA did not sneak a peek. Owners of Hondas and other seven- or eight-year old cars with Takata airbags were left in the dark about the risk of being sliced and diced by their safety equipment.

On May 6, 2010, less than three months after RECALL NUMBER THREE, by itself, should have set off alarm bells and four months after President Obama's chosen NHTSA Administrator, David Strickland, was sworn in, the federal vehicle safety watchdog yawned and rolled over. NHTSA terminated its investigation. The bureaucrats' only stated reason for sticking their heads where the rising sun doesn't shine was that they had *"insufficient information* to suggest that Honda failed to make timely defect decisions on information [Takata] provided." It's no wonder NHTSA lacked information; the Office of Defects Investigation did not wait for Takata to supply documents they requested. The Obama Administration's vehicle safety agency rushed to call it quits. NHTSA unequivocally declared *"there are no additional vehicles to be investigated."*

Gross bureaucratic incompetence might explain the sudden closure of the Takata investigation, but there is a darker possibility. The real "root cause" of the Takata fiasco probably lies in a Washington phenomenon called the "revolving door." Earnest people who take government jobs to "do good" often leave to "do well" – in other words, they can make far more money working for businesses they once regulated. Their personal relationships with government decision-makers offer "back-channel" communications that frequently are never written down, not even in text messages.

Before NHTSA closed its investigation, America's auto safety "watchdog" asked Takata point-blank whether it had "sold any inflators similar to those covered by the 2008 and 2009 recalls" to manufacturers other than Honda. One of Takata's American engineers tried to tell the truth, that BMW, not Honda, had experienced the first rupture in Switzerland, in 2003. He was silenced. His superiors told him the company's NHTSA lawyers advised it was fair to interpret the agency's imprecise question about "similar" inflators as applying only to units *manufactured during October* 2001, not any other month of production.[53]

Of course, Takata's lawyers were not just NHTSA lawyers – they were *NHTSA's* lawyers – as in, lawyers who previously worked for the government and, presumably, for the benefit of the American public. Erika Z. Jones was Administrator Raymond Peck's "special counsel" from 1981 to 1985, when they led the unsuccessful effort to kill the airbag mandate. From 1985 to 1989, Jones was NHTSA's Chief Counsel, the agency's top lawyer. Jones parlayed that job into a partnership at the Chicago law firm Mayer Brown, which also later hired Ken Weinstein, a Yale-educated lawyer who spent 17 years as the top official in charge of the "watchdog's" bark and bite as NHTSA's top litigation counsel from 1988 to 1997 and as the agency's enforcement chief from 1997 to 2005. Jones and Weinstein were not just former colleagues of the NHTSA defect investigators who were supposed to figure out what was behind Honda's limited airbag recalls. They were their former leaders.

The government lawyers and investigators who met with Takata's lawyers knew that the Mayer Brown law firm or its client, Takata, were potential employers when their turn came to pass through the "revolving door." One NHTSA investigator, Christopher Santucci, proved how tempting the revolving door could be. Santucci was investigating Toyotas that ran away with them-

125

selves and killed people in 2009 and 2010. Toyota's "face man" was Christopher Tinto, another former NHTSA employee. On two weeks' notice, Santucci also went to work at Toyota – under Tinto! – on an investigation that uncovered corporate lies about deadly cases of unintended acceleration and ultimately resulted in Toyota paying a record-setting $1.2 billion fine. NHTSA did not prohibit Santucci from negotiating a job with the same manufacturer he was investigating.

Takata's 2003 and 2004 "field ruptures" received absolutely no public attention. Jim Takada, by contrast, received special attention on June 6, 2005 – a "Special Award of Appreciation" from NHTSA for his "leadership" and "tireless work in promoting automobile safety" and for his "continuing support of NHTSA." The Associate Administrator who handed Takada the heavy plexiglass plaque credited him for employing the "best scientific talents." The Secretary of Transportation – Norman Yoshio Mineta, a California politician who spent his formative years in an internment camp for Japanese immigrants during World War II – was on hand to be the first to congratulate the first-ever Japanese component supplier to receive such an award. The accolades were a curiously oblivious way to acknowledge rampant destruction and manipulation of test results by Takata's "best scientific talents," the engineers who were busy at that moment "XX-ing" unfavorable data to hide the propensity of Takata's airbag inflators to slaughter people.

 Mineta, who was 75 years old when he left government service, was still a popular, personable and bi-partisan fixture of American government. Over many years, whenever he visited the Home Islands, he joined Jim Takada and his wife, Akiko Yamada, in a round of golf. In 2006, after serving longer than any other Secretary of Transportation, Mineta passed through the "revolving door" between protecting the public interest as a government official and manipulating the government to serve private interests. In his new job as Vice Chairman of Hill + Knowlton Strategies, Inc., a global public affairs firm known for the "reputation management" services it provided to such clients as the Church of Scientology, he remained close to Akiko, not only as a golf buddy, but also as a trusted and well-paid advisor on all things American. Translation was never needed; both Akiko and Norm were equally comfortable speaking English and Japanese.

Mineta's main job for Takata, as soon as he stopped regulating Takata, was to help the company trade on its recent "Special Award of Appreciation" and avoid trouble with the NHTSA officials who dared to open the 2009 investigation into Takata's first round of airbag recalls.

2011-13

Washington

In April 2011 Honda admitted in RECALL NUMBER FOUR that the previous recalls failed to include thousands of cars that received inflators produced in the era of rampant manufacturing screw-ups. However, the new Defect Information Report did not mention the Griffin, Parham or Rathore horror stories and there is no indication anyone at any level of the NHTSA bureaucracy was aware of their grisly deaths.

RECALL NUMBER FIVE, filed in December 2011, also was limited to 2001 to 2003 model cars, but it more than doubled the admitted number of vehicles with potential pipe bombs to more than 2.5 million. For the first time, Honda mentioned to NHTSA that Takata's airbag inflators had experienced benign-sounding events they called "energetic dis-assemblies." They left out any mention of the airbags ripping people's throats out. These deaths did not result from the same inherent problem, dating back to the 1970s, of vehicle occupants who were out-of-position when their airbags inflated "taking one for the team." "Punch-out" deaths had been deemed a reasonable risk to car occupants on the theory that some people got polio from the polio vaccine. Still, neither the shocking news that airbags were killing people in unheard-of ways nor the gigantic, five-fold expansion of the 2008 recall prompted NHTSA to reopen its investigation.

For five years, NHTSA took comfort that the defective inflators affected only Hondas. Takata gave the agency that impression in 2010, before investigators closed their investigation into Honda's 40,000-car initial recall. In Honda's RECALL NUMBER SIX, filed in the Spring of 2013, the recall population swelled by another half-million of their vehicles. The big shock to NHTSA was that other makes – Toyota, GM, Nissan, Mazda and BMW – together added 1.3 million more. Takata's already massive recalls were making history and, before the end of 2013, swept up two additional Japanese carmakers, Subaru and Mitsubishi.

Motorists driving four million recalled cars had no idea they were playing Russian roulette every time they got behind the wheel. None of them died during 2012 but several Americans found out what an "energetic disassembly" of a Takata airbag felt like. In March 2012, within days of each other, Angelina Sujata, a 2001 Civic owner in Columbia, South Carolina, took a piece of shrapnel in her chest, so deep that her breastbone was exposed. In Jacksonville, Florida, Sharonda Blowe's 2001 Accord planted a chunk of shrapnel in the middle of her forehead big enough to fracture her skull.

By 2013, it did not matter much whether any particular vehicle was formally included in a "recall population." Inflators that were made years after the supposed end of Takata's "siesta" problem also began to explode. Floridian Joseph Nasworthy suffered devastating eye and nose lacerations requiring 1,000 stitches when his eight-year old 2005 Civic blasted him on August 6, 2013. NHTSA callously dismissed Nasworthy's injuries as "minor." Just three weeks later, a Destin, Florida, woman suffered a similar blast. Unbeknownst to her, the Takata airbag in Air Force Lt. Stephanie Erdman's 2002 Civic had been under recall for four years. During that period, she took the car to her Honda-certified dealer for service three times. They never offered to replace her defective airbag inflator. It blew out her right eye and mangled her face, but she survived. Less than 48 hours later, on September 3, 2013, police in Alhambra, California, were dispatched to a parking lot to investigate a gruesome homicide in a 2002 Acura. Hai Ming (Devin) Xu, 47, had just gotten off work at a restaurant when someone took a shotgun to his face, or so the police thought. It took them several days to figure out that chunks of his airbag inflator hit him so hard, reverberations inside his skull scrambled his brain. Honda's website gave conflicting information whether the airbag in Xu's Acura had ever been recalled. Spokesmen for Honda and Takata initially disclaimed any knowledge about Xu's death. A Chevy Cruze driver, 25-year old Brandi Owens, was blinded by her Takata airbag in October 2013.

Despite a dearth of national publicity about the airbag explosions, plaintiff's lawyers were mobilizing to recruit more victims as clients. Those who had not yet settled with Honda and Takata were frustrated, however. The manufacturers were denying liability but quick to write settlement checks, so "discovery" requests, including "interrogatories" (a set of written questions requiring sworn answers) went unanswered. They tipped off Reuters correspondent Ben Klayman and shared with him a list of 67 thorny questions. Exactly what role did Honda play in the design, development, manufacturing and quality control of the Takata airbags? Why was Takata the only airbag manufacturer to use ammonium nitrate? Will other recalls be needed as the AN degrades over time? Was there a problem with Takata's corporate culture? Klayman, an experienced business reporter, considered the inquiries fair game.

Honda, having received nothing of substance in response to the basic question its U.S.-based leader, Hidenobu Iwata, put to Shigehisa Takada in 2009 – "Why does it explode? I want to know the truth!" – passed the hot-potato questions along to Takata. Takata's personal injury defense lawyers dismissed the questions as a back-door way for plaintiffs to get responses to discovery requests. In an effort to satisfy its biggest customer, Takata shared draft answers with its public affairs advisors. They noted that the proposed responses were clumsily evasive. The Takada family had an easier way to deal with the challenge. Akiko went straight to her "go-to" guy in Washington. Hill + Knowlton Vice Chairman and former Transportation Secretary Norm Mineta interceded with Honda. Takata's biggest customer withdrew their demand that Takata answer the "67 questions." By December 2013 Klayman rightly figured he would never hear back from Honda. He sent three simple queries directly to Takata: Are more recalls coming, and will they involve younger cars? Are airbags blowing up in cars that have never been recalled? Did Honda pressure Takata to produce more inflators, faster?

Takata Corporation's North Carolina-based Executive Vice President, Frank Roe, got wind that Klayman had phoned former Takata executives and told them the gist of the "special report" he was writing. The article would be published in the opening days of 2014. Roe knew it would be no puff piece. Ominously, Klayman was interviewing chemists about Takata's decision to switch to ammonium nitrate as the inflator propellant.

Roe started canvassing for someone who could cook up a public affairs strategy for dealing with potential revelations about the destruction and fabrication of test data and the other ugly truths he saw coming. He needed a Washington veteran who had a strong, pro-auto safety reputation, hands-on experience with the automotive industry and vehicle safety recalls, unassailable professsional credentials and good media sense. Most importantly, he needed someone who would not be afraid to burst the bubble in Tokyo and explain why Akiko Takada's personal and client relationship with Secretary Mineta was no longer a magic bullet.

On January 10, 2014, he found me.

2014

Washington

Frank Roe was Takata's most senior executive in the United States but he knew that counted for little in Japan. Whenever he attended meetings in Tokyo with the corporation's other top leaders, he told colleagues, Roe felt outranked by the Japanese guy with an embroidered towel over one arm who served tea in the conference room.

The day he hired me as a consultant, we spoke by telephone late into the evening. He seemed deeply worried about the impending Reuters article but also hoped its publication would be a wakeup call to his company's leadership in Tokyo.

Roe knew all the details about what Takata's defective airbag inflators were doing to people. He told me with a quavering voice how Ashley Parham's death in Oklahoma five years earlier often drove him to tears. Roe assured me the unfortunate "field ruptures" resulted not from a design error but from a series of manufacturing screw-ups that rendered a small, easily identified portion of propellant supplies unusually sensitive to moisture. The problem was financially manageable, Roe added, because the company's personal injury defense lawyers had proven adept with the same 1950s approach to vehicle defects that Ralph Nader railed against in *Unsafe at Any Speed*. Takata wrote big checks to get victims to clam up. Every time that happened, "discovery" requests, including at least one notice to take Shigehisa Takada's deposition, evaporated and nobody got wiser about why people were getting slaughtered by equipment that was supposed to save their lives. Even where there could be no doubt that someone got butchered by an exploding airbag inflator, Takata never once had to admit liability, much less acknowledge the existence of any sort of "defect related to motor vehicle safety" that would trigger the expensive process of warning people and fixing their cars. How much – or how little – it valued victims' lives in dollars and cents was forever kept top-secret.

Roe assured me the corporation finally was on top of its chaotic manufacturing process – going forward, at least. Investors were glad the company had enough insurance to survive the litigation expenses resulting from three wrongful death settlements and eight personal injury lawsuits that were pending when Takata signed me up in early 2014. Unfortunately, an unpredictable number of additional people inevitably would be killed or injured by airbags in old Hondas. Only about three out of four newly recalled vehicles ever get fixed, and I knew that ratio flips to less than one out of four when cars get old, like the vehicles that killed Parham and Rathore in 2009 and Xu in 2013. The chronically low "repair rates" for older cars are bad news for drivers but pure gold for car manufacturers. Nothing compels them to do *anything* to follow up on their initial, "snail-mail" notices, even though only a fraction of them ever show up in current owners' mailboxes.

Roe was confident Takata could ride out a few more scattered lawsuits involving manufacturing defects but he seemed less sanguine about any suggestion that ammonium nitrate was inherently unsafe. Roe worried that the impending feature article would be a major exposé. He knew Klayman interviewed chemical engineers who might portray the deaths and injuries that had occurred through 2013 in eight- or 10-year old Hondas not as the factory goofs Honda described in its formal defect reports but as the result of environmental degradation that would, sooner or later, turn their entire production of more than 200 million inflators into potential pipe bombs. My first assignment, then, was to create a cogent, reassuring statement that ammonium nitrate was a safe choice. Roe put me in touch with Al Bernat, who had retired as Takata's Vice President of Engineering in 2012 but was returning to the company as its new Senior Vice President for Product Development. The input I got from Bernat by email came with a disclaimer. He said the information was "drawn from interviews of Takata personnel (primarily Paresh Khandhadia)," a chemical engineer who bragged that his lab at Takata's Armada, Michigan, facility developed and launched the AN-powered inflators.

I boiled ammonium nitrate's supposed bona fides down to a "one-pager" that proclaimed Takata's explosive to be "the best propellant available" because of its efficiency in pumping more gas and less toxic smoke and dust into airbag cushions and because the raw material was less likely to blow up in transit. The document we drafted made two misleading statements. The first was that "improper deployments [one of the euphemisms Takata used for pipe bomb-like explosions] resulted from certain specific manufacturing issues that arose only between 2000 and 2002." The second was that "improved manufacturing processes" were enough to protect the public because, *while properly sealed inside an inflator unit, AN is stable and ready for lifetime use.*"

Roe was thrilled with the results of my collaboration with Bernat. Finally, he had responsible corporate officers on record that the company could assure the public that AN was a safe design choice. The looming questions Takata wanted me to address were how, when and to whom Takata should communicate this information.

Reuters published Klayman's "special report" on January 13, 2014, and it was tough.[54] It highlighted Takata's admissions in NHTSA filings that its Mexican workers "improperly stored chemicals ... botched the manufacture of the explosive propellants ... [and] kept inadequate quality control records." Klayman suggested that Takata had "lost its grip on quality" and presented a "case study in how a lapse in quality control rigor can prove extraordinarily costly." He wondered whether the recalls might undermine the company's financial viability and quoted Jim Takada's observations in 1985 that Takata Corporation would be crossing a "dangerous bridge" if it got into the airbag business and that "one mistake could ruin the company." Klayman quoted experts who wondered out loud whether the choice of ammonium nitrate could turn out to be that fatal, "one mistake."

I sent Roe the outline of a crisis communications action plan hours after the Reuters story broke. He phoned me at 9 p.m. and asked me to travel the next morning from my office in Washington, D.C., to Takata's U.S. corporate headquarters in Auburn Hills, Michigan.

"I expect you to work very closely with Rob [Fisher] and Tim Healey," Roe instructed. "We want to be absolutely accurate and are depending on Mr. Al Bernat [to] fact-check" any executive talking points Takata executives might use.

2014

Auburn Hills, Michigan

Snow was falling steadily when my flight touched down at the Detroit Metro Airport. Such weather would have shuttered government offices in Washington, but Michigan drivers were nonplussed. I followed the icy ruts left by their tires all the way to Auburn Hills.

I sloshed my way inside Takata's low-rise U.S. corporate headquarters. Robert Fisher, the president of TK Holdings, the American subsidiary of the Japanese parent, greeted me with a warm smile. Timothy Healey, Fisher's predecessor and mentor, wheeled in on a scooter designed to keep him off of the leg on which he had recent surgery. Alby Berman, the Vice President of Corporate Planning and Communications, introduced himself as an electrical engineer, not a PR guy. "Japan thought I would fit corporate communications because the corporation does not communicate with the public," he said, "and I plan to retire soon."

Paresh Khandhadia, the engineer who "perfected" the ammonium nitrate-powered airbag inflator, was a no-show. Al Bernat, who was my source on the point paper extolling the virtues of AN as an airbag propellant, made a point of saying we would just have to *assume* Khandhadia had conclusive technical data to show that the company's decision to use ammonium nitrate in the inflator was beyond reproach. That precluded any discussion about what the company would need to say if the inflator design itself turned out to be defective.

I presented company leaders with a "Crisis Communications Action Plan to Affirm the Safety of Takata's Airbag Inflators and Their Propellant." The Reuters special report that prompted our urgent meeting was somewhat technical but we assumed it would get "pickup" beyond financial media. The purpose of the strategy I laid out was to "minimize pressure on regulators to encourage [vehicle manufacturers] to widen their recall campaigns" beyond the first two million vehicles. The most urgent tactical need, I advised, was for Takata to establish a single point of contact, an American "voice of Takata." When I suggested Fisher, with his 30 years in the industry and degrees from the General Motors Institute and a business school in Auburn Hills, should claim that role, every man in the room shot sideways glances at the others. Fisher, a tall man with broad shoulders and the first wisps of gray hair rising from his high forehead and temples, was first and foremost a "sales guy," representing the company to its carmaker customers. Bernat and Berman had no experience in the spotlight and Healey seemed happy to be easing out of corporate leadership. At least one American executive needed to tell the world, with credibility and authority, that whatever went wrong with Takata's airbags has been fixed and whatever might yet go wrong will be fixed. That person needed to develop a simple, clear consistent and concise "base message," which I described as a set of "Takata Truths." After Bob Schubert's name came up, Fisher adjusted his glasses, studied a spot on the floor between us for a full minute and then announced that lunch was being brought in.

"I hope you like sushi."

The senior Takata executives in Rob Fisher's office that snowy January day knew remarkably little about how airbags got mandated in cars. They seemed surprised to hear that vehicle manufacturers had warned everyone who fought in the airbag wars of the 1970s and 1980s that airbags would kill some people, even if they inflated exactly as designed. They had not seen the disgusting film clips Detroit's lobbyists took to Capitol Hill, in which live baboons stood in for children and petite women who could be out-of-position during a normal airbag "punch-out." The consensus was that a civilized society does not withhold a vaccine and sacrifice a large number of people just because the vaccine will also kill a tiny number of unfortunate individuals. Only Bernat seemed aware that, in the early days, airbags killed a child every week of the year and that, for quite a while, airbags that deployed normally killed more kids than they saved.

Car manufacturers in the 1990s did not recall vehicles because of punch-out deaths. Instead, partly at Bernat's urging when he chaired an industry trade group earlier in his career, they improved airbag designs and reduced wrongful death litigation costs by reducing the number of unneeded deployments and designing airbags that pushed a person who was out-of-position away an instant before the more violent punch-out happened. In fact, Bernat emphasized, Takata's switch to ammonium nitrate helped make those "dual stage" airbags possible. Takata's inflators were both cheaper and smaller than its competitors' so there was more room in the dashboard and the budget to incorporate extra features. New NHTSA standards set in 2006 boosted Takata's sales of "smart" airbags. Fisher and his colleagues remembered NHTSA's administrator, David Strickland, presenting Takata's chief research engineer, Ryoishi Yoshida, an

Award for Safety Engineering Excellence in May 2013 for designing solutions to the punch-out problem.

I applied the "vaccine" story to the federal safety statute. Nobody in the Government considered those early, deadly airbags to pose an "unreasonable risk" to safety. Instead, they were simply a sad part of the process of achieving the greater good. Assuming the truth of the point paper Bernat and I drafted, the three known deaths that had occurred before our meeting – and others likely to occur in vehicles that would crash before they got repaired – also could be seen as part of the process of making airbags safer, overall. There were plenty of experts-for-hire who could characterize the handful of ruptures – and I was told to assume there would only be a handful – as growing pains associated with the development of smaller, dual-stage inflators. At the end of our four-hour meeting Fisher asked me to flesh out the plan. He said he would present it to Takata's Chairman, Shigehisa Takada, by telephone that night, when it would be early morning in Tokyo.

"Proceed as we discussed," Fisher instructed me after he phoned Tokyo.

2014

Tokyo

The Reuters' special report contained more innuendo than outright allegations of wrongdoing, but we figured Reuters' investor-oriented readership would be shocked by any suggestion that Takata's airbag recalls could threaten the company's financial viability. To our surprise, "general interest" media almost entirely ignored the Reuters report and Takata's stock price was unaffected. A Takata director, John J. O'Brien, made sure all of Takata's top officers, including Fisher, Bernat, Berman, Roe and Chairman Takada himself, received a message from John Mendel, American Honda's Executive Vice President. Mendel wishfully told Honda dealers the Reuters article "is referring [only] to … certain 2000 through 2003 model year vehicles." Without naming any names, Mendel assured them that the 2013 explosion that ripped Joseph Nasworthy's face apart "is not related to the issues that led to the earlier recalls." My work continued at full speed until Healey expressed doubt that Tokyo was still fully on board with the plan. A week later, Roe forwarded to Fisher and me another message from Takata's O'Brien. It read, "Honda is not making an issue of this…. Best to just *lay low and don't talk about it*."

I argued that O'Brien's approach was dangerously short-sighted. "The lack of a response," I worried, "will be taken as an admission." The Reuters story fizzled but it obviously would not be the last. Takata had an urgent need to put someone in charge of a "truth squad," I advised, a "Mr. Right Now, if not a Mr. Right."

Berman traveled to Tokyo on January 28, 2014, where he presented the merits of my proposed "truth squad" directly to Chairman Takada. Berman reported by email that Takada was intrigued by the notion of media training but declared my work a "temporary assignment." He instructed Berman to rely instead on CNG Advisors, LLC, the consulting firm Secretary Mineta joined after he retired from Hill + Knowlton. CNG was owned by Greg Basye, a former spokesman for the Transportation Department who had also worked at Hill + Knowlton. Chairman Takada said Mineta was "excellent in supporting Takata during the painful stage of *convincing Honda not to answer the 67 questions*" Klayman had posed a few months earlier.

A week after Chairman Takada personally nixed my proposed truth-telling project, Fisher told Roe and me he was "cleaning up some files" and forwarded a guest editorial by a public relations pundit. Under the headline, "The Surprising News About Product Recalls," its author opined that "product recalls … present [companies] a unique opportunity … to demonstrate they *care more about the safety of their customers than their own profits*." Takata's then-Senior Vice President for Sales and Marketing, Kevin M. Kennedy, had shared the article with Fisher and the company's other top American executives in 2010, not long after NHTSA abruptly closed its initial Takata investigation. The pundit's general advice seemed less applicable to motor vehicle recalls because the trade association for the new car dealers had commissioned studies showing that safety recalls tarnish a car brand only when they are "tied to numerous injuries or deaths and media attention is widespread."[55]

Months went by with no progress on the proposed "truth squad." In June, Berman told me it fell victim to Takata's *directed cost-avoidance mode of operation*." As Chairman Takada complained in the company's Annual Report, "we are not satisfied with our current operating profit margin."[56] To me, this made Takada's actual first priority crystal clear. Berman added that the "truth squad" was a tough sell, given Honda's "preference to stay quiet. Several people here want us to stand down until the next wave of recall remedy changes occur." Still, Berman added, "we may need some help with forming the Takata 'truth squad' for when Rob [Fisher] and I go to DC to meet with NHTSA head and possibly [Transportation] Secretary Foxx." I heard no more about it because Takata sent the opposite of a "truth squad" to those Washington meetings.

Despite his earlier complaints about falsification of data, Bob Schubert led the delegation of Takata's American engineers to NHTSA headquarters, which occupies one wing of a massive office building a few blocks southeast of the U.S. Capitol. Skipping over the fundamental design issues presented by their use of ammonium nitrate, Takata's brain trust told the government's safety experts on May 20, 2014, that it would take them another year-and-a-half to figure out why airbags with no known manufacturing errors were killing people. Only then, they told the government, it *might* make sense to recall additional vehicles.

NHTSA's side in the discussion included three division chiefs – Greg Magno from Defects Assessment, Scott Yon from Vehicle Integrity and Jennifer Timian in Recall Management – and a roomful of agency "wall-sitters." They got some big surprises. Schubert, Al Bernat and D. Michael Rains, Takata's senior safety engineer, admitted that half a dozen additional inflator ruptures occurred in late 2013 and early 2014. None of those exploding Hondas, Toyotas, Nissans or Mazdas had ever been recalled and half of them did not show up in Magno's central vehicle-defect data repository, known as ARTEMIS (a cute acronym for NHTSA's Automotive Recall, Tire and Equipment Management Information

System). Nobody mentioned that the staffer responsible for monitoring airbag recalls had been told to stop.[57] Half of the newly disclosed ruptures occurred on the driver-side and half on the passenger-side.

The propellant in all those exploding airbags was identical to what Takata used in the millions of cars that had already been recalled but there was no indication that any of those explosions resulted from production errors. This belied Takata's wishful assumption that all of the ruptures resulted from *manufacturing*, not *design* defects. The Takata delegation admitted that "environmental exposure" contributed to the explosions but insisted ruptures *could not occur* without a concurrent "compromised manufacturing process." Even in those yet-to-be-identified circumstances, they said, "moisture intrusion" could be a secondary factor, but only in places like Florida, with "high absolute humidity." Takata was doing research to figure out whether "a *combination* of long-term exposure to high absolute humidity environment and processing issues … may have influenced aging stability," but Schubert and his colleagues told NHTSA not to expect the results of Takata's science project for another 18 months. They did not mention 14 years of internal test reports showing the inherent unpredictability of ammonium nitrate's explosive power.

With Takata's lawyer, former NHTSA enforcement chief Ken Weinstein, looking on, Magno gently suggested Takata might want to consider a "regional" recall, aimed only at cars in the most humid states. According to Takata's internal report on the meeting, Magno also requested monthly updates on Takata's extended research project.

The NHTSA meeting lit no fires under Takata to confess the real reason its airbags were killing people, even after a sudden uptick in ruptures that wrecked the lives of a new round of victims. Just nine days after Takata's presentation to NHTSA, Corey Burdick, a 26-year old forklift operator and father of two little boys, got blasted by the airbag in his 2001 Honda Civic in a 15-mile-per-hour collision. The vehicle had not been recalled, but the airbag inflator split the right side of his face wide open and scooped out his right eyeball.

Within weeks after Berman told me Shige Takada had personally nixed the "truth squad" project, almost a dozen other Honda drivers got blasted. A Takata airbag maimed Claribel Nunez in Florida. An AN-powered inflator of a different Takata configuration killed Law Suk Leh and her unborn baby in Malaysia. Four additional Southeast Asians died from airbag explosions that summer in a model called the Honda City.

On September 7, 2014, Jewel Brangman, a 26-year old aspiring actress who dated Hollywood icon Clint Eastwood's son, Scott, was rendered brain-dead in a rented Honda on a California freeway, leaving her father to make the emotionally excruciating decision to "pull the plug" on her life support. It took Honda more than nine months to acknowledge that a Takata airbag killed Brangman.

Days later, the death of Hien Tran stirred publicity in Orlando, Florida. Police were convinced that the 51-year old Vietnamese immigrant was stabbed to death as she drove home with a wad of cash from her nail salon. The money was left in the car, so robbery did not appear to be the motive. Homicide investigators recognized the airbag as the culprit only after they stumbled across an article in *Car and Driver* magazine that described the horrendous fate of Devin Xu a year earlier. A recall notice for Tran's 2001 Accord arrived at her home a week after she died.

NHTSA first broached the notion of a scaled-down recall campaign, limited to humid states, with Takata's car-maker customers two weeks after Takata's May 20, 2014, presentation. Takata's second-biggest customer, Toyota, panicked. The company was still scraping together the historic $1.2 billion criminal fine it agreed to pay just weeks earlier for its own dissembling about its cars running away with themselves when improperly installed floor mats trapped accelerator pedals. More than 100 people had been killed or hurt by a problem Toyota said was impossible. One young driver was sentenced to years in prison for vehicular homicide when a jury found it inconceivable that Toyota sold him a car that could run away with itself and kill someone.

No Toyota drivers had been killed by a Takata airbag, but the last thing Toyota needed was headlines and investigations brought on by airbag deaths. Takata told NHTSA it would support only "regional field actions," not a recall. Takata was willing only to yank more inflators out of cars in Florida, Puerto Rico and certain individual counties known to experience "high absolute humidity" for its proposed 18-month "root-cause" project. Toyota forced Takata's hand on June 10, 2014, when it recalled another 700,000 of its vehicles across the United States. Within days, Honda issued another million-car recall, BMW pulled back another 600,000 vehicles and four other manufacturers joined them. It was the auto industry equivalent of yelling "fire" in a crowded theater. Chrysler, Ford and five other carmakers recalled another 4.2 million cars, but only if they were registered at that moment in places they considered "humid." A NHTSA press release spread incorrect information about the numbers, makes and models of cars that were covered by manufacturers' recall filings. The result was mass confusion among 15 million affected vehicle owners. Just check our website, the agency told the public, not realizing that it, too, was the victim of a different sort of crash. It was not scaled to handle that much traffic so NHTSA launched a new online tool designed to allow worried owners to type in their vehicle identification numbers and see whether their cars might contain a killer airbag. NHTSA also persuaded vehicle manufacturers to make this "VIN-Lookup Tool" available on their own sites.

The unique sizes and customized designs of Takata airbag inflators – the reason for their stunningly quick conquest of the American market – generally meant there would be no replacements until Takata could make them. Upham, Takata's former marketing chief shocked reporters by observing that "you cannot just plug and play a new inflator." [58] A larger canister could require reconfiguration of the entire airbag module, which could only be installed after months of testing. When they figured out that no timely fix was available, Toyota told its vehicle owners not to allow anyone to sit in the passenger seat and to post a sign on the dashboard, saying "DO NOT SIT HERE." Toyota owners who paid for four-seater cars and ended up with three-seaters sued to recover the loss of value of their cars.

Chaos reigned, especially after NHTSA reopened its investigation of Takata in July 2014. Takata could have put the situation in perspective by zeroing in on what it called "Alpha" inflators – the haphazardly made units that were installed in 2001-03 Hondas and Acuras. Carmakers could have concentrated on mitigating the risk to drivers of those cars but Takata fervently maintained its "preference to stay quiet," volunteering nothing in public. Even customers like BMW, who urgently demanded access to Takata's test results in October 2014, got shut out.

An old-fashioned media "feeding frenzy" – the only type of event known to make a safety recall hurt carmakers' reputations and sales – started overnight, early in the Fall of 2014. The *New York Times* amplified a consumer advisory NHTSA issued on October 21, 2014. After network and cable television news shows started making "Takata" a household name, Takata paid me to supervise a high-tech video news clip monitoring service to compile every "media mention" on its airbags and the carmakers who had installed them. It was painfully obvious with each weekly report that nobody was swallowing the pablum Berman was spooning out – "Takata's dream of zero fatalities … still drives the company."[59] People started to doubt his rote assurances that the company "will continue to cooperate fully with any inquiries or requests from regulators."[60]

An internet parody worthy of *The Onion* announced the launch of Takata's new "weapons division," whose "exacting military specifications" made airbags discharge "razor-sharp … projectiles." Harking back to a Ford engineer's quip in the 1960s about placing a Claymore mine under every driver's seat, the morbid jokester noted that drivers who think their airbag will protect them were "more lax about how they drove" but the prospect of catching "metal spikes … if they screwed up would make drivers pay more attention."

Japanese financial analysts, known for their understated confidence in any Japanese company, turned only a bit bearish on Takata. In the face of a "quality problem," Yusuke Ueda of Merrill Lynch said, the response will be measured by "how promptly you disclose your information. Takata has not understood this well." Kasuyuki Terao of Allianz Global Investments said, "it is not good for the CEO to keep silent in a critical situation like this." Shintaro Niimura at Nomura Holdings mildly added, "Takata's management may have underestimated the fallout."[61]

Even Takata's own Japanese executives started begging their chairman to step up to the plate. One warned Takada, in broken English, about "many notes start to coming out on internet." The uproar "will combine directly to the increase of pressure for immediate massive recall and Congress movement. We have to prepare these situations." The note suggested nothing the company should do to protect people from death or grievous injury.

Instead of making its executives available for interviews, Takata kept issuing more pablum – Takata "works closely every day with its customers." The company's new president and chief operating officer, a Swiss named Stefan Stocker, seemed more open. Craig Trudell, a Bloomberg News reporter in Tokyo, emailed Stocker directly after receiving no response for months from Chairman Takada. Trudell offered Stocker an opportunity to defend the company "on or off the record." Berman floated Stocker's proposed reply by me, former Secretary Mineta and Takata's newly hired criminal defense attorneys, including a former top Justice Department official named Steven G. Bradbury. Over my objections, Takata chose to send yet another stiff-arm email. Despite the opportunity to show that the company had the situation in hand and public safety in mind, Stocker could only say "we welcome the chance at a later date to tell our story." Trudell's scathing article appeared under the headline, "Warning: This Airbag May Contain Shrapnel."[62] Weeks later, after just 18 months on the job, Stocker quit.

Roe and I, of course, realized Takata had never developed its "story" and had trained no one to tell reporters, government officials or anyone else the explosive truth about the likely future scope of its airbag recalls. Still, he was optimistic that Chairman Takada, who had just sliced his own $2.3 million a year salary in half, was finally beginning to see the urgent need to do *something*. My "truth squad" rubric had bombed in Tokyo in January, so Roe asked me to propose a system for "strategic information management" that would develop and vet company statements and put factual disclosures to the public into an order that could quell the growing panic, especially among Takata's car-making customers. I started casually questioning Takata lawyers about rumors that, just before they hired me, Takata executives told former U.S. Secretary of Transportation Rodney Slater and their other Washington lobbyists at the Patton Boggs law firm that company engineers had manipulated and falsified test results from the get-go and senior management had known about it at least since 2009. The lobbyists had also advised Takata to make a full disclosure, so the rumor went, but Tokyo refused and Roe tried to hedge the company's bets by hiring me.

Was this why my truth squad proposal had languished for 10 months, I asked? Wasn't the need to disclose the truth more urgent than ever? Yes, I was told, Honda and Toyota were also pressuring Takata to "repair its battered image" but my colleague told me company executives were struck dumb when Bradbury's team of "white-collar" criminal defense lawyers at the New York-based Dechert law firm issued a stern warning: Bradbury's former employer, the Justice Department, had cited Toyota's mealy-mouthed public statements to customers and investors in the run-away car cases when it nailed them earlier in 2014 for a felony called "wire fraud." Over a late-night drink in the Detroit Airport Marriott Hotel, I asked Ross Hamilton, the lawyer Frank Roe put in charge of the "Oriental Project" in 2009, point-blank whether anyone at Takata destroyed or manipulated the results of tests to assess the suitability of ammonium nitrate as a propellant. Hamilton's off-hand reply gave me no comfort: any documents showing such conduct, he said, "would have been written in Japanese." Why weren't we getting Rob Fisher, the president of the American company, ready to stand up and tell the truth about what happened and how Takata would fix it? Fisher was no longer running the American company, I was surprised to learn. The last thing Shunkichi Shimizu, the Japanese executive who had taken over most of Fisher's responsibilities, wanted to do was to speak to me about a "truth squad" or "strategic information management."

October 2014

Armada, Michigan and Tokyo

Roe sent me back to Michigan in October 2014 to get educated on the technical details concerning which inflator designs were and were not included in the piecemeal regional recall NHTSA had suggested five months earlier. He also asked me to meet with Kevin Kennedy, a Senior Vice President who had inherited some of Fisher's duties. Kennedy agreed to the meeting but said he was unavailable while I was in Michigan. I set up shop in Hamilton's former "Oriental Project" war room at Takata's Armada facility, where frantic, muttering Takata engineers ran in and out. Elsewhere in the building, they were test-firing airbags pulled from hundreds of Toyotas. One frazzled employee told me a stunning *ten percent* of the units he tested had turned out to be pipe bombs.

"One in ten million is one thing," the grim-faced engineer in his mid-30s told me, literally tearing at his hair. "One in ten is impossible to justify."

The day I left Takata's Armada facility and headed back to Washington, Takata's Chairman had two diametrically opposite proposals on his desk. Roe's plan, which featured my insistence on preparing "individual company executives … who have the credibility, temperament and communication skills to get the truth across," had languished since January. My rebranded "truth squad" proposal landed on Chairman Takada's desk on October 24, 2014. That same day, Takada received an entirely different proposal from his mother's friend, Secretary Mineta. The stated subject of Mineta's eight-page memo was the "Current Media and Political Environment in the United States." It consisted of news clips about the most recent deaths and the nascent criminal investigation. Mineta's proposal, which was addressed to Chairman Takada, Executive Officer Shunkichi Shimizu and Berman, was a masterful example of Japanese doubletalk. It took only a little reading between the lines to understand Mineta's two main action

145

items. The first was to avoid more recalls by exploiting NHTSA's weaknesses. Although "NHTSA has come under increasing pressure to intensify fines and … issue subpoenas … in reality the regulatory agency has lost a considerable amount of power and its reputation has become tarnished." Takata's most pressing need, Mineta continued, was to examine "how to … work with NHTSA while also thinking through how to expand [Takata's] network of allies and confidants inside Washington. NHTSA is … ripe for a facelift."

Mineta offered his personal leadership to make Takata "part of the conversation versus standing by idly while others make important decisions that will greatly impact the future of Takata's business." The federal criminal investigation made it urgent to line up those "allies and confidants," Mineta added, because the investigation was putting "intense pressure" on Takata's biggest customer, Honda. The former Secretary did not seem to think anyone at Takata was at risk of going to prison, but he predicted that a Justice Department investigation of Honda's "accident reporting practices … may very well occur," especially now that unnamed former Takata "employees have gone rogue."

Mineta also identified a "more complex and multi-dimensional" angle of attack against both NHTSA and the Justice Department. America's former top official responsible for motor vehicle safety told Takata it must "examine important stakeholder relationships, protect its business … and also identify the right paths where it can *grow new relationships in Washington*." All Mineta said he needed was "additional resources" meaning, presumably, more money, to put Takata "on a path toward *protecting its reputation and business interests*." The proposal included not a single word about warning ordinary American drivers about the mortal dangers they faced.

I learned on October 25 that Shige Takada had immediately opted to implement the Mineta plan and that Berman, the head of corporate communications, would let me know "how best … to use/integrate" my services into that effort. "Puh-lease," I fired back, disgusted. I mimicked Mineta's "new relationships in Washington" mantra and said his firm "would have told Caesar to beware the Ides of March on March 16."

NHTSA's reputation was tarnished, for sure, but the Safety Engineering Excellence Award the agency gave Takata just 16 months earlier was also getting stained. Ken Weinstein started picking up ugly vibes in the hallways where he spent his own lengthy government career. The agency's new Assistant Chief Counsel for Litigation, Timothy H. Goodman, had told Weinstein he would "not allow claims of privilege to prevent [NHTSA] from obtaining information it needs to carry out its safety mission."

Negative publicity about Takata was at a fever pitch and the Takada family stood to lose hundreds of millions of dollars as Takata's stock price took one hit after another. Having known nothing other than limitless wealth and privilege, Shigehisa Takada's technical degree from Keio University and lack of work experience outside his family company left him ill-prepared to deal with an existential public, customer, legal and government relations crisis. One insider told Reuters Shige was "paralyzed to make decisions on his own." Even worse, Reuters humiliated him with a report that "Shige went missing for a few hours" on November 30, 2014, "after a row with his mother. Nobody knows where he went."[63]

A few years earlier, in 2007, Juichiro and Akiko Takada had named Shige president of the company when he was just 41. That same year, Takata Kabushiki Gaisha (Takata Corporation) started selling stock to the public. When Jim died a billionaire in 2011, Shige inherited the additional role of chairman even though, behind his back, top people in the company derided him as "Shige-chan" ("Little Shige"), a puppet for his mother. Akiko, who had close ties to Japanese royalty, was known to everyone in Takata's inner circle as "O-Okusan" ("Big Wife") because she dominated everything in her grasp, including minute details of company decision-making.

"Big Wife" dropped off Takata Corporation's board of directors. Nevertheless, Akiko, high-cheeked and attractive into her 70s, maintained absolute control of the company with the modest-sounding title, "special advisor." The family essentially owned 80 percent of the stock and Big Wife ruled the family.[64] Nobody could be more "special" than that.

What "Big Wife" hammered into "Little Shige" in the proverbial woodshed has not been reported but, just hours after the row with his mother, the son began to implement Secretary Mineta's strategy of "growing relationships" in Washington. By December 2, 2014, Takata Corporation had hired, on top of Secretary Mineta and Secretary Slater, two more former American Cabinet secretaries who were Akiko's generational contemporaries – 76-year old Samuel Skinner, a Chicago lawyer who was Secretary of Transportation and White House Chief of Staff under President George H.W. Bush, and 75-year old John W. Snow, who at various times served as Deputy Secretary of Transportation, NHTSA Administrator and Treasury Secretary. Takata also recruited two more former NHTSA Administrators and two additional experts who had not served in government. Former NHTSA Administrator Marion Blakey's high profile was more current because she had recently chaired the National Transportation Safety Board and ran President George W. Bush's Federal Aviation Administration on her way to the revolving door that made her CEO of the Aerospace Industries Association and, later, President of London-based Rolls-Royce's American operations. Takata also hired Dr. Jeffrey Runge, an emergency room physician who became NHTSA Administrator in 2001. With great public fanfare, Takata described the assignment for its blue-ribbon, "Independent Takata Corporation Quality Assurance Panel." Their job, ostensibly, was to publish an "unbiased review" titled "Ensuring Quality Across the Board," on Takata's "safety, quality, design and manufacturing practices."

In February 2016 the Quality Assurance Panel reported the bleeding obvious. Takata needed "significant improvement across the quality spectrum," especially "in addressing quality-related concerns, ensuring quality in Takata's design and manufacturing processes and promoting quality." However, "no link" should be inferred "between the gaps in quality processes … and the failure of products covered by Takata's current recall campaign."

Takata presented it as a "we've seen the light!" type of moment and Skinner sunnily declared that "the Takata team … has not only met the Panel's expectations but … has set a new standard for the industry."[65] Their report was studiously consistent with Takata's big lie, that its airbags killed people only because of a few early *manufacturing* mistakes, not a *design* that was inherently defective. It mentioned nothing about Takata's falsification of test reports because Takata placed blinders on the esteemed panel members. All of the nominally "independent" experts agreed up front *"not to evaluate* the products that prompted the current recalls or the processes employed when the products of concern [Takata's killer airbags] were manufactured."[66]

November and December 2014

Capitol Hill, Washington

On November 6, 2014, under the headline "Takata Saw and Hid Risks in Airbags in 2004," the *New York Times* falsely accused Takata's most senior engineer, Al Bernat, of masterminding secret airbag inflator tests in 2004 and destroying the results. The Gray Lady got that wrong. The only urgent testing done in 2004 dealt with torn cushions, not inflator ruptures – but Takata was in a poor position to set the record straight. Secretary Mineta's firm drafted a statement the next day and Roe ran it by me, criminal defense counsel Steve Bradbury and NHTSA counsel Ken Weinstein. It called the *Times* out on its sloppy falsehoods – Bernat was not, as the *Times* said, a *former* Takata employee – and branded the story "fundamentally inaccurate." Instead of denying the most devastating allegation – that Takata had deep-sixed test results showing inflator ruptures – Mineta's draft response whined that Takata was "fully entitled to explain … to the appropriate government authorities before the media reaches any conclusions." In other words, Takata would tell the public what it wanted them to know when it wanted them to know it.

Takata offered a slightly more detailed rebuttal a week later, saying the *Times* confused "multiple events occurring at different times and for different purposes and thereby tells a story that is simply untrue."[67] Takata, of course, still did not reveal that the Japanese engineers who validated the company's ammonium nitrate inflators in 2000 had manipulated data, hid instances when the test inflators exploded or that they got promoted for doing it, even though top management had been aware of their criminal conduct for several years.

The *Times* was correct, however, to report that Takata was under federal criminal investigation. Working with the Criminal Division of the Justice Department, the U.S. Attorney for the Southern District of New York had just served Takata with a grand jury subpoena.[68] Takata's usual "network of allies and confidants" – the people Secretary Mineta told Chairman Takada just days earlier he needed more of – started running for cover. Market analyst Scott Upham, who remained in close touch with Takata's top executives throughout the crisis and tipped them off about the Reuters special report prior to its publication in January 2014, was convinced his former employer could ride out the controversy until the *Times* story hit. "I was confident [Takata] was too big to fail, but this is really shaking my analysis," Upham said. Criminal prosecution threatened "Takata as a continuing operation."[69]

I refrained from jumping into the internal email storm over the *Times* exposé. Roe noticed my uncharacteristic reticence.

"You have been quiet," he wrote me on November 7, 2014.

I responded bluntly. If it did not cut the flow of pablum and stop trying to hide behind "appropriate government authorities" and its paid coterie of "allies and confidants inside Washington," Takata was doomed. It could survive only by matching "real facts against the media miasma." If Takata was finally ready to face the truth, I said, "we can create an overall strategy to save the company." In essence, I repeated, it was essential for Takata to "choose an executive to say what needs to be said – either (a) this didn't happen or (b) we are vigorously investigating what happened or (c) it happened and I have the authority to do whatever it takes to make sure it never happens again." Roe instructed me to prepare a new strategic communications plan based on that advice and tried to schedule a presentation for Takata's leadership in Michigan. Not one of the company's other executives wanted to hear it, even after Congress started demanding testimony from Takata under oath.

"I am a voice in the wilderness," Roe wrote me, exasperated, on November 12, 2014. "In my heart I know we are good guys and try to do the right thing, yet we seem paralyzed."

As it turned out, paralysis would have been superior to the approach Big Wife and Little Shige chose. They were still actively trying to keep a lid on a scandal that, by that point, stunk to high heaven.

The Senate Commerce Committee had re-established its historic role as the policy-making core of motor vehicle safety early in 2014, after General Motors precipitated a crisis of its own by suddenly announcing a massive recall of cars with faulty ignition switches. More than 1,400 people had been killed or injured in the late 2000s and early 2010s when power to their Chevy Cobalts and other cheap GM models – more specifically, power to their steering wheels, brakes and airbags – got cut by an ignition switch that would turn the engine off with the slightest brush of a driver's knee or a chance encounter with a pothole. GM voluntarily recalled 8.7 million of those cars, but only after 114 people died. Fearing greater scrutiny of unrelated steering problems and other types of defects, GM set about rewriting the narrative by voluntarily recalling a total of 25 million vehicles by mid-2014 – almost as many in six months as the company had produced in the previous ten years, combined.

The Committee Chair, Bill Nelson (D-FL), called GM on the carpet. With the Justice Department, NHTSA and other federal agencies breathing down her neck, GM CEO Mary Barra handily beat back outraged Senators. Barra took responsibility for essentially nothing GM had done and glossed over numerous occasions when her company – or, at least, its pre-bankruptcy doppelganger, "Old GM" – had deliberately concealed a deadly safety defect. She did, however, assure Committee members that the faulty ignition switch had been fixed under her leadership at the post-bankruptcy "New GM" and she would take personal responsibility, going forward.

Several weeks later, on November 20, 2014, it was Takata's turn to face Senate Commerce. I urged Roe to use Barra's bravura performance as a template and reiterated my advice that the "voice of Takata" needed to be an American executive who could take responsibility for what the company did wrong and assure law-makers that a proper "fix" was at hand.

To my horror, Takata did the exact opposite. The company flew in a Japanese witness. At first, I thought Takata was sending Shunkichi Shimizu, the Executive Officer who had taken over management of the American company from Rob Fisher. Barely one month earlier, on Saturday, October 25, "Shun" had set off a panic among Takata's American advisors when he forwarded a draft news release "for dissemination to the Tokyo Stock Exchange" on Monday, the 27th, Japan time. The company planned to tell investors that the number of Takata airbag-equipped cars subject to recall "has not increased" and, therefore, there was no reason to worry about Takata bearing higher warranty costs. The proposed release went on to say that "media reports that federal prosecutors have begun investigating Takata are false."

Ken Weinstein saw Shimizu's draft release first and went ballistic. All three statements were palpably false. He sent Shun a Toyota announcement that they were *increasing* the number of vehicles subject to their airbag recall campaigns. Takata also could not truthfully state that warranty costs will be limited "because the final scope of the ongoing field action is not known." Weinstein knew from his recent experience with runaway Toyotas that prosecutors went after them because they thought "Toyota had made false or incomplete statements to the public about the safety of its vehicles in an effort to prop up its stock price." Weinstein sternly warned Takata not to deny that a criminal investigation was underway. Takata "should not be perceived as attempting to minimize the severity of the problems it is facing," Weinstein warned. To the relief of all of us on the American team, Takata spiked "Shun's" news release in the nick of time.

Takata's witness for the Senate hearing turned out instead to be a mid-level executive, Hiroshi – not Shunkichi – Shimizu. Hiroshi's claim to fame within Takata arose from his management of inflator production at Monclova. Under his watch, the plant cranked out 300,000 inflators with botched welds and crammed them into a leaky warehouse known as "the swamp." When the plant fell behind in its deliveries to automakers, according to senior inflator engineer Kevin Fitzgerald, many were fished out, sent along to vehicle assembly lines and installed inches away from drivers' faces. [70]   Fitzgerald, who watched the Senate Commerce Committee hearing on C-Span from his home in Michigan, was aghast. Takata's presentation of Shimizu, of all people, to the U.S. Congress as Takata's global head of quality assurance made it "evident that the company was doing what it could to limit the scope of the recall."

I knew from my own correspondence with him that Hirochi was not fluent in English. That made it difficult for Steve Bradbury, who sat at his right elbow while victims told the Committee their horror stories, to whisper any last-minute advice. Hirochi, sporting a comb-over above his furrowed brow, glasses and broad nose, brought an interpreter with him to the witness table.

Senators had burning questions. Would Takata agree to a national, not just a regional, recall of vehicles equipped with airbags it recognized as dangerously sensitive to moisture? Hiroshi dithered, then was finally cornered into saying no.[71] Had the rising death toll led the company to change its manufacturing processes? "Every time it happens," Hirochi unhesitatingly responded, "we address all the issues and they are taken care of."

Senator Dean Heller (R-NV) gave Hirochi Shimizu the perfect opportunity to do what I had told Takata for months had to be done: to take responsibility for the half-dozen deaths its product had already inflicted and to move quickly to assure not just the recall but the expedited replacement of its most immediately dangerous airbags. Heller asked, point blank, did Takata take full responsibility for the growing airbag fiasco? Something apparently did not translate well during a lengthy aside with Hirochi's interpreter. After offering several nonsensical responses, Shimizu finally replied in heavily accented English that the company "was not necessarily to blame for all of the reported fatalities." My "media mention" reports showed that, in their news shows that evening, network television producers had to put English subtitles on the screen so viewers could understand Shimizu's response.

Shimizu's denial was consistent with the pablum Berman and Takata's other corporate flacks were still dishing out. Echoing six years of bogus defect information reports, they were still insisting the deaths "all had completely different causes that led to recalls" and that there was no "causal relationship between them." At the hearing, while still under oath, Shimizu doubled down, claiming that Takata was "confident in the integrity of our engineering and our current manufacturing processes," and "we continue to work closely with the automakers and with NHTSA." Senator Marco Rubio (R-FL), whose state had racked up the highest number of casualties, felt compelled to ask, essentially, whether Takata had used the *Fight Club* formula, deferring life-saving recalls until the math was in their favor. Shimizu denied it but the question did more damage than the answer.

The whole Commerce Committee wanted Takata's head but had nobody to wield the ax. President Obama had left the top job at NHTSA vacant for 343 days prior to the hearing, so Deputy Administrator David Friedman was in the hot seat. Friedman, who became Acting Administrator in May 2013, had already embarrassed himself during the "GM show" by failing to answer basic questions about such subjects as the extent of the agency's subpoena power. One Senator pointed out in that earlier hearing that GM's lawyers had established policies to avoid using the word "defect" to shield information about their faulty ignition switch under attorney-client privilege and NHTSA had let them get away with it.

The man who ran the agency when that happened, former Senate Commerce Committee staffer David L. Strickland, had escaped blame by dashing through the "revolving door" in 2013. Strickland joined a Washington law firm that represents motor vehicle manufacturers, auto auctions and other auto industry clients. Strickland's government service swan song was a guest editorial full of praise for NHTSA's "vigilance and professionalism" as it used "real data, sound science and careful engineering." He claimed he left the agency "laser-focused on safety," but all he really did was set the stage for the sharpest two-year bump in highway fatalities in 53 years.[72] The largest year-over-year percentage rise in motor vehicle deaths in 50 years occurred in 2015. Nationwide, a total of 37,757 Americans – disproportionately young people, as usual – ended up in body bags in 2015. That was a 7.2 percent rise over 2014. The largest-ever, annual percentage increase was only slightly higher – 8.1 percent from 1965 to 1966, the year Congress felt compelled to pass the first national vehicle safety laws.

The overall death toll in 2016 was even more appalling. Well over 40,000 people died in traffic accidents – six percent higher than in history-making 2015 and 14 percent higher than in 2014. A third of those killed were aged 15-29.[73] The Obama Administration's "laser-focused" NHTSA helped make America's road-safety record the worst in the developed world, with deaths equivalent to driving 800 fully loaded school buses off a cliff each year. In 2015, Americans perished in car crashes at a rate more than three times the death rate in Germany.[74]

The gross number of corpses was not the most shocking statistic during 2016. The absolute number of deaths was, to some extent, a function of cheap gasoline and a corresponding increase in the number of miles people chose to drive. Two other measures take such variables out of the equation. The "annual *mileage* death rate" – expressed as the ratio of the number of dead people for every 100 million miles traveled by all the vehicles in America – also took a sharp upward turn, to 1.22 in 2015 and 1.25 in 2016. That set two records in a row for the worst mileage death rate during the 2010s. Another yardstick for measuring the Obama Administration's stewardship in auto safety is called the "annual *population* death rate." It shot up seven percent from 2014 to 2015, to 11.87 deaths for every 100,000 people in America, then rose another five percent, to 12.40, in 2016.[75]

Senators who attended the Takata hearing in 2014 demanded to know the real reason Strickland's NHTSA had been in such a rush to close its 2010 Takata investigation. Friedman said he would look into it but never provided an explanation. No Senator from either political party took seriously NHTSA's idea of allowing Takata to conduct a "regional recall," which would limit repairs to vehicles that were currently registered in a handful of hot, humid states and territories. Chairman Nelson bluntly told Friedman that it was time for NHTSA to "start socking it to the folks that are dragging their feet, not answering questions."[76] Senator Danforth's successor in the Senate and on the Commerce Committee, Senator Claire McCaskill (D-MO), joined other members in demanding that Takata be "held fully accountable, not just with financial penalties, but also with criminal charges."

Committee Democrats later declared in unison that "Takata operated with an utter disregard for safety."

I told Roe the hearing was the worst disaster I had seen in a committee room in my 41 years as a Hill-watcher – and I was in the Senate Caucus Room when White House Counsel John Dean sank the Nixon Administration at the height of the Watergate hearings. Takata and I parted company five weeks later.

I considered Takata a "dead man walking" at that point but had no inkling of the fateful drama that was simultaneously unfolding in Michigan. While I was in Ross Hamilton's former "war room" in Armada, Takata's president, Stefan Stocker, decided it was time to put Shiniki Tanaka, the Japanese engineer who presented the fake test results to Honda in 2000, in charge of all of Takata's inflator operations. Kevin Fitzgerald was told he would report to Tanaka. Fitzgerald flatly refused and reportedly told Stocker "Shin" should be "charged with a felony," not promoted. Fitzgerald quoted Stocker's off-hand reply: "people change and we need to move on."[77]

Fitzgerald decided to fight back. He hired lawyers and collected ammunition. A colleague in Takata's Moses Lake operation was able to lay hands on the fraudulent validation report for the earliest AN-powered inflators and sent it and the truthful version, the Sheridan Report, to Fitzgerald. Still hoping to save his own job – or at least thwart Tanaka's promotion – Fitzgerald refused to show up at his office. Instead, he carefully laid out his case in a letter to the head of Takata's Human Resources Department. "Shin committed fraud that knowingly put inflators into production vehicles that had exploded during validation testing," Fitzgerald revealed. "I wrote the factual report and made sure that everyone who signed the first fraudulent one knew what really happened. They all ignored it." Fitzgerald suggested this should not come as news to corporate leadership because "I talked to [Ross Hamilton and other] lawyers representing Takata twice in 2009 and told them the entire story and who was responsible."

Fitzgerald stayed home from mid-October 2014, watched the horrifying Senate Commerce Hearing in November, then sat through a House Energy and Commerce Committee hearing on December 3. As Hirochi Shimizu offered the House of Representatives the same lame excuses and denials, Steve Bradbury was perched over Shimizu's right shoulder; another Takata lawyer, former NHTSA Chief Counsel Erika Jones, loomed near Shimizu's left ear. The performance was as disastrous as the Senate Commerce hearing a few weeks earlier.

Takata Corporation had plenty of incentive to negotiate with Fitzgerald but chose instead to roll over him. A week after the House hearing, on December 11, 2014, Takata's lawyers threatened Fitzgerald and demanded that he surrender any work-related documents. Fitzgerald's lawyer matter-of-factly responded that she was keeping a copy of the fake engineering reports because the Justice Department had subpoenaed them. Days later, Fitzgerald was in the FBI's Detroit field office, handing six federal investigators an arsenal of "smoking guns." In the middle of the document dump, Frank Roe phoned Fitzgerald and left a message promising him a better job at Takata. Fitzgerald understood the message not as witness tampering but an indication of just how far out in the wilderness the company had left its highest-ranking American executive.

After Takata pled guilty and declared bankruptcy, Fitzgerald asked himself "why would Takata keep such an incriminating document after the great lengths they took to cover up the events it describes?" His answer was simple. "Because they are idiots, that's why."

Fitzgerald had no way to know what I knew. For decades, Takata had watched the motor vehicle industry cow federal regulators and apply the *Fight Club* formula with impunity. Even after the lid on their stinkpot shot skyward, Little Shige and Big Wife still believed the network of "allies and confidants" Secretary Mineta had recruited for them in Washington, D.C., could avert the looming catastrophe.

PART 6

Asleep at the Wheel

1970s-1980s

Washington

From the day vehicle safety regulators claimed their desks at the new Department of Transportation in 1970, Detroit set out to block them from implementing the 1966 National Traffic and Motor Vehicle Safety Act. The agency's mandate was to force vehicle manufacturers to develop and install new safety technology, especially passive health interventions, such as the airbag. Even after waging decades of trench warfare over the airbag mandate, the carmakers were ready for more. They fought the agency's safety engineers over nearly every proposed new safety standard, arguing to federal judges that they were not "practicable" or were not "stated in objective terms," as required by provisions they had lobbied into the statute.

In the 1970s, Detroit's lawyers triumphed over the rules and highly technical safety standards NHTSA's engineers proposed. The courts, oddly enough, put far greater stock in evidence the agency offered to justify recalls. NHTSA felt so compelled to "lawyer up," the agency's Office of Chief Counsel quickly leapfrogged every other office in the agency hierarchy. NHTSA created an Office of Defects Investigation ("ODI") in July 1971. When consumer complaints about vehicle defects doubled, so did ODI's staff.

Detroit did not appreciate NHTSA's "help" identifying safety defects much more than their "help" designing cars. Through the 1970s and 1980s, the carmakers and the regulators engaged in two epic battles. One involved a Ford model known as the Pinto, which tended to burst into flames when it got rear-ended. Another was the tread-shredding "Firestone 500" steel-belted radial tire. A half-dozen other carmaker goofs spilled blood on the highways and made headlines.

Even before the Reagan Administration took control of NHTSA in the 1980s, an unholy relationship had already developed between the car industry and the agency that was supposed to protect people from their products. It was based on two rules of thumb. The first tacit agreement was that if a defect involved a sufficiently massive number of cars, industry could get away with *promising to warn* car owners about a safety defect instead of actually removing the threat. In 1977, for example, Nader's Center for Auto Safety shined a light on Fords made in the late 1960s and early 1970s that tended to jump into "reverse" and run over people. Nobody seemed able to put a finger on the exact cause but thousands of "park-to-reverse" cases were reported. NHTSA's then-Administrator, Joan Claybrook, eventually started an investigation based on a 1975 federal court decision that "a significant number of failures alone in normal use is a sufficient basis for a recall *without determination of a precise cause of failure*."[78] In 1978, however, even Claybrook balked at ordering a recall that necessarily would involve 23 million vehicles. That was more than twice the total number of new vehicles sold annually in America at that time. Recognizing the political impact of such a massive step, NHTSA swung into action by issuing a press release telling drivers it was a bad idea to leave the engine running when they step out of their cars.

Multiple consumer lawsuits in the late 1970s and early 1980s seeking court orders to compel NHTSA to stop the runaway Fords proved fruitless. Claybrook held hearings during the final weeks of the Carter Administration that revealed 23,000 complaints, 6,000 accidents, 1,710 injuries and 98 deaths. Claybrook tipped off then-Secretary of Transportation Neil Goldschmidt that she intended to order a slimmed-down, 10 million-car recall. Just days before his Reagan Administration successor, Drew Lewis, took over, Goldschmidt traded Claybrook's proposed recall for a Ford pledge to mail out 23 million 5½-inch-by-1¼-inch black-on-silver decals, suitable for gluing on dashboards. Under the headline "Important Safety Precaution," minuscule print told drivers to "make sure the gear selector is engaged in Park." Unfortunately for drivers, the mechanical defect made it impossible to know whether teeth inside the lever fully engaged the Park gear. When they took over NHTSA, President Reagan's Administrator, Raymond Peck, and Peck's special counsel, future Takata lawyer Erika Jones, refused to revisit the issue and effectively brought all of the other safety defect investigations they inherited from Claybrook to a halt. Deaths and lawsuits from what NHTSA called "unintended powered rollaways" continued into the 2010s.

This convenient precedent for industry was not lost on Takata when, in 2014, deaths from its defective airbags began to spike and NHTSA got pressured to order a nationwide, not just a regional, recall of the 8 million cars with inflators the company had already declared unsafe. If a 23-million car recall was off-limits in the 1970s, surely NHTSA could not order a total recall of 70 million vehicles with Takata airbags, even as it became obvious that all of them were potential pipe bombs. The 1975 court ruling that a large number of unexplained failures was enough to order a recall remained good law but Takata remembered how easily political influence trumped a NHTSA recall, even under a Democrat president and a die-hard, consumer-oriented administrator.

The second rule of thumb NHTSA established with carmakers was that they could avoid ruinous government penalties even where they knew their products were defective and failed to report them, so long as they eventually confessed and agreed to fix them promptly without causing NHTSA too much embarrassment for its cluelessness. Between 1996 and 2000, 81 percent of vehicle safety recalls began before NHTSA detected any reason to investigate.[79] Always good at math, the manufacturers figured out that delayed self-reporting saved them a great deal of money, even if they got caught, eventually. They could *agree to fix* all the defective vehicles *without actually fixing them*. In 1999, for example, manufacturers ended up paying for repairs on only one out of three newly recalled vehicles.

Nobody took greater advantage of this cozy arrangement than Takata. In the 1990s, company leaders in Tokyo said nothing to NHTSA when they learned seat belts they installed in the mid-1980s were popping open in mid-crash. Who was to know that people who were injured or killed *actually did* buckle their seatbelts before a collision occurred? Emergency responders could see only that vehicle occupants shot forward into steering wheels and windshields and their seat belts were unbuckled. As years went by and the unverifiable complaints accumulated, Takata seatbelts deteriorated so badly that they could not be buckled at all or, in some cases, unbuckled. Such pre-crash failures forced Takata to admit what they and Honda had known for at least five years – that the cheap plastic they used in the buckles deteriorated over long-term exposure to sunlight. By that point, NHTSA had received so many accident reports and consumer complaints that it had to admit there was a potentially deadly defect in Takata equipment that was supposed to protect occupants.

In May 1995 Takata and 11 of is vehicle manufacturer customers, including Detroit's Big Three, recalled almost nine million 1986-91 model cars. As of that date, it was the second-largest vehicle safety recall in history. For Takata, however, the gigantic campaign was a mere hiccup. Repair costs were low because so many eight- and nine-year old cars had been sold and resold and the recall notices never caught up with current owners. The law specified snail-mail so, two years later, fewer than one in five vehicle owners had brought the cars in to be fixed. By illegally waiting five years to warn motorists about their potentially deadly safety equipment, Takata saved vastly more than the measly $50,000 fine NHTSA imposed for the "late notification." The lesson for both Takata and Honda was unmistakable – NHTSA would go easy on them if the defect took several years to manifest itself, multiple millions of cars were involved and Takata initiated a recall before the agency compelled them.

1990s-2000s

Washington

Takata was not the only company to learn from NHTSA's milquetoast response to the "park-to-reverse" defect of the 1970s and the deteriorated seat belt buckles of the 1980s. Ford Motor

Company was riding high in the 1990s with a top-heavy SUV they called the Explorer. For tires, they turned to a company based in Tokyo, Japan. Named after its founder, Shojiro Ishibashi (in English, "Bridge of Stone"), Bridgestone had much in common with Takata Corporation. When its first huge customer, the Imperial Japanese Army, surrendered in 1945 the company desperately needed a new market. Like Takezo Takada, Ishibashi considered America the promised land.

Ishibashi's big break came in 1985, when an American business icon, Firestone Tire & Rubber Company, faced bankruptcy because of defects in the "Firestone 500" steel-belted radial tires it sold in the 1970s. The Japanese company gladly scooped up Firestone's American assets and its century-long business relationship with Ford. Bridgestone/Firestone USA supplied Ford with almost 25 million "Firestone Wilderness" and similar tires. Poor manufacturing processes made the Wilderness, like the Firestone 500s, fall apart at highway speeds. Hundreds of Ford Explorers flipped upside down. Those and other tire-failure crashes killed 271 Americans and crippled another 823.

Without breathing a word to NHTSA, Ford started yanking back tires on cars they sold in Saudi Arabia in 1999 and Malaysia in early 2000. It did not start recalling the Firestone tire-equipped Explorers in America until August 2000, and only included those with tires produced in some of Bridgestone/Firestone's manufacturing plants. Congress had already noticed the widespread deaths and injuries. Senate Commerce, headed in 1999 by Senator John McCain (R-AZ), tore into the Clinton Administration's appointees at NHTSA. He demanded to know how such a horror could happen and what NHTSA intended to do to keep it from recurring. The agency's response was classic. They were so outgunned by the auto manufacturers, they complained, only a huge increase in taxpayer resources would protect them from being blindsided again. Congress fell for it; they passed the Transportation Recall Enhancement Accountability and Documentation ("TREAD") Act just before the Clinton crew packed their bags and turned the Transportation Department over to President George W. Bush's appointees. Bush's NHTSA finally ordered additional recalls in October 2001, five years after the agency first learned about the deadly defect.

The Bush Administration inherited an utterly useless system for collecting and analyzing data that could spot defects before manufacturers reported them. NHTSA's database, appropriately named the Defect Information Management System or "DIMS," could better be described as a defec*tive* information management system. It could not match even the most basic types of data by topic and was guaranteed never to spot the 3,000 reports of Ford Explorer deaths, injuries and property losses before or after they occurred.[80]

Congress threw the book at NHTSA. TREAD imposed 22 new legal requirements, some on NHTSA and others on the automobile industry.[81] All of the supposed reforms depended entirely on agency guidance and enforcement.

Senator McCain and other Congressional leaders were appalled by NHTSA's inability to use the information available to them but somehow decided the agency needed even more of it. They threw the checkbook at the problem, doubling ODI's budget. Congress also told NHTSA to ditch DIMS and replace it with a 21st Century database that would receive and analyze the expected flood of incoming quarterly reports of deaths, injuries and other "early warning data" TREAD obligated the manufacturers to provide.

NHTSA ignored statutory deadlines and dragged its heels instead of quickly adopting regulations to implement TREAD. When the agency finally set out to build an Advanced Retrieval Tire Equipment and Motor Vehicle Information System, it laid ARTEMIS' foundation on quicksand. The Transportation Department's Inspector General implored NHTSA not to transfer the garbage data from DIMS into ARTEMIS but the agency did it anyway. NHTSA also ignored government-wide requirements for the procurement of new information technology infrastructure. When the Transportation Department's watchdog criticized NHTSA's refusal to use "generally accepted cost-estimating techniques," Jeffrey Runge, President George W. Bush's choice to run the agency, stiff-armed them. Runge was an emergency room physician with no experience in government, much less in managing a hugely expensive and complicated computer infrastructure procurement, but he insisted that "NHTSA is confident

[ARTEMIS] will be completed on time and within the allocated budget."[82] As it turned out, ARTEMIS cost almost twice what Runge promised and took twice as long before they could even pretend that it was operational.

Almost five years after Congress passed the TREAD Act, NHTSA still lacked "advanced analytical capability ... to help point analysts to potential safety defects." ARTEMIS could not "link deaths to an alleged defect or identify relationships between categories of early warning report information." Analysts could run the same exact search in ARTEMIS twice and get completely different results. A search for problems with "brakes" returned one set of results and a search for "braking" returned different results. NHTSA managers did not consider such discrepancies to be a problem. The agency continued brushing off the Inspector General's complaints, even after he reported in 2015 that ARTEMIS could not perform any of the "advanced trend and predictive analysis" Congress demanded in the TREAD Act.[83]

NHTSA's failure to create a useful data tool didn't matter much because the agency hired nobody capable of using it. ODI increased its staff by 39 percent in 2001 but did nothing to train them. Even when the agency started hiring contract trainers, it did nothing to make sure the training "took" and gave no one responsibility for implementing or auditing training programs. Staff responsible for interpreting statistical test results had no training or background in statistics. The agency assigned no one to verify the accuracy or completeness of early warning reports coming in from vehicle manufacturers. As a result, the carmakers gamed the reports they submitted by "routinely mis-characteriz[ing] safety incidents" to "mask potential trends." For example, fires would be reported as "strange odors."

When people were dying from its ignition switch defect, General Motors started sending its early warning reports to NHTSA in a computer file format the agency could not read or use. Nobody at NHTSA noticed.[84] NHTSA's associate administrator for enforcement saw some early reports about the GM switch defect and told an ODI staff member to monitor new reports closely. Soon after, the staffer left the agency and the task was never reassigned.[85]

Another vehicle manufacturer stopped filing *any* early warning reports in 2004. NHTSA did not notice the lapse for 10 years, until 2014.[86]

In 2003, when Takata airbags started exploding, Honda started miscoding data and avoided sending 11 years' worth of death and injury reports – 1,729 of them, to be exact. In 2011, ODI asked Honda to explain discrepancies in their reporting but did nothing until Honda admitted to the lapse in 2014.[87] Eight Takata airbag ruptures were among the hidden reports.

The agency assigned screeners in 2008 to review airbag issues, but they had no engineering or automotive background, much less airbag training. Even where the screeners passed suspected defects up NHTSA's bureaucratic chain, possible recalls were thwarted by disagreements among NHTSA's Chief Counsel, the Chief of the Defects Assessment Division and the Director of the ODI on fundamental questions about what standards should apply in opening an investigation. If an investigation miraculously led to a recall, the manufacturers decided for themselves how many cars would be included; their reports often omitted key remedy and scope information but ODI had no procedures in place to compel compliance.

Writers at *Car & Driver* magazine kept tabs on a series of internal audits that laid bare NHTSA's persistent neglect. "The agency responsible for overseeing the nation's vehicle safety is full of incompetent, mismanaged staff who are practically set up by their superiors to fail," they wrote. "Yes, NHTSA really is that bad."[88]

Agency incompetence in designing and using an information infrastructure made the Takata fiasco not only possible, but inevitable. In the 15 years leading up to the Takata airbag crisis, NHTSA failed to get ahead of defects in Ford SUV tires, sticky accelerators in Toyotas and faulty ignition switches in GM's cheapest sedans that killed hundreds of people and injured thousands more. Nobody at NHTSA got fired or disciplined for their incompetence and not a single executive in any of those automotive companies was ever charged with a crime. Government fines never put more than a dimple in company profits. That made Takata overconfident and unprepared for the coming catastrophe.

2015

Washington, New York and Tokyo

Immediately after I stopped working for Takata, the bloodbath got deeper. Red flashed on all fronts from the first day of 2015, with more unsuspecting drivers chopped up by their airbags and red ink staining Takata's balance sheet. Red-faced NHTSA bureaucrats were forced to grapple with the impossibility of removing killer airbags from American cars any time soon and the overwhelming political pressure to allow vehicle manufacturers to continue installing them in millions more new cars.

On New Year's Day, 2015, one woman lost half her right ear in a 2002 Honda Civic. Two weeks later, a Texan was injured in another Honda brand, a 2002 Acura. In March 2015, an airbag shredded the driver of a 2003 Honda Civic, then the 20-year old driver of a far newer car, a 2006 Nissan. Oklahoma high schooler Ashley Parham, Virginia soccer mom Gurgit Rathore, two Californians, restaurant worker Devin Xu, actress Jewel Brangman and Florida nail salon owner Hien Tran were already in their graves, thanks to Takata airbag explosions in 2001 Civics, Accords and Acuras. The body count started anew on January 18, 2015, when a young Houston dad, Carlos Solis, died in a 2002 Civic. Kylan Langlinais, a 22-year old woman driving a 2005 Honda in Louisiana, died next. Her family received a recall notice while she was fighting for her life in a hospital for nearly a week in April. A 13-year old boy died when a passenger airbag exploded in another Honda in Pennsylvania. Takata closed out the year in macabre fashion just before Christmas, 2015, when South Carolina welder Joel Knight was beheaded in his 2006 Ford Ranger pickup by an airbag that had never been recalled. Of the 11 Americans killed by the end of 2015, seven were driving 2001 or 2002 Honda Accords or Civics equipped with Takata's earliest and most dangerous ammonium nitrate-powered airbags.

Big Wife's "keep a lid on it" strategy was making investors nervous, even though only a handful of new deaths and injuries made the news during 2015. The company's stock price declined by two-thirds in 2014 to a five-year low, then dropped by half from January to December 2015.

Takata faced more than 70 wrongful death and personal injury lawsuits in federal and state courts. The carmakers, too, were accused of "reckless, deceptive conduct" and of being "far from innocent, unsuspecting victims." Plaintiffs accused them of having "independent knowledge ... that Takata's airbag inflators were not safe well before installing them in millions of vehicles."[89] By year's end, the federal cases were consolidated before U.S. district judge, Federico A. Moreno. The new "multi-district litigation" was designed to consolidate pretrial discovery before the individual cases went back to their home districts for trial but, more than two years after the cases were consolidated, Takata still had not produced thousands of requested documents. The co-lead attorneys who control the discovery process and plaintiffs' lawyers appointed to an "executive committee" will split a percentage of whatever the carmakers end up paying, so there is naturally more incentive to secure quick settlements than to punish guilty companies.[90]

Takata also had to deal with class actions for economic losses, claims that did not arise from injuries or deaths. Fifty million "similarly situated" businesses and consumers, including parts suppliers who were stuck with inventory they could not sell, brought fraud claims against Takata, Honda, Toyota and other manufacturers seeking compensation for financial losses they suffered on account of the Takata recalls. Those "economic loss" cases also were consolidated before Judge Moreno on February 15, 2015.

By May 2015 a federal grand jury in New York had finished its work and referred the Takata criminal investigation to a U.S. Attorney in Michigan, where prosecutors were already poring over Kevin Fitzgerald's "smoking gun" documents and interview transcripts. The local District Attorney already knew her way around Takata's U.S. headquarters in Auburn Hills. The FBI had raided the building in February 2011 and hauled away incriminating documents tying Takata Corporation to a huge, decade-long criminal conspiracy to violate the Sherman Antitrust Act by rigging the prices Japanese auto manufacturers paid for seat belts in cars Honda and others sold to American consumers. Barely seven months after the raid, Gary Walker, a senior executive in Takata's American subsidiary, TK Holdings, Inc., pled guilty and began a 14-month prison sentence. Two weeks later, the Japanese parent corporation declared itself a criminal for the first time and paid a $71.3 million fine. As part of its plea deal, the company fingered three of its own U.S.-based Japanese executives, Yasuhiko Ueno, Saborou Imamiya and Yoshinobu Fujino, all of whom pled guilty in late 2013 and were still incarcerated in a federal penitentiary as their former employer's airbag disaster was starting to unfold.

All Takata's spokesman, Alby Berman, could say in 2015 about the rapidly deteriorating situation was that "we are highly focused on cooperation with NHTSA and the government investigation." Takata had little choice. The government was "highly focused" on them.

Shigehisa Takada made his first public statement on his company's existential crisis on June 15, 2015. As he was leaving a shareholders meeting, Shige bowed and whispered into a microphone that "the company that should be offering safety to the users ended up hurting them. It grieves me most deeply." Seven years after the first recall, Shige assured the American people that their safety, not his family fortune, was his "number one priority." He wanted the world to believe his company was "cooperating fully," working "to facilitate the required recalls" and "doing everything we can to ensure uncompromised safety."

Behind the scenes, of course, Takata was still doing the exact opposite. Shortly after Bob Schubert told NHTSA there would be no more recalls until Takata finished its 18-month "root cause" science project, the agency formally opened a new defect investigation in June 2014 and upgraded it to a more threatening "engineering analysis" a few weeks later. Over the next five months, the agency demanded a massive number of documents. Takata's NHTSA lawyers stonewalled their former employer until the company's criminal defense lawyers took over. NHTSA's reputation was "tarnished," as Mineta put it, but the agency still had legal authority under the Motor Vehicle Safety Act that even four former Cabinet Secretaries and multiple former NHTSA Administrators couldn't blunt. Takata was compelled in May 2015 to extend its regional recalls nationwide.

Bradbury and his team at Dechert must have recognized how dangerous it would be for Takata also to stonewall the Justice Department's criminal investigation, which was proceeding apace on a separate track with help from Kevin Fitzgerald and other former Takata engineers. The "lid" was coming off, so Takata worked out a half-measure that would assure future availability of important materials to the government, plaintiffs' lawyers and other stakeholders without actually having to turn much of it over any time soon. Takata attorney Steve Bradbury and Executive Vice President Frank Roe offered NHTSA a Preservation Order and Testing Control Plan. Starting on February 25, 2015, Takata would preserve not only the documents the agency requested, but it would also collect and warehouse inflators that were removed from vehicles, regardless of whether they had ruptured or were being replaced as part of a recall campaign. The Preservation Order established a process by which hundreds of litigants and engineering experts could take inflators out of the stockpile and conduct their own tests. Mark Rosekind, NHTSA's brand-new Administrator, a quintessential technocrat and former member of the National Transportation Safety Board, accepted Takata's offer. It was a logical first step because everyone was sick of Takata's whining about their inability to identify a "root cause" of the inflator ruptures. As Scott Upham, Takata's former marketing chief, sardonically put it, Takata had become the industrial equivalent of O.J. Simpson, promising to "go out and find Nicole's killer."[91]

Ten of Takata's carmaker customers had already pooled their money to form what they called an Independent Testing Coalition and hired bona fide rocket scientists at Orbital/ATK. It did not take them long to confirm what Takata's own consultant, the Fraunhofer Group, hinted at the year before. The number one factor in the deadly ruptures, Orbital concluded, was Takata's choice of ammonium nitrate as the propellant. Sloppy construction of inflator assemblies was another problem; exposure to heat and humidity made everything worse. NHTSA sent three other research organizations out to hunt down Takata's elusive "root cause." They, too, quickly identified the design choice of ammonium nitrate, based on science that was readily available the whole time Takata claimed it was looking for a "root cause." This led to an official NHTSA conclusion: the root cause of the inflator explosions was "a function of time, temperature cycling and environmental moisture and that, at some point in the future, *all non-desiccated* ... inflators will reach a threshold level of degradation that could result in the inflator becoming unreasonably dangerous."[92] The agency conveniently bypassed the question whether *desiccated* inflators – in which a drying agent called Zeolite was sprinkled in with ammonium nitrate tablets – also would eventually degrade or might pose other, yet unknown risks.

Administrator Rosekind's most urgent job was to stem the political damage from his acting predecessor's embarrassing performances on Capitol Hill and the agency's persistent obeisance to Takata and its politically powerful friends and customers. Being well-acquainted with "probable cause" determinations during his four years at NTSB, the Stanford and Yale graduate quickly recognized the extent of Takata's efforts to *avoid* identifying the fundamental design defect in its inflators. Takata had turned over 3.3 million documents and Rosekind promised the impossible, that NHTSA was "reviewing each of these documents carefully" to see if Takata's actions "constituted violations of the Motor Vehicle Safety Act." Rosekind also ordered Takata to explain how "it will use traditional media, new media and individual contacts to inform customers and boost [recall repair] rates."

A reckoning was long overdue, but Rosekind had to strike a delicate balance between punishing Takata and killing it. In one respect, Takata had NHTSA over a barrel. The company made as many as 285 million inflators between 2000 and 2015 and roughly half of them were installed in cars sold in America. Driver's side inflators were "toroidal" (shaped like a hockey puck) and passenger inflators were "cylindrical" (resembling a pipe). The devices for both sides were additionally customized to fit into 19 different makes and dozens of models of cars. A total recall involving so many variations would likely cost Takata $24 billion and swamp the company. The safest and most effective option would be to stop Takata from selling – and their carmaker customers from installing – any new inflators powered by ammonium nitrate, but that solution would have virtually shut down huge portions of the U.S. auto industry, idling thousands of American assembly-line workers for months on the eve of the 2016 presidential election. Takata's only two serious competitors – Sweden-based AutoLiv and ZF TRW in Germany – were working at near-full capacity to supply their own carmaker customers, who had wisely rejected Takata's questionable product. The Europeans could run their own production lines 24/7, but their inflators could not fit into or otherwise work with Takata's down-sized airbag modules.

Even if vehicle manufacturers could find a way figuratively to jam Takata's square pegs into the carmakers' round holes, the redesigned airbags could not be installed without first undergoing 18 to 24 months of testing. Apart from the production of inflators for new cars, millions of defective units in cars already on the road – some far more dangerous than others – urgently needed to be replaced. Only Takata could supply replacements and it would take them almost three years to build an adequate supply.

NHTSA decided to blow the lid off Big Wife's stinkpot just before Thanksgiving, 2015. By that time, Roe was out of the picture and Takata's NHTSA lawyers at the Mayer Brown firm got eclipsed by Bradbury and the Dechert firm's federal-prosecutor-turned-hedge-fund-defense-lawyer, Andrew Levander. According to Dechert's promotional materials, the firm specialized in "scandals that force [clients] to talk under oath while also under scrutiny from law enforcement authorities and plaintiffs' lawyers."[93] Bradbury knew all about forcing people to talk. He was one of three Justice Department attorneys in the George W. Bush administration who authored memos justifying the CIA's use of torture on suspected terrorists.

Throughout the Summer of 2015, Takata's top American executive, Kevin Kennedy, kept insisting that the company had always "acted responsibly, without undue delay." The recalls "go well beyond the scope of the safety risk," Kennedy insisted, because "it is not the case that all of the inflators covered in the [recalls] are 'defective.'"[94] Within five months, Dechert convinced Takata to do an about-face. It was time to confess "that it did not satisfy the notice provisions in the Safety Act" and that it had deliberately misled NHTSA for years. In a convoluted, 33-page Consent Order, issued November 3, 2015, NHTSA announced that Takata would pay the Government $200 million, the largest civil fine the agency had ever assessed in its half-century of existence.

The "root cause" of the airbag defect had not yet been officially established, but NHTSA and Takata built their Consent Order on two vague assumptions: first, that moisture was the culprit; and second, that new recipes that included a drying agent in the explosive wafers might ameliorate the defect. Takata could dodge most of the record-breaking fine if it cooperated with agency efforts to identify the nature of the problem more precisely and worked assiduously to replace the older, defective units. The first chunk of the fine, $70 million, was due in six installments, with three years to pay the first half and the second half not entirely due until late 2020. Carmakers were counting on Takata to supply millions of new – but indisputably defective – ammonium nitrate inflators under *existing contracts*. The Consent Order did not cancel those contracts or prohibit the resulting installation of millions more defective airbags. Instead, NHTSA threatened to impose an additional $60 million fine if Takata did not phase out its "non-desiccated" ammonium nitrate inflators in favor of "desiccated" explosives before the end of 2017. The remaining $70 million fine would be due only if Takata ever entered into any *new contracts* with automakers for the sale of non-desiccated inflators.

Takata's own engineers were testing the new inflator design and found that all eventually ruptured.[95] Nobody at NHTSA was convinced that any type of desiccant could make ammonium nitrate inflators safe in long-term use, so Rosekind left a sword dangling over Takata's head. "Absent proof that the desiccated inflators are safe, Takata will be required to recall them."[96] NHTSA recognized a total recall of Takata's AN-powered inflators – including original equipment and "remedy" units – would push the total number of affected vehicles from at least 30 million to 70 million – roughly one out of every four cars on American highways.

The Consent Order imposed three additional, non-contingent obligations on Takata. For starters, the company had to fire certain unnamed employees. Takata then had to improve its "internal safety culture," in part by paying *its own lawyers* at Dechert LLP to submit a "detailed written report ... regarding the history of the rupturing inflator issues ... [including] a summary of the facts, internal discussions and decision-making, safety lapses that Takata has uncovered and steps taken by Takata to mitigate the risk." Takata's criminal defense lawyers would, of course, avoid adding fuel to the criminal investigation. Takata's product had killed almost a dozen people by that point but Bradbury, who transmitted the report to NHTSA, said the Dechert team's job was to identify "events that led to the production of ... inflators that *may* pose a safety risk."[97] Takata's competitors had rejected ammonium nitrate as a propellant because it was unstable, yet Dechert described the problem as a "previously unrecognized and unanticipated phenomenon." Giving no credence to Takata's former engineers and other whistle-blowers who were already coming out of the corporate woodwork, Dechert did not say Takata engineers falsified testing data; they simply "encountered issues during moisture testing." The tests, including a crucial "process validation report" that Takata gave Honda on June 23, 2000, were not fraudulent; they just "inaccurately reported [the ammonium nitrate inflators] as showing compliance when in fact they were not compliant." No worries, though, Dechert assured NHTSA. Takata had developed and funded a vigorous "Get Out the Word" campaign to maximize recall completion rates.

The Consent Order contained an additional obligation – to abide by a separate agreement NHTSA had worked out with Takata's carmaker customers. The Coordinated Remedy Order, also dated November 3, 2015, was designed to jumpstart the process of replacing essentially every airbag inflator Takata had ever made. It compelled the affected manufacturers to accept "like-for-like" interim replacements for the most dangerous units that remained on American highways. In other words, carmakers were allowed to replace old, spongy, non-desiccated inflators with new but equally spongy inflators.

The Coordinated Remedy Order, in turn, created a Coordinated Remedy Program ("CRP," for short) under which recall campaigns would proceed in four tranches. At that point, 12 carmakers were known to have 19 million cars with killer airbags in them. NHTSA, in fluent bureaucratese, said it had little choice but to implement "a principled, rational risk mitigation-based approach for the prioritization and phasing of recall plans" that would put older, spongy driver-side inflators at the head of the queue for replacement but defer any action to prevent explosions on the passenger side. The result was a matrix that took into account an inflator's age, its location in a car and the climate in the geographic location where the car was registered. Replacement inflators would go first to cars in model year 2008 or *older*, but only if they were registered in *humid* locations and had already been recalled. PRIORITY GROUP 2 included *newer* cars in *humid* locations. PRIORITY GROUP 3 included *passenger* inflators in *newer* cars in *non-humid* locations. Millions of new spongy inflators that were used as "interim" repairs would themselves have to be replaced so PRIORITY GROUP 4 was designed not as a recall but as a *re-recall* to replace those newer but defective replacements with a presumably non-defective "final remedy."

NHTSA's "rational risk mitigation-based" plan was almost impossible to explain or justify to the driving public, so the agency didn't try. The bottom line was embarrassing: even if the carmakers carried out NHTSA's CRP to the letter, millions of Americans would be driving around with potential pipe bombs in their faces for four or more years. For example, the owner of a PRIORITY GROUP 1 vehicle might get a new, non-desiccated AN-powered inflator in December 2015 but the vehicle manufacturer would not have to issue a recall notice, much less actually replace it with a less spongy, AN-powered inflator, until December 2019. The only way any owner could learn where he stood in line for the lifeboat was to check an Annex to the CRP, which listed specific makes and models by Priority Group.

NHTSA's two Orders produced another result that left car owners and drivers in the lurch. By mid-2017, 8.8 million vehicle owners had received recall notices advising that their airbag could kill them but replacements were not yet available. In effect, they were being told, "try not to die in the meantime." Barely half a dozen of the 19 affected vehicle manufacturers offered to put their endangered customers in free loaner cars. By 2018, replacement inflators were plentiful, but for one chilling reason: many owners had not bothered to bring their cars in for the free fix. Many did not receive snail-mail recall notices because they were sent, not to them, but to long-lost first owners. Others could not read English or mistook the letters as some sort of scam or spam. Many who diligently responded to the first recall notice could not fathom why an airbag that got replaced last year must be replaced a second time this year, so they just trashed the second notice.

Takata and the vehicle manufacturers committed in the CRP to seek a 100 percent recall "completion rate" by the end of 2017 for the most dangerous inflators. Takata's lofty commitment to rid the world of their so-called "alpha" inflators was pure lip service. NHTSA already knew from eight years of experience that vehicle owners had been no more responsive to the Takata recall campaigns than any others. Despite enormous publicity, the repair rate for GM's defective ignition switch topped out at 70 percent. Even before the biggest Takata recalls were announced, there were 70 million cars on American highways with open recalls for one or another type of safety defect.[98] It was no wonder; the agency did not follow its own procedures to address low completion rates in any of the earlier Takata recalls.[99] The 2017 deadline came and went, with fully half of Takata's ticking time bombs still out there, inches from drivers' faces.

Congress also noticed that drivers in general were not taking recall notices seriously. Only 15 percent of recalled vehicles more than 10 years old ever get fixed. The average age of cars and light trucks on American highways hit an all-time high in 2016 – 11.6 years. By 2021, analysts predict we will have to deal with 30 percent more vehicles aged 16 or older – 81 million of them. In that ocean of clunkers, almost one-fourth will be a quarter of a century old. Even in the midst of the Toyota, GM and Takata fiascos, overall completion rates were moving in the wrong direction, from 74 percent in 2010 to 60 percent in 2014.

New legislation, the Fixing America's Surface Transportation ("FAST") Act, required NHTSA to reverse the trend and submit a self-report card every two years.[100] NHTSA's first report, published in May, 2017, gave the agency a big, fat "F" because 65 percent of all recalled vehicles were still on the road, just as dangerous as the day they were recalled.[101] NHTSA's Recall Management Division relies entirely on ARTEMIS for information on recall completion rates and does nothing to verify information they receive from vehicle manufacturers about the number of repairs completed, the number of vehicles that got scrapped before they were repaired, which models were being fixed or whether the unavailability of repairs left owners "frustrated or apathetic after attempting to obtain a remedy." It was obvious, however, that some manufacturers were much better at repairing their safety-related defects than others but NHTSA insisted it could not hold any particular manufacturer's low completion rates against it.

NHTSA also knew that it lacked sufficient resources to enforce the long list of requirements in its Consent Orders against a flailing supplier and a growing list of affected carmakers. The agency required Takata to fund an "independent monitor" to review and assess "progress of the Coordinated Remedy Program" and Takata's compliance with all the other obligations. The Monitor was given no authority to require action by anyone. Former Deputy Attorney General John D. Buretta and his New York City firm, Cravath, Swaine & Moore, won the financial windfall that came with the otherwise thankless and powerless assignment.

The "allies and confidants" Secretary Mineta recruited for Takata could not keep Mineta's successor, Secretary Anthony Foxx, from lashing out the day NHTSA unveiled its incomprehensible November 3, 2015, Orders.

"For years, Takata … refused to acknowledge that … [its inflators] were defective," Foxx charged. The company "provided incomplete, inaccurate and misleading information to NHTSA, to the companies using its inflators and to the public. Those failures put millions of Americans at risk." Foxx added that Takata's "refusal to acknowledge the truth allowed a serious problem to become a massive crisis."[102]

181

Takata pretended NHTSA's Orders and Foxx's damning remarks were good news, providing them "a clear path forward."[103] The question was, forward into what? Foxx found only one word to describe what Takata and his own Department had agreed upon.

"It's a mess," he admitted.

2016

Washington

Secretary Foxx's bloody "mess" got even bloodier in 2016. The media carried heart-wrenching reports of more Takata airbag deaths. On March 31, Huma Hanif, a 17-year old high school student in Texas was in a minor fender-bender on the way to her after-school job. Her airbag shot a twisted metal fragment through her neck, severing her carotid artery and jugular vein. She stepped out of her 2002 Honda Civic and bled to death on the spot. The car had been recalled five years earlier, but her family swore they never received any notice.

In June, 81-year old Ramon Kuffo was repairing a 2001 Accord in his driveway. The airbag inflator exploded and killed him.

NHTSA reacted to these back-to-back tragedies in typical bureaucratic fashion – they issued a press release just before the Fourth of July holiday weekend. It instructed 313,000 Americans who owned older Hondas and related makes and models to *STOP DRIVING THEM NOW*. Drivers of those cars had a 50/50 chance of being *killed, not saved*, by their airbags.

NHTSA's warning did not reach 50-year old Delia Robles. On September 30, 2016, she died in Corona, California, on her way to get a flu shot. Her son told reporters she was an exceedingly cautious person. She was driving her 2001 Honda Civic just 25 miles per hour with her seatbelt securely fastened when a Chevy turned in front of her and caused a minor collision. Robles' car was included in the original 2008 recall but she never received any of the 20-plus notices Honda claimed it sent to registered owners over the intervening eight years.

As if to prove how jinxed Takata was, a transport truck rushing replacement inflators to dealers from Takata's plant in Monclova, Mexico, overturned in the middle of the night on August 22, 2016, on a highway outside a home in Quemado, Texas. The ammonium nitrate inside the inflators exploded all at once and incinerated 69-year old Lucila Robles (no relation to Delia), who was sleeping inside. It took investigators two days to find her charred remains. The Transportation Department took no steps to tighten safety regulations governing shipments of new inflators or the millions of defective units that were being removed from recalled cars.

Public confidence in NHTSA's CRP also was incinerated within months. Four car manufacturers – Mitsubishi, Toyota, GM and Chrysler – got caught putting spongy, non-desiccated Takata inflators in brand-new cars. Those 2016 and 2017 models got recalled days after their owners drove them off their dealers' lots. The carmakers had installed 8.4 million replacement inflators by mid-2016, half of them supplied by Takata's competitors who did not use ammonium nitrate. The other half came from Takata with the unquestionably defective AN-powered design and half of those – 2.1 million "repair" units – were the spongy kind. Law-makers were astonished to see that the fine print in NHTSA's Orders allowed car manufacturers to replace older time bombs with newer time bombs. When German automakers also got caught installing new, spongy inflators in place of old units, they re-recalled nearly a million brand-new VW's and Audis. BMW recalled another quarter-million of its newer cars when it realized its dealers might have used spongy inflators as spare parts.

Despite the string of embarrassments, Administrator Rosekind did not abide criticism of "NHTSA's aggressive actions in 2015." He damned his own efforts with faint praise, pro-nouncing the Takata situation "already a year ahead of where it would have been." His press office falsely claimed credit for uncovering the Takata defect. Rosekind reluctantly admitted that

NHTSA had only "encouraged," not required, the auto manufacturers to let owners know they were only getting an "interim"
fix. Rosekind insisted that NHTSA's Office of Defect Investigations "leads the world in protecting the driving public from vehicle
safety defects." Clarence Ditlow, the long-time president of the
Nader-founded Center for Auto Safety, offered a different take: "If
NHTSA had done the right thing and really probed Takata, they
could have caught it a lot sooner" and kept Takata from
committing "the most colossal blunders in the history of the
industry."[104]

Honda eventually said it was shocked – shocked! – to discover
that Takata had "manipulated" test results for inflators "in several
instances." Chairman Shige Takada initially responded with a
half-hearted denial. "We did not do it. I don't think."[105] Although
Japanese engineers led the fraud, Takada tried to blame the
American subsidiary. Takata Corporation eventually admitted
that its "data integrity problems ... were entirely inexcusable and
will not be tolerated or repeated," but it gratuitously added that
the fakery – including the deletion of test results showing the
earliest inflators exploding like hand grenades – was "not related
to the root cause of the airbag inflator ruptures."

In September 2016 Takata's biggest customer said it was
"disappointed and troubled."[106] Honda dropped Takata as a
supplier of new or replacement units. With his flagship customer
sunk, Shige promised to resign once a "new management regime
has been selected," but he was too busy trying to pump some life
back into Takata's stock price. The defect, according to Takata's
2016 Annual Report, involved only "a small percentage of inflators" and the company would "determine as soon as possible
the root cause." Takata's foremost objective was "ensuring the
continuation and growth of the airbag business." The company
had suffered two consecutive years of net losses but Takata's
overall operating income was up nearly 28 percent. Net sales and
ordinary income were also trending upwards.

Takata's sales were not growing as fast as the number of
affected vehicles, however. By the end of 2016, NHTSA had to
amend its Coordinated Remedy Order three times and triple the
number of repair Priority Groups from four to 12. The number of

vehicle manufacturers in the CRP swelled from 12 to 19. The CRP was dealing with *61 million defective inflators*, not 23 million. The new Plan gave vehicle manufacturers a big break, however, while increasing the risk to their car-buying customers. Carmakers would have until the end of 2020 to start replacing new spongy inflators that had replaced old spongy inflators.

NHTSA's CRP failed Joel Knight, who was beheaded in his 2006 Ford Ranger. Ford did not consider South Carolina a "high absolute humidity" area and was not required even to have on hand a replacement for the inflator that killed him, much less to replace it, until a year after Knight died. When Ford finally reported Knight's death, six months after the event, NHTSA responded by requiring all manufacturers to consider South Carolina and California "humid" and criticized the vehicle manufacturers' persistent foot-dragging in implementing the Remedy Plan.

The carmakers also stiffed John Buretta, the Independent Monitor NHTSA appointed to assure compliance with the CRP. They denied him information about the status of their recall campaigns and avoided using the modern, more effective, means of communication he recommended to notify drivers that their airbag could kill them. The Monitor recognized the deadly risks posed by recalled airbags but vehicle manufacturers actively discouraged owners from going in for their free fix by "indicating that the remedy is not important or the recall is not serious" even in light of 220 confirmed ruptures by December 1, 2016. "The risk for injurious or lethal ruptures … increases each day," Buretta added

By Christmas, 2016, federal prosecutors in Michigan had interrogated Takata's Bob Schubert and served subpoenas on his bosses, Al Bernat and Paresh Khandhadia. None of them were charged. Bernat and Khandhadia invoked their Fifth Amendment right against self-incrimination and refused to testify. A grand jury returned criminal indictments against the three Japanese engineers with whom Kevin Fitzgerald had tangled for more than a decade. It was time for Takata Corporation to cop a plea.

2017

Washington

As the calendar rolled around to 2017 and grandstands were going up around Washington to celebrate the Inauguration of Donald Trump as President of the United States, the Obama-appointed Justice Department leadership had two high-profile corporate crime cases on their list of unfinished business. They were not about to turn either of those prosecutions – the Volkswagen emissions fraud or Takata's killer airbags – over to Trump appointees.

The George W. Bush and Obama administrations had set records for imposing criminal fines on corporations. In March 2014, just before the lid popped off the Takata scandal, Toyota paid the biggest criminal penalty for a car company in history, $1.2 billion, but neither the corporation or anyone who ran it pled guilty to any crime and no one went to jail for intentionally hiding information about its runaway cars or for making deceptive statements to protect Toyota's brand image. Even Japanese executives, it seemed, were "too big to jail."

Barbara McQuade, the U.S. Attorney in the Eastern District of Michigan, spent 2016 trying to nail Volkswagen for selling 600,000 supposedly "clean" diesel-engine cars in the United States with a device designed to defeat federal air pollution control tests. The charges included conspiracy to defraud the United States, wire fraud, violations of import regulations and obstruction of justice. McQuade was not satisfied with the prospect of punishing only the German company. She had already won indictments of seven VW executives based in the United States and Germany, including Oliver Schmidt, a Takata neighbor in Auburn Hills. Schmidt had falsely told U.S. regulators in 2014 that the vehicles complied with American environmental regulations before he moved home to Germany, a country that generally will not extradite its citizens. When FBI agents interviewed him there, Schmidt forthrightly described the fraud and incriminated other, higher-level VW executives, so he thought he was off the hook. No such luck. Schmidt made the mistake of visiting Florida over Christmas 2016. McQuade had him arrested at the Miami airport on January 7, 2017, dragged him into court in shackles, handcuffs and an orange jumpsuit, then locked him up in a Michigan prison with no hope of bail during the two years that would likely pass before trial. Schmidt copped a plea after another VW executive, an American named James Liang, was sentenced to three and a half years in prison in August 2017. The judge who presided over both cases, Sean Cox, endorsed prosecutors' argument that "unless individual actors are also punished, future corporate executives and con-tractors may be tempted to justify their criminal behavior as just 'doing their job' or 'following orders.'"

The charges against Schmidt, Liang and VW must have sent a shudder down the spines of Takata executives. Much like Takata, the German company executed a "strategy of concealing … [its wrongdoing] from U.S. regulators while appearing to cooperate" and "continued to offer … 'fixes' and explanations without revealing the underlying reason" why its product failed to meet federal requirements. According to McQuade, VW's il-legal conduct was directed by the company's executive manage-ment, who chose not to "advocate disclosure … [but] instead authorized its continued concealment."

On January 11, 2017, Volkswagen pled guilty and agreed to pay $4.3 billion in criminal and civil fines, easily topping Toyota's previous record of $1.2 billion. VW spent more than $20 billion more to settle civil cases filed against them. The corpora-tion's capitulation did nothing to help Schmidt, however. Even though he had cooperated with U.S. investigators and prosecutors in almost every way, and even though the lies he told did not kill or maim anyone, Schmidt was sentenced to seven years in prison. His bosses wisely stayed in Germany.

Takata's lawyers – Bradbury, Levander and the Dechert team – saw an opportunity to negotiate a deal with McQuade that would be more favorable to the Takata executives who had worked so hard to keep a lid on the corporation's stinking mess. They had cornered their client into cooperating fully with the investigation in January 2016 and a plea deal was starting to take shape by August.[107]

It would have been a stretch to expect the outgoing Obama team to let the corporation off without admitting it was guilty of any crime, given criticism the Justice Department suffered when it entered "non-prosecution agreements" with General Motors and Toyota. The fine would have to appear to be in the same billion-dollar range as Toyota's and the prosecutors would need to claim some scalps – or at least make it look like some individual wrongdoers might also be punished.

The top Takata executives who had resisted expansion of the recalls were luckier than their neighbors at VW. Bradbury held not just a trump card but a Trump card in the negotiations. Before he was a torture-memo author in the George W. Bush Administration, Bradbury was a law clerk in 1992 to Supreme Court Justice Clarence Thomas. That credential guaranteed that the 56-year old graduate of Stanford and the University of Michigan Law School would be popular with the incoming Trump White House, which was preparing to nominate a slew of former Thomas clerks to federal judgeships.

With the clock running out, McQuade had few options. The corporation was willing to plead guilty and offer up cash. It could also identify three fall guys who, conveniently, could never be compelled to testify against any other Takata executives in Japan or the United States. McQuade made a show of indicting the three Japanese engineers who started falsifying the test reports Takata gave Honda 16 years earlier, in 2000, and kept on "XX"ing bad results. Shinichi Tanaka, Hideo Nakajima and Tsueno Chikaraishi were accused of wire fraud and conspiracy but they retreated to Japan and the Justice Department has never requested their extradition.

In the finest *Fight Club* tradition, the Justice Department agreed to make the case a simple matter of dollars and cents without any particular emphasis on the 11 deaths and 184 grue-some injuries that had been recorded by the end of 2016. The real crime, according to the plea deal, was purely financial. Takata pled guilty to a single count of wire fraud. The criminal fine was just $25 million, barely enough to cover the government's cost in bringing the case and a fraction of the civil fine NHTSA had announced a year earlier. It was pocket change compared to the $4.3 billion assessed against VW for misdeeds that did not kill or injure anyone. The Takata plea deal was all about reparations for those the U.S. Government considered the real "victims of [Takata's] fraud scheme, that is, those auto manufacturers" who padded their own profits for an entire decade by purchasing and installing Takata's cheap airbags. "Individuals who suffered (or will suffer) personal injuries caused by the malfunction of an ... airbag inflator" were mentioned only in passing. The vehicle manufacturers were awarded "restitution" of $850 million. To make sure Honda, Toyota and the other car companies got their figurative pounds of flesh, the plea agreement expressly required payment no later than March 4, 2018 – or else. The "else" being that non-payment would free Justice to pursue additional criminal charges and penalties against the Japanese parent company "or any of its ... subsidiaries." Justice also remained free to initiate "prosecution of any natural persons, including any officers, directors, employees, agents or consultants."[108] Either way, Takata was obligated to "disclose all factual information not protected by a valid claim of attorney-client privilege or attorney work-product."

For innocent people who were horribly injured or who lost loved ones, Takata agreed to deposit a mere $125 million in an "Individual Restitution Fund." The Justice Department's priorities were clear. Prosecutors assured the corporate "victims" almost seven times the compensation they set aside for the human beings whose lives had been lost or wrecked.

On January 13, 2017, just two days after VW's deal was announced – and with exactly one week left in the Obama Administration – McQuade went before the television cameras and boiled the whole case down to dollars and cents. Takata, she said, "falsified and manipulated data because they wanted to make profits on their airbags."[109] Investors realized that Takata had gotten off easy. They immediately bid up Takata's shares on the Tokyo Stock Exchange by 16.5 percent. Takata was still cranking out replacement inflators, half of which on the passenger side were still the spongy type, at full speed.[110] Its main competitors – AutoLiv, Daicel and TRW – had supplied 15 million replacement inflators and taken orders for another 15 million. No doubt about it, criminal conduct that sent no one to jail was good for everybody in the airbag business.

Takata's criminal acts were not, by any measure, good for the broader auto industry. Automakers could claim their respective shares of the whopping $850 million restitution fund but they knew every penny was already spoken for. As the appalling scope of the Takata recalls became apparent in 2017, class action lawsuits rained down on vehicle manufacturers, whose franchised dealers and their retail customers had to front a fortune to replace so many millions of Takata airbags. Consumers, too, sought reimbursement of their own out-of-pocket costs, ranging from rental fees paid while their cars were out of service, towing to dealerships, lost wages and childcare. Scrap yards wanted to be reimbursed for the "diminution of value" in airbags they kept in inventory for sale to repair shops.

The car companies were desperate to give their own shareholders a more definite idea what size financial "hit" they would take in the economic loss cases. Some were quick to sit down with claimants' lawyers, work out a number, set up a payment mechanism and – most importantly for themselves – extinguish future claims by anyone who failed to join the "class" in time. The first big settlement, in May 2017, earmarked $553 million for some of the people and businesses that lost money on the Takata recalls. Toyota kicked in $278.5 million of that amount and three other manufacturers contributed the rest. By August, Nissan forked over $97.7 million, including seed money for an "outreach program" to get more of its customers to take their vehicles in for airbag replacements. Honda eventually started paying economic damages claims and created an online claim form.[111] Ford settled for $299 million in 2018.[112] Not all of the money went to aggrieved plaintiffs, however; their lawyers took $166 million of it in fees.

State government officials also wanted a piece of Takata. Several state attorneys general, flush from victories in the VW emissions fraud cases, rushed into their local courts to collect fines for defrauding their citizens. One of them convinced a judge to order Takata to put $8 million in escrow "forthwith," even before liability was established.

The victim compensation line grew longer even before U.S. District Judge George Caram Steeh approved Takata's criminal plea deal on February 28, 2017, and picked Harvard Law School Professor Eric Green to divvy up $125 million among the hundreds of individual victims who had not yet settled their claims against Takata. On February 2, Diane Moulton of Dearborn, Michigan, died from injuries she sustained several months earlier, when the airbag in her 2002 Honda CRV exploded in a parking lot. Weeks later, 18-year old Karina Dorado exposed a huge gap in NHTSA's Coordinated Remedy Program. The agency had known for decades that unscrupulous repair shops padded their profits by charging for *new* repair parts when, in fact, they were actually installing much cheaper parts salvaged from cars previously "totaled" by insurance companies. NHTSA's 2015 Orders did nothing to keep defective salvage airbags from adding to the Takata death toll. Dorado was driving a 2002 Honda in Las Vegas. She had a fender-bender and the airbag shot a chunk of metal through her trachea. The car was not among the 11.4 million Hondas then under recall because NHTSA had no way to trace the defective salvage inflator to her car. Honda had bought 60,000 Takata inflators from salvage yards to get them out of circulation but they missed the hand grenade that went off in Dorado's steering wheel.

In July 2017, George ("Rob") Sharp, 60, of Baton Rouge, Louisiana, was killed in a 2004 Honda Civic equipped with an airbag salvaged from a 2002 Civic. Sharp will not be the last to die from a salvage airbag. In early 2020, hundreds of original equipment inflators, including Takata's most deadly "alpha" inflators, were readily available for purchase on eBay and no statute expressly prohibited mechanics from reinstalling them in unsuspecting people's cars.

Sharp was just one of four people killed by Takata airbags in July 2017. Steven ("Mike") Mollohan, 56, was off to a holiday weekend in Martinsburg, West Virginia, in his beloved 2006 Ford Ranger, the same make, model and year as the Ranger that beheaded Joel Knight in December 2015. NHTSA had not required Ford to issue a recall notice because the agency did not consider West Virginia sufficiently humid to pose any imminent risk of

Mollohan's inflator degrading and blowing his head off. But his driver-side inflator was a virtual twin of the inflator that decapitated Knight 18 months earlier. In fact, Mollohan's pickup came off the same Ford assembly line, right behind Knight's. The inflators in Ford Rangers were built from an unusual Takata design, different from the airbags in the Hondas that had already killed at least a dozen Americans. It was, however, the same design Honda installed in a model it sold in Asia, the Honda City. Before Mollohan died, it had already killed five people in Malaysia, including a pregnant woman. Ford did nothing to keep it from happening again until February 2018, when it warned 3,800 Ford Ranger owners not to drive their vehicles. The manufacturer also made a point to remind them that "Ford Motor Company is not providing long-term loaner vehicles." Another 323,000 pickups were under recall, but Ford did not warn owners to stop driving them because, as a company spokeswoman put it, "we respond to the data."

Two weeks after Mollohan died, a 58-year old man in Sydney, Australia, was killed by the airbag in his 2007 Honda CR-V. That same week, on July 19, 2017, in Holiday, Florida, Nicole Lynn Barker was enjoying a hot, humid summer with her two young children and her mother. When the airbag in her car exploded in a 30-mph collision, her family was there to witness the results first-hand. The vivacious 34-year old died from a six-inch by three-inch gaping wound to her left temple that fractured her skull and caused her brain to bleed.

The scent of death was on Takata Corporation, but Little Shige and Big Wife seemed to be the only people on the planet who could not pick up the smell. One type of corporate death, reorganization in bankruptcy, had become a popular way for automotive companies to escape or limit their responsibility for safety defects. In May 2009 Chrysler Corporation transferred its assets into a company it called "New Chrysler." Death and injury claims could be filed only against "Old Chrysler." A month later, General Motors transferred its assets to what it called "New GM." The remaining "Old GM" renamed itself "Motors Liquidation Company" and retained liability for safety defects, but only for deaths and injuries that occurred before the date of the restructuring.

Months after the corporation pled guilty to federal crimes, Takata was still more-or-less promising investors that it would not go bankrupt. "It is the judgment of the company's management there are no material uncertainties regarding the company's viability as a going concern."[113] The Takada family was convinced they had the world over a barrel in 2017 to the same extent that they had rolled NHTSA in 2015, when the agency allowed them to keep selling their unquestionably defective, spongy inflators, not just as replacements but also as components of brand-new cars. Much of that confidence was based on the new formula Takata was using to make "desiccated" inflators. Takata put a drying agent called calcium sulfate in inflators that were installed in almost three million cars between 2005 and 2012. Ford refused to recall cars with calcium sulfate, arguing that inflators containing that desiccant posed an "inconsequential risk" to drivers. The whole time Takata was using calcium sulfate, one of their top inflator engineers, Kevin Fitzgerald, carefully documented every time he warned them it would not work. Takata finally admitted in July 2017 that Fitzgerald was right, that those inflators were equally dangerous and all the affected cars had to be recalled.

Takata Corporation was part of a classic Japanese "*keiretsu*," a financial spider web of interlocking corporate directorships and investments that make it nearly impossible for any Japanese company to go belly up. Shige Takada hired Lazard, Ltd., a global investment bank, to work with those other Japanese companies, mostly carmakers and commercial banks, to "re-structure" the corporation. Takada was not shy about reminding Honda and other Japanese carmakers, who were also among his biggest shareholders, that they had to cooperate with him if they wanted to protect their supply of replacement airbags and their investments in the company that made them. Takada was confident that, even if Honda wouldn't take a big financial "haircut" in the restructuring, Japanese banks would bail him and his family out. At first, airbag market analyst Scott Upham gave him a 70 percent chance of pulling it off. Even if Honda and Nissan bailed, Upham believed, the Japanese banks would step in and impose a GM- or Chrysler-style metamorphosis on Takata. The reorganiza-tion would keep Takata alive but he estimated that its share of the global inflator market would drop from 22 percent in 2015 to 10 percent by 2020.

Before the criminal conviction, Upham advised that "the chances that Takata completely implodes is remote," no more than 10 percent. Lazard managed to line up five potential bidders, but none of them would touch the company unless it got restructured in a way that would insulate them from seemingly endless liability for the defective airbags; in other words, they might pay good money for Takata's untainted assets, such as its seat belt production facilities, which made one-third of the world's supply, but only if the company first discharged all of its liabilities from the tainted airbag operations in bankruptcy. That was not what the Takada family wanted to hear.

Privately, Honda and Nissan listed explicit reasons why they refused to bail Takata out. The first was Takata's catastrophic decision, contrary to the advice Frank Roe and I provided, to deny responsibility for killing people during its Congressional testimony in 2014. The second was more a matter of *keiretsu* loyalty. In the Dechert report and some public statements, Takata tried to blame *their customers* for failing to notice that it had lied to them about inflator test results. They also considered it unforgivable that Shige Takada had refused to implement any sort of crisis communications plan, like the "truth squad" Roe and I presented to him in January 2014, before the lid blew off the scandal. The Japanese carmakers knew they would be throwing good money after bad if they tried to bail out a company whose share price had dropped 84 percent, whose "market cap" had withered from $2.7 billion to less than $300 million and whose balance sheet showed $10 billion in liabilities from the airbag recalls and perhaps another $40 billion in other liabilities.

Even as bankruptcy loomed, Shige Takada spent the first part of 2017 shooing away any potential bids from the world's biggest airbag maker, AutoLiv. At one point, he threatened to fire anyone who provided information the Swedish company might use in preparing an offer. The only eager buyer of Takata Corporation's assets was Key Safety Systems, owned by China's Ningbo Joyson Electronics Corp. Nobody in Japan could stomach the idea of putting Takata's turnaround in Chinese hands or giving China 25 percent of the airbag market and making it, overnight, the world's second-largest supplier. Takada had twice considered buying Key, but the tables had turned. For once, Shige found *himself* over a barrel. The Chinese calculated exactly how much cash Takata needed for the criminal and civil fines and their up-front restitution payments. If Takata failed to meet the March 4, 2018, payment deadline set in the criminal plea deal, the Justice Department could unwind it and file new charges against individual Takata executives.

A "structured liquidation" of the entire company was the only way out. The simultaneous June 27, 2017, bankruptcy filings in Tokyo and Wilmington, Delaware – the largest ever by a Japanese manufacturing company – started a mad, global scramble among Takata's creditors. The company was like a majestic, twelve-point buck, lying mortally wounded on a forest floor. It had valuable assets – think of prize antlers – but it would never rise again. Somebody needed to put it out of its misery and organize a way to divide the rest of what it had to offer. Otherwise, buzzards would get there first and ruin the venison, the pelt and anything else that could be turned into cash.

The bankruptcy court established nine different classes and 35 subclasses of creditors. Mortgage and lien-holders were put at the head of the line; people killed or injured by ammonium nitrate inflators were well down the list, but seven subclasses ahead of people who got killed or injured by other Takata products, including defective inflators that did not contain ammonium nitrate. Three of Takata's former engineers threatened to hold up the bankruptcy until the government paid them a $1.7 million whistleblower reward for helping the Justice Department press the criminal prosecution.[114]

Federal law also gives bankruptcy judges the priestly power to absolve a dying corporation of its sins. They can enjoin affected parties not to file suit against whatever may be left of the corporation or whomever might have purchased its assets. The Takata case was assigned to Judge Brendan Shannon, who promptly approved the issuance of 80,000 bankruptcy notices on postcards with microscopic print advising creditors how to get in line for the opportunity to pick at Takata Corporation's bones. Takata had many valuable assets in its seat belt production facilities and related intellectual property but anything connected in any way to its ammonium nitrate-powered airbags was toxic. The Chinese were not about to expose themselves to any of Takata's governmental obligations or financial liabilities. Takata had paid only $20 million and still owed American taxpayers $50 million of the noncontingent portion of the fine NHTSA had announced with great fanfare in 2015. Takata's carmaker customers had $850 million coming to them from the restitution fund set up in criminal plea agreement but it was a drop in the sea of expenses Takata planned to dump on them. The Chinese were eager to acquire Takata's assets for a "fire sale" price of $1.6 billion, but not until the court entered a "channeling injunction" that barred any claims individual victims of airbag explosions might make against them. Vehicle manufacturers were stuck with billions in costs to replace inflators in their own customers' cars. Economic loss claimants could recover only from the carmakers. Takata Corporation was gone, but the Takada family got away, free and clear.

The Dechert firm was rightly proud of its work. Steve Bradbury and the team made sure no individuals at Takata ended up in a prison cell next to Oliver Schmidt, their former neighbor at VW. In fact, the only Takata employees who were formally threatened with prosecution – and who presumably could be pressured to "sing" or "compose" about the actions of their bosses – were in Japan, conveniently outside the reach of U.S. prosecutors. The criminal plea deal was also popular with Japanese car manu-facturers because it guaranteed them more than half of the "restitution" amount. Dechert's negotiations with NHTSA never led to criminal fines for violating the Motor Vehicle Safety Act but they made it possible for NHTSA to pat itself on the back for issuing a $200 million civil fine and for Takata Corporation to get away with paying only one-tenth of that amount.

Big Wife and Little Shige's family fortune was much reduced but, unlike the families of people who got shredded by Takata airbags, none of their beloved was missing from the dinner table at family celebrations, nobody had bandages on their face from their most recent facial reconstruction surgery. The Takadas apologized to people who lost money by investing with them but had nothing to say to the hundreds of people who had already been killed and maimed or the additional 2,000 people likely to get blasted in the future, all of whom were left with no legal recourse against the Takadas or their bankrupt company. Akiko made clear what gave her "heart-wrenching sorrow" for Takata's failure: "I am deeply sorry for all the shareholders."[115] Shige was similarly sentimental. "I deeply apologize from the bottom of my heart to all the relevant people and creditors who have been supporting and cooperating with us."[116]

For his part, Steve Bradbury took another spin through Washington's revolving door. Dechert paid him $1.2 million, including an $800,000 bonus, for 16 months of work on the Takata crisis.[117] In his former job at the Justice Department, it would have taken him more than *six years* to earn that much. Just months after he out-lawyered the government attorneys at NHTSA, Bradbury headed back into public service with enthusiastic support from auto industry lobbyists. The Trump Administration sent NHTSA's career staff an unmistakable message. In late February 2015, NHTSA's Chief Counsel, O. Kevin Vincent, called Bradbury out on Takata's failure to comply with Special Orders the agency had issued. A few months later, Trump nominated Bradbury to be General Counsel of the Department of Transportation, where he would take effective charge over Vincent and every other NHTSA lawyer responsible for making Takata and the carmakers comply with their obligations under the deals Bradbury had struck on behalf of the industry. Senate Commerce approved Bradbury's nomination on August 2, 2017, after a bitterly contested confirmation hearing and a party-line, 14-13 vote. Two years later, President Trump made Bradbury the Acting Deputy Secretary of Transportation as well as General Counsel. Bradbury's Deputy General Counsel, James C. Owens, became Acting Administrator of NHTSA. Takata's former lawyer thereby took total control over crucial decisions to enforce – or ignore – the commitments Takata and the carmakers made in 2015 to recall and repair 70 million cars equipped with killer airbags.

Takata's website remained online for a short while after the company filed for bankruptcy. It offered the world a sickening *sayonara*: "We hope the day will come when the word 'Takata' becomes synonymous with 'safety.'"

2018-19

Wilmington, Delaware and Washington

Individual victims of Takata airbag explosions fared no better in bankruptcy court than in the criminal proceedings. Judge Shannon could figure out how many landlords and suppliers deserved a piece of Takata's remains but no one could predict how many more people would end up in line for the $125 million – minus millions that likely will be spent to administer the fund – that was set aside in Takata's criminal plea deal. Takata Corporation was about to disappear as a legal entity and the Chinese buyers were proclaimed "protected parties" who were taking on none of Takata's past or future liabilities for personal injury or wrongful death. As a matter of due process in such cases, the bankruptcy judge was required to appoint a "Future Claims Representative."

The FCR's job is not to prosecute claims for the victims but to make sure money is set aside for them. Judge Shannon created a Takata Airbag Tort Compensation Trust Fund but Takata offered to contribute nothing to it. The vehicle manufacturers were not feeling especially generous, either. They offered to chip in less than $4 million. The lawyers Shannon chose to act as the FCR used the only leverage they had – to hold up and possibly wreck the sale to Key Safety systems. The vehicle manufacturers and Takata's insurers eventually agreed to match the $125 million that Takata had deposited in the Individual Restitution Fund established in the criminal case. Nearly 80 percent of that "donation" came from Honda, Toyota and Nissan. As of February 21, 2018, victims had a total of $250 million to recover against but no way to know how many other people would fall into the same line or how long it would take for Professor Green to release any of the money.

Three more people died and dozens more were maimed in 2018 while Takata's creditors bickered in bankruptcy court. Honda's

Asian model, the City, which contains the same inflator config-uration that beheaded Joel Knight in 2015 and Steve Mollohan in 2017, killed more Malaysians on January 1 and again on May 27. An American, 55-year old Armando Ortega, bought a Honda Civic in May 2018 in Buckeye Arizona, apparently without knowing it had been recalled in 2014. His Takata airbag exploded just weeks later, on June 8, and killed him. Honda said nothing about it in public for nine months, until the end of March 2019. The Takata airbag in a BMW killed another man in 2019.

As in other mass tort cases in which the perpetrators used bankruptcy proceedings to escape responsibility, Green had to develop a methodology for dividing an essentially fixed amount of money among an unknown number of eventual claimants. The number of killed and injured, of course, would be determined by the number of inflators that blew up in people's faces. That number, in turn, is a function of how many recalled airbags will get replaced before they blow up. Green hired economic con-sultants in New York City, who looked at the manufacturers' poor repair rates and initially forecast that at least 922 – and perhaps as many as 1,769 – would get blasted by Takata airbags.[118] That meant Green had to stretch the $250 million in the two compensa-tion funds to cover claims approaching $1.7 billion.[119] In October, 2019, Green figured he could finally start disbursing some of the money to people who had endured multiple surgeries, who were rendered unable to work or whose families had lost their bread-winners over the previous six years. On October 3, 2019, the judge from the criminal case approved payment of just $11 million to some of the victims – just 6.5 cents for every dollar they likely would have been able to recover from Takata had it not gone bankrupt. In other words, in the initial payments, a victim who deserved a $1 million damage award so far has received just $65,000.

Future payments to victims, of course, will be reduced every time another Takata airbag explodes in someone's face. Professor Green's economic consultants confirmed in late 2019 that Takata airbags will keep killing and maiming people throughout the 2020s and 2030s because the manufacturers will actually repair only a fraction of the cars they have recalled. NHTSA has authority to verify completion rates reported by manufacturers, but they do not use it. Instead, the agency has allowed carmakers to omit important information from three-fourths of their recall reports.[120] NHTSA has clear statutory authority to direct the manufacturers to take action to improve low recall completion rates but has not used it. As a result, a quarter of the most dangerous Takata inflators – in 2.9 million cars made by 12 manufacturers – were still on the roads at the start of 2020, despite NHTSA's assurances that all of them would be fixed by the end of 2017. The supposedly less dangerous inflators were still in 30 million cars in 2018. Public confidence in the recall repair program took a hit in 2019, when Honda admitted that its dealers had installed many thousands of the new inflators backwards.

From the agency's perspective, Takata airbags are just part of the problem. A record total of 53.2 million cars were recalled in 2016 and another 900 recall campaigns began in 2018, compared with 450 new campaigns in 2009. More than half of the 264 million vehicles operating on American highways in 2017 were under a safety recall.[121] Nearly 26 million of those potential deathtraps will remain on the road until their wheels fall off. A congressional watchdog, the Government Accountability Office, told NHTSA in 2011 it should develop a plan to identify best practices in recall campaigns. Seven years and four GAO audits later, NHTSA had not developed or implemented any plan "to follow up on Takata recall completion rates."[122]

The only person President Trump ever nominated to run NHTSA during his entire first term, former Office of Management and Budget analyst Heidi King, understated the agency's failure in 2018, when she testified to Senate Commerce that "overall completion rates are not where we want them to be." King resigned as Acting Administrator in frustration a few months later. Her acting successor, James C. Owens, who reports directly to Steve Bradbury, Takata's former lawyer, made clear that his own priorities for the agency are "regulatory reform efforts" and "reducing unnecessary burdens" on the motor vehicle industry.[123] When the Transportation Department's own watchdog, the Office of Inspector General, exposed NHTSA's abdication of its responsibility to make manufacturers actually fix vehicles they had recalled, King chided them for a report that "may leave the public with misconceptions regarding NHTSA's oversight of recalls in general and the Takata recalls in particular.[124] King stuck to the bureaucratic party line, that NHTSA was "dedicated to continuous improvement of the risk-based processes addressing potential safety defects and recalls."[125]

2020

Washington

Any sense of urgency about Takata's killer airbags died in 2020. When NHTSA created its Coordinated Remedy Program in 2015, the agency established an Independent Monitor to do what it knew was beyond its own capabilities – to shine a light on the carmakers and report whether they were making good on their promises to do what was necessary to remove the threat to American drivers. Just before *Killer Airbags* was published, the Independent Monitor essentially surrendered.

The Monitor, New York lawyer and former Justice Department official John D. Buretta, is better known for his representation of Burisma, the infamous Ukrainian gas company. Buretta started his work related to the Takata scandal by publishing a facebook of Americans who had been chopped to death by their airbags. He also issued a forthright warning that the "severity of potential death or serious injury is un-precedented."[126] He reported that, 18 months into NHTSA's supposedly Coordinated Remedy Program, the vehicle manufacturers had repaired fewer than half of the most dangerous cars.[127] In his second report, for 2018, Buretta said "the clock is ticking for drivers and passengers with defective inflators still in their vehicles" and expressed disappointment at the "stagnation" of repair rates at 60 percent and alarm that the process of repairing even the most dangerous vehicles "has slowed." [128] Buretta's report for 2019, by contrast, nonchalantly noted that 15 of the 19 affected carmakers had not replaced up to 30 percent of the potential car bombs they had planted inches away from their customers' faces.[129] Buretta seemed not to notice that, of all the recall campaigns Takata kicked off between 2008 and 2015, 81 percent of them showed repair rates below 30 percent nine months out and 92 percent of them fell below 65 percent 18 months out.[130] Buretta seemed equally unaware of a brand-new estimate, commissioned by the trustee of the Takata victims compensation funds, that more than 1,000 people likely would get blasted by their airbags. Instead, Buretta congratulated the carmakers for making "substantial progress."

The recall repair rates Buretta described involved only vehicles for which recall notices were mailed during 2019. It did not take into account the *ten million* additional recall notices that were issued in January 2020. Nor did it take into account 30 million additional vehicles with inflators that Takata claimed in 2015 were safe – and declined to recall – because they contained a desiccant called Zeolite. Buretta mentioned in his first report that all of those cars would also have to be repaired if the car industry failed to prove them safe before December 31, 2019.[131] NHTSA apparently received no such evidence by that deadline, and the former Takata engineers who designed the desiccated inflators publicly declared that no such evidence could exist because all desiccants will saturate. Nevertheless, Buretta's report for 2019 failed to mention the prospect of a massive new wave of recalls or the number of people who eventually will be killed or maimed when the desiccated inflators start to explode.

In his earlier reports, Buretta criticized the vehicle manufacturers for failing to issue recall notices that would motivate their customers to arrange for repairs. Technical jargon about "inflators" and "propellants" and "over-pressurization" does not motivate car owners; they are far more likely to respond to stories, illustrated with color graphics, about the hundreds of fatalities and injuries that have already occurred. Despite the horrifying consequences of an airbag rupture, Buretta said, car-makers were treating it as "just another recall" and did not bother to measure the performance of their dealerships or provide any financial incentive to maximize the number of customers who bring their vehicles in for the free repair.

A year later, in the Independent Monitor Report for 2018, Buretta said the manufacturers still were not communicating urgency to their customers. With few exceptions, they have stubbornly insisted on "single channel" communications (i.e., "snail mail") instead of electronic notices or targeted mass media. Manufacturers were not refreshing vehicle owner information, even though half of their current owner records were wrong and correct information was readily available from state DMVs and other sources. Recall letters generally included no "call to action," little or no information about how or where to schedule a repair or what amenities, such as loaner cars or extended service hours, would be available to make a recall repair appointment more convenient. Standard recall letters included no eye-catching graphics and they failed to emphasize that, by law, the car companies were required to complete the repair at no cost to the vehicle owner. Buretta listed more than a dozen specific steps vehicle manufacturers were failing to take to get killer airbags out of people's faces.

Buretta also revealed the extent to which new car "dealers view themselves as detached from recalls." They did not always offer customers a loaner car, even if the manufacturer would pay for it. They often told customers "replacement parts were not available when parts were, in fact, available." They promised customers they would let them know when recall parts became available but failed to follow up.

New car dealers and their service departments are not the only automotive organizations shirking their responsibility to protect people from killer airbags. Honda, which has been the most aggressive about repairing its vehicles, warned Congress in 2018 that we face "an unprecedented public health challenge that requires unprecedented action from other stakeholders ... to find and notify customers." [132] Buretta's 2018 report named and shamed used car dealers, independent repair shops, auto auctions, car insurers and state vehicle registration and licensing authorities for their lack of cooperation.

The first priority for used car dealers, Buretta noted, is to move vehicles from trade-in or acquisition at a wholesale auction to retail sale "as quickly as possible." Outstanding safety recalls, including Takata airbags, may be noted in the fine print of sale contracts, but used car dealers almost never consider it their responsibility to repair them before customers drive their cars off the lot. AutoNation, American's largest used car retailer, stopped selling cars with open airbag recalls in 2015 but went right back to it after the Federal Trade Commission ruled that it was not an unfair trade practice for used car dealers to advertise and sell as "safe" vehicles with unrepaired safety defects. NHTSA offered only lip service in opposition to the FTC ruling, noting that "all safety recalls ... present an unreasonable risk to safety and ... it is inappropriate to suggest some defects are not risky enough to require repairs." [133] By 2019, one of every nine cars on Auto-Nation's lots contained unrepaired Takata airbags or other safety-related defects.[134] Almost a third of the cars in CarMax's inventory had open recalls in 2017. They typically ask buyers to sign purchase contracts and then demand a waiver of any liability should the safety-related defect kill or maim anyone. Rental car companies also are allowed to fix safety defects when and if they see fit and are not required by law to disclose to customers that a vehicle is subject to an open recall.

Wholesale auto actions are the biggest single source of used-car inventory. Millions of cars with defective airbags cross their blocks every year. Buretta described a demonstration project that produced a 90 percent repair rate for those cars but the auctions generally do nothing to keep killer airbags away from their buy-side dealers or the dealers' retail customers.

Repair shops that are not affiliated with franchised car dealerships handle millions of vehicles every year with killer airbags but they are not authorized to repair them and make no money by referring their customers to a nearby dealership. These independent repair facilities usually do not bother checking to see whether a customer's car has been recalled. Even when mechanics mention an outstanding recall to a customer, Buretta reported, barely 20 percent of their customers follow up with a repair.

Motor vehicle insurers – Allstate and the other companies that lobbied so long and so hard to mandate the installation of airbags – have turned their backs on their own customers. Insurers, who collect $230 billion in auto insurance premiums each year, almost always know how and where to reach their own insureds but they refuse to help vehicle manufacturers deliver re-call notices. According to Buretta, they have "concerns regarding legal risks or liabilities associated with sending recall notifications and potential impacts on their own brands."[135]

State departments of motor vehicles issue millions of new titles and registration documents for cars infected with killer airbags. None of Buretta's reports mention how effective a ban on registration of cars with unrepaired safety defects would be or that Honda had endorsed that solution.[136] In his 2018 report, Buretta described them only as "highly effective messengers for recall outreach."

Buretta's report for 2019 is starkly different from the two earlier reports in almost every respect. The 2017 report, which ran 101 pages, full of colorful graphics and urgent language, was written and edited to Supreme Court brief standards. The comprehensive and well-written 2018 report was half as long at 51 pages but it provided additional insight into the behavior and motivations of a host of organizations that could take specific action to rid the roads of killer airbags. The 2019 report was filed late, compared to the first two, and looked like it was written by an associate who got stuck with the assignment after being passed over for partnership. Its scant 30 pages do not tell us manufacturers have seen the light, that their franchised dealers have made killer airbags a top priority or that owners of relatively new cars now understand why the airbag repairs are so urgent or how easy and convenient it can be to bring them in for replacement. To the contrary, Buretta's report for 2019 recites how "franchised dealers have turned away affected vehicle owners ... or failed to repair a defective Takata airbag [during] ... an unrelated repair," how "dealers sometimes fail to check for a recall or notify the vehicle's owner about a recall" and that some dealers were still quoting unacceptably long wait times ... and placing vehicle owners on hold for extended periods ... or transferring calls to voicemail."[137] Nothing in the report suggests that NHTSA or anyone else is doing anything to stop such resistance and neglect by the very businesses that profited most by opting to install Takata's cheap airbags.

Instead of helping to get the word out to consumers, the vehicle insurers are still "citing concerns" about their own legal risks. One wholesale auto auction worked with two manufacturers to prove how easy and economical it would be for mobile repair teams to replace killer airbags before cars go over the block – but none of the industry leaders are actually doing it. The state DMVs also are still refusing to protect people they are supposed to serve. Honda has publicly begged for help from state officials but Buretta has never floated the idea of prohibiting the registration of cars with killer airbags. He congratulated them for writing warning letters but acknowledged that fewer than half of the states participated, despite impressive results in states that conducted airbag-specific mailings.

By claiming "substantial progress" in protecting consumers from killer airbags when the Takata's recall campaigns are failing so miserably, Buretta has betrayed everyone NHTSA's Coordinated Remedy Program was supposed to protect. The motor vehicle manufacturers benefit by controlling information about their own performance and hiding the extent to which they are delaying or avoiding repair costs. As the Transportation Department's Inspector General recently pointed out, "neither [NHTSA] nor the Takata [Independent] Monitor verifies [the reported] recall completion rates or the accuracy of the information submitted by manufacturers."

Buretta remained silent when NHTSA refused to initiate a recall of 30 million additional cars with inflators containing a drying agent called Zeolite. NHTSA promised in 2015 that those vehicles would be recalled unless Takata could positively prove them to be safe. On May 7, 2020, NHTSA slipped a "Q&A" into the agency's website. Based on secret test reports and without consulting any of the Takata engineers who designed those inflators – all of whom vehemently insist that the affected vehicles are *not* safe – NHTSA gave the automakers a pass. The likely result is that a new wave of people will be chopped up by their airbags, long after the victim compensation funds have run dry.

Just as they did in the 1950s, the car manufacturers still hold all the cards. Despite hard-fought wins in legislation and regulation over two generations and despite taxpayer investments of a billion dollars a year to run NHTSA, auto safety remains a do-it-yourself proposition.

PART 7

Do-It-Yourself Auto Safety

Action Item # 1

Don't wait for postal delivery of a recall notice!

Virtually none of the people killed by Takata airbags received any warning. Joel Knight, the South Carolina welder who was beheaded in his 2006 Ford Ranger just before Christmas, 2015, is a classic example. Takata acknowledged months earlier that the inflator in his vehicle was dangerous but it negotiated a deal with NHTSA to delay issuing a recall notice. The government gave other inflators higher priority. Joel's widow received a recall letter a few weeks after she buried him. Florida nail salon worker Hien Tran's recall notice arrived at her home shortly after she died from what police initially thought was a shotgun blast to the face. Kylan Langlinais lay dying in a Louisiana hospital when her parents received a recall notice for the Takata airbag that slashed their 22-year old daughter's throat.

Many Takata victims got blasted because car manufacturers sent recall notices not to them, but to businesses that lacked any financial incentive to protect people. Stephanie Erdman took her car to a dealership four times after Honda declared it unsafe. Service departments do not profit from "free" repairs and Erdman's dealership passed up all four opportunities to replace her airbag. They never mentioned the recall to her, so she learned about it when it shredded her face and partially blinded her. Jewell Brangman, the young actress who was rendered brain-dead by a Takata airbag on a California freeway, was driving a rental car. The rental agency could have obtained a free repair from any Honda dealer, but it chose not to take the vehicle out of revenue service long enough to get the job done.

Always assume that any car you drive is (or soon will be) subject to a safety recall. From 2001 through 2019, carmakers put Takata's killer airbags in 70 million American cars. That amounts to one out of four vehicles across 19 different brands. When Takata admitted in 2015 that its supposed lifesavers could turn into life-takers, the Japanese corporation convinced the U.S. government to allow them to replace *older* defective airbags with *newer* defective airbags. Those newer defective airbags, in time, also will have to be replaced. Unless you are one of the lucky vehicle owners whose replacement inflator did not come from Takata, you should expect recalls, re-recalls and re-re-recalls. Your manufacturer will do the bare minimum to let you know when your turn for each of those replacements rolls around again. Never assume one replacement was enough.

Recalls so far involve only about half of all killer airbags. More than 40 million notices have been mailed but another 30 million cars have not been recalled yet because Takata added a certain drying agent to inflators it made more recently. The Takata engineers who designed and built those inflators insist that they, too, will eventually explode. If NHTSA has its way, by the time those recalls start, the affected vehicles will have been resold and the manufacturers will have lost track of where to send all the recall notices. Fewer customers will actually receive notices, which means fewer repairs will be made. That arrangement will save the manufacturers a fortune but it leaves millions of Americans at risk.

Motor vehicle safety is a Do-It-Yourself project. Your vehicle manufacturer might conveniently fail to warn you but there are two other reasonably reliable ways to find out for yourself whether you have a killer airbag. The first is a bit cumbersome. You can find your vehicle's unique identification number – its VIN – on your insurance card or by standing outside your car and peering through your windshield at a tiny plate on the driver's side. Carefully write down all 17 digits – letters and numbers – then type them accurately into a dialogue box you can find on this government website : https://www.nhtsa.gov/recalls If any safety recall applies to your car at that moment, you will get a "hit." Remember that the Takata recalls and re-recalls will come in waves, so you will have to request future electronic alerts or manually enter another query regularly – say, every three months. Your vehicle manufacturer also offers an online VIN-matching service. Honda's site – http://hondaairbaginfo.com/# – conveys urgency and it's easy to use. One caveat, though; Honda's website has been known to report vehicles that have not been repaired as being safe.

Fortunately, there's a mobile phone application for this process. Search the Apple Store for the term "airbag recall" and install the app. Use your phone to snap a photo of the license plate on your car – or a car that you are about to rent – or on your neighbor's car – and the app should automatically associate it with the car's VIN and run the recall match against NHTSA's database. The Airbag Recall app provider shows as "TK Holdings, Inc.," one of the Takata entities that liquidated in 2017, so its reliability and longevity are unclear.

Action Item # 2

Do not drive any car with an outstanding safety recall – take it straight to a franchised dealer for repair!

Never buy a car with an unrepaired safety-related defect! Your government has done nothing to prevent a used car salesman from passing a killer airbag along to you. Franchised dealers – places that sell *new* Hondas, Fords, and so forth – are currently required to have on hand everything they need to remove killer airbags from cars they handle. That includes inventory on their "previously owned" sales lots. Nevertheless, they will generally take a trade-in or buy a car at a wholesale auction with unrepaired safety defects, then pass it along to a used-car buyer in the same dangerous condition. Independent dealers – who sell *only used*, not new cars – also could easily rid their lots of killer airbags. They could refuse to acquire cars with unrepaired safety defects at auction or by calling on the vehicle manufacturers to send field repair teams to replace the defective parts on-site. Non-traditional dealers also will put you and your family in mortal danger. Recent surveys revealed that a shocking percentage of cars for sale at AutoNation and CarMax come equipped with killer airbags and a host of other potentially lethal defects. If any of these businesses or a private seller offer you a car that fails the VIN-check described above, just say no!

Any dealership that sells your brand of vehicle owes you a free fix. It makes no difference if you did not buy your Ford – or Honda or Toyota or whichever – at your neighborhood Ford or Honda dealership. They are obligated by law to replace killer airbags in any car of their brand for free. Some dealerships will try to put you off by claiming they have no repair parts or appointment times available. If you ask for a loaner replacement while you wait for them to fulfill their repair obligation, they might try to turn you down, even though the vehicle manufacturer has agreed to pay for a loaner. Remember that one of the last people to die before *Killer Airbags* was published was just two days shy of his scheduled replacement. Don't take no for an answer. Call your local legal aid office. Better yet, if you drive, say, a Nissan, try to get your repair done by a more reputable Nissan dealer.

Many dealerships will try to sell you a newer car while you're in the showroom, waiting for service to complete your repair. Think about it as you would any other purchase – but remember that, as much as you might love your old car, it might be subject to multiple recalls and replacements of Takata airbags. Better to own a car that never had a killer airbag in it.

Action Item # 3

Forget about suing Takata!

The normal rules for personal injury and wrongful death suits do not apply to Takata airbag explosions. If you get injured when your defective brakes fail, you go to a personal injury lawyer in your community and she files your claim in a nearby state or federal trial court. Not so with Takata airbag cases. Most of the claims against vehicle manufacturers have been consolidated before a federal judge in Miami, Florida. You will end up on a long list of plaintiffs represented by a small group of lawyers you will never meet because they were chosen by other lawyers and the judge. To learn more about this "multi-district litigation," visit this site: https://www.motleyrice.com/personal-injury-wrongful-death/takata-airbag

You can no longer sue Takata. The Japanese corporation and its American subsidiaries liquidated in 2018 and the bankruptcy judge issued an order that essentially prohibits suits against Takata entities or successor corporations.

Get in line for pennies on the dollar from the Takata victims compensation funds. Before Takata went bankrupt, the airbag maker and its carmaker customers deposited a total of $250 million in two separate trust funds. The law professor empowered to divvy up the money over the next 20 years recently estimated that victims will be lucky to collect about ten cents for every dollar of compensation they would have received if Takata had not gone bankrupt. If vehicle owners across the country do not become much more vigilant about replacing their airbags, of course, more people will end up in the compensation line and future payouts will shrink accordingly. To apply for compensation, go to this link: https://restructuring.primeclerk.com/takata/EPOC-Index

Action Item # 4

Demand government action!

The government's auto safety watchdog has been asleep for years. Congress unanimously passed the National Traffic and Motor Vehicle Safety Act in 1966 and created an agency, NHTSA, to enforce it. Had the agency done its job, there would be no killer airbags in our cars and hundreds of Takata victims would be alive or unharmed today. Fewer people will be killed and maimed over the next 10 years if NHTSA would just wake up. Congress appropriates a billion dollars a year to NHTSA but oversight committees in the House and Senate have failed to get satisfactory answers to several life-and-death questions. For example, why are there still tens of millions of killer airbags on U.S. highways when there are virtually none in cars driven in other nations that were big Takata markets, such as Germany, Japan and Australia? Is NHTSA helping manufacturers overstate the number of vehicles they have repaired by choosing not to audit their reports? How can dealerships get away with discouraging vehicle owners from claiming their free fix? Why do state motor vehicle administrators readily issue new titles and registration documents for cars they know contain unrepaired killer airbags and other safety defects instead of requiring owners to fix them first? Who can stop used car dealers from passing deathtraps along to their customers?

Fundamental statutory changes are also needed to re-balance the economic interests of corporations and the human beings who make them rich. Congress should ban nondisclosure agreements ("NDAs," for short) that allow vehicle manufacturers to gag their victims – to pay them extra in an out-of-court settlement not to warn others of the danger. Motor vehicle safety defects are public hazards, dangers to people's general health and safety but NDAs make it too easy for carmakers to squelch warnings.

Autonomous vehicles should include autonomous safety. The U.S. Supreme Court observed when it unanimously upheld the airbag mandate in 1983 that the manual seat belt was inherently flawed because it required "an affirmative action of the passenger." True lifesavers, the Court added, would have to be "automatic or passive devices that require no action by vehicle occupants." Vehicle manufacturers have moved technology in that direction by developing "driver-assist" safety systems, giving their cars minds of their own when it comes to braking, staying in a lane and maintaining highway speeds without the driver touching a gas pedal. Defects have already popped up in such high-tech, automatic safety devices but carmakers cling to in-effective, 20th Century ways to warn their customers. For example, when Chrysler discovered a defect in more than five million of its cars in June 2018, the company posted letters – in "snail mail"! – telling owners to keep driving their cars but never engage the cruise control, because their vehicle could run away with itself. Half those owners probably never received the warning; the half that opened their recall letters were assured that Chrysler will eventually patch the defective software, if it can ever figure out what went wrong. Recall repairs can and should be essentially automatic, requiring little or no action by vehicle owners. Why not require manufacturers to use electronic signals to illuminate automatic warning lights on dashboards when the manufacturer issues a recall? Better yet, why not require that self-driving cars *drive themselves* to repair shops as soon as the manufacturer signals a killer defect?

There is a crying need for leadership in the public interest. The Takata fiasco shows how prescient Ralph Nader was to worry that industry might "capture" the safety regulators. No matter which political party controls Congress, the Senate regularly consents to the appointment of industry operatives to run NHTSA. Secretaries of Transportation and NHTSA Administrators of both parties have made far more money for themselves as advisors and lobbyists for car companies than they could make in a lifetime of government service. The Trump Administration took this "revolving door" to a whole new level when it gave Takata's lawyer effective control over every government official who could take aggressive steps to stop killer airbags from killing people.

The Takata airbag scandal is, without doubt, the worst disaster in automotive history. Unless all the American businesses who profited from Takata's cheap knockoffs of crucial safety equipment pay a price for their own involvement, we've set ourselves up for an even bloodier vehicle safety crisis in the future. The only way we can teach them otherwise is to leverage the existing legal requirements by making the carmakers replace the killer airbags in *all 70 million* affected vehicles. That's a job for readers of *Killer Airbags* – and anyone else who is willing to let them know, we're not taking this anymore. The lives we save may be our own.

ACKNOWLEDGMENTS

The fight to get car manufacturers to put airbags in cars in the 1980s and to get them to take Takata's killer airbags out of cars in the 2020s are bookends for a big chunk of my career. Two people stood by me, literally and figuratively, during both of those wars. The first is my wife, Victoria, my moral compass and love of my life, who deserves a Ph.D. in angst management. The second is Jon DiGesu, a talented corporate communications professional and, more importantly to me, a trusted source of personal encouragement and friendship through the many drafts of this book.

Three people helped me sharpen my recollection of the last battles that led to the airbag mandate. I thank U.S. Senator Jack Danforth for the opportunity to work on such an important issue and, much more recently, for reviewing the portion of the book that recounts our work together. Former U.S. Secretary of Transportation Elizabeth Dole was kind to share her retrospective observations on the lives we saved by forcing the airbag rule. Chandler Howell took the time to describe to me in vivid detail his 1976 accident, which resulted in the world's first airbag deployment in a compact car and cemented Allstate's commitment to the airbag mandate.

Dennis Wholey, my friend of nearly 30 years and a *New York Times* best-selling author, provided invaluable guidance and encouragement. He also introduced me to his friend of nearly 50 years, Ralph Nader, an auto safety icon and undaunted provocateur for consumer safety. Ralph saw my nose sticking out of a tent, grabbed it and helped make sure my story got out.

Several friends of longstanding who coincidentally got involved in the Takata mess and helped me understand its most complicated aspects deserve huge credit – but I do not dare mention their names.

Anecdotes offered by Kevin Fitzgerald and other engineers who warned Takata twenty years ago that its inflators would kill people and who found the courage to blow the whistle on their former employer greatly augmented my description of Takata's decades-long fraud. John Keller deserves particular credit for recognizing the continuing dangers and devoting so much of his own time and money to get the word out.

Jay Hamilton, my friend and Forerunner Foundation co-founder, provided invaluable practical advice on how to tell the story in plain English. He and David Flory also raised my spirits at crucial moments.

Thanks also go to Chris Calhoun and Bob Roe for believing in the project. Now, it's up to my publicist, Jeremy Murphy, to prove the experts wrong by raising a hue and cry about a defective device that will kill and maim thousands more American drivers unless they receive and heed the urgent warnings presented in this book.

BIBLIOGRAPHY

Books

Ralph Nader, *Unsafe at Any Speed: The Designed-In Dangers of the American Automobile*, New York: Grossman, 1965.

Lance Cooper, *Cobalt Cover-Up: The Inside Story of a Deadly Conspiracy at the Largest Car Manufacturer in the World*, Grand Rapids: Zondervan, 2020.

Martin Albaum, *Safety Sells: Market Forces and Regulatory Development of Airbags*, Insurance Institute for Highway Safety, 2005.
https://www.iihs.org/media/186adabe-9ef4-479c-ad37-36b9f0e7fca1/Ka0wWQ/Albaum_Safety_Sells.pdf

Kevin Fitzgerald and David Schumann, *In Your Face: An Insider's Explosive Account of the Takata Airbag Scandal*, Delaware: Recall Awareness, 2019.

Periodicals and Podcasts

"Takata Airbag Recall – Everything You Need to Know: What This Recall Means to You and What Actions You Can Take," *Consumer Reports*, March 2, 2017.
https://www.consumerreports.org/car-recalls-defects/takata-airbag-recall-everything-you-need-to-know/

Craig Trudell, "Sixty Million Car Bombs: Inside Takata's Air Bag Crisis: How the Company's Failures Led to Lethal Products and the Biggest Auto Recall in History," *Bloomberg*, June 2, 2016.
https://www.bloomberg.com/news/features/2016-06-02/sixty-million-car-bombs-inside-takata-s-air-bag-crisis

Ben Klayman & Yoko Kubota, "Deadly Airbags Backfire on Firm That Crossed 'Dangerous Bridge,'" *Reuters*, January 13, 2014.

Russell Mokhiber, "Jerry Cox on Takata, Honda and the Growing Toll of Gruesome Deaths and Injuries by Killer Airbags," *Corporate Crime Reporter*, October 18, 2019.
https://www.corporatecrimereporter.com/news/200/jerry-cox-on-takata-honda-and-the-growing-toll-of-gruesome-deaths-and-injuries-by-killer-airbags/

Jerry W. Cox, "Takata Airbag Recalls: Survival Tips for Automotive Remarketers," November 11, 2019, *Used Car Week* Presentation
https://usedcarweek.biz/ucw-2019-content/

Jerry W. Cox, *Used Car Week, Auto Remarketing Podcast*, "Expert Describes What Could be Next in Takata Recall"
https://www.autoremarketing.com/print/trends/podcast-expert-describes-what-could-be-next-takata-recall

Television Coverage

CBS News
https://www.youtube.com/watch?v=_W7DcKnPhbg
https://www.youtube.com/watch?v=JZJwAgUxxBU

60 Minutes Australia
https://www.youtube.com/watch?v=WkT3YMAcHlo

Congressional Proceedings

U.S. Congress, Senate Committee on Commerce, Science & Transportation, "Examining Takata Airbag Defects and the Vehicle Recall Process," November 20, 2014.
https://www.commerce.senate.gov/2014/11/examining-takata-airbag-defects-and-the-vehicle-recall-process

U.S. Congress, House Committee on Energy & Commerce, Subcommittee on Commerce, Manufacturing & Trade, "Takata Airbag Ruptures and Recalls," June 2, 2015.
https://docs.house.gov/Committee/Calendar/ByEvent.aspx?EventID=102776

Consumer Resources

Product Liability Litigation
In re: Takata Airbag Product Liability Litigation, Docket No. MDL 2599 (S.D.Fla.), https://www.docketbird.com/court-cases/In-RE-Takata-Airbag-Products-Liability-Litigation/flsd-1:2015-md-02599

Plaintiffs Lawyers
https://www.motleyrice.com/personal-injury-wrongful-death/takata-airbag

https://www.podhurst.com/landmark-cases/

Bankruptcy Proceedings
https://restructuring.primeclerk.com/takata/

Takata Tort Compensation Trust Fund
http://takataairbaginjurytrust.com

Airbag Recall App
https://apps.apple.com/us/app/airbag-recall/id1225620929

"Investigation Finds One in Nine Used Cars for Sale at AutoNation Have Unrepaired Safety Recalls," USPIRG, October, 2019.
https://uspirg.org/news/usp/investigation-finds-1-9-used-cars-sale-autonation-have-unrepaired-safety-recalls

Government Resources

NHTSA "Spotlight" & VIN Lookup
https://www.nhtsa.gov/equipment/takata-recall-spotlight#takata-air-bags-vehicles-affected

Independent Monitor of Takata and the Coordinated Remedy Program, *The State of the Takata Airbag Recalls,* November 15, 2017, *Update on the State of the Takata Airbag Recalls,* December 21, 2018, and *Update on the State of the Takata Airbag Recalls,* January 23, 2020.
http://www.takatamonitor.org

NHTSA/Takata Consent Order
https://www.nhtsa.gov/sites/nhtsa.dot.gov/files/documents/nhtsa-consentorder-takata.pdf

NHTSA/Car Industry Coordinated Remedy Order
https://www.nhtsa.gov/sites/nhtsa.dot.gov/files/documents/nhtsa-coordinatedremedyorder-takata.pdf

Public Service Announcements

Featuring Morgan Freeman
https://www.safeairbags.com

Featuring Stephanie Erdman
https://www.youtube.com/watch?v=m1tV-05EmGA

NOTES

PART 2   Killing the Messengers

[1] Ralph Nader, *Unsafe at Any Speed: The Designed-In Dangers of the American Automobile*, New York: Grossman, 1965 ("*Unsafe*"), pp. vii, viii, 88-89, 114-15, 117, 124.
[2] Martin Albaum, *Safety Sells: Market Forces and Regulatory Development of Airbags*, Insurance Institute for Highway Safety, 2005 ("*Safety Sells*"), pp. 2, 8, 13 n.42, 24 n.19, 26 n.27, 28, 33, 36, 55, 222.
[3] Insurance Institute for Highway Safety, *Background Manual on the Occupant Restraint Issue* ("*IIHS Manual*"), June 1, 1978, pp. 51, 55-56.
[4] *Safety Sells*, p. 75.
[5] *Ibid.*, pp. 77 n.151, 80.
[6] *Ibid.*, pp. 83, 84 n.6.
[7] *Ibid.*, p. 89.
[8] *IIHS Manual*, p. 5.

PART 3   The Vaccine

[9] U.S. Congress, Senate Committee on Commerce, Science and Transportation, Subcommittee on Surface Transportation, 97th Cong., 1st Sess., *Government Regulations Affecting the U.S. Automobile Industry,* January 28, 1981.
[10] *Safety Sells*, pp. 46, n.31, 54, 59.
[11] Telephone Interview with Chandler Howell, August 9, 2016.
[12] *Safety Sells*, p. 106.
[13] *Ibid.*, p. 110.
[14] U.S. Congress, Senate Committee on Commerce, Science and Transportation, Subcommittee on Surface Transportation, 97th Cong., 2d Sess., *Oversight of the National Highway Traffic Safety Administration*, March 31, 1982.
[15] *Safety Sells*, p. 75 n.146.
[16] *Chrysler v. Dept. of Transportation*, 472 F.2d 659, 671 (6th Cir. 1972).
[17] *Pacific Legal Foundation v. Dept. of Transportation*, 593 F.2d 1338, 1344-45 (D.C. Cir. 1979).
[18] *Safety Sells*, p. 116.

[19] "Takata Airbag Recall – Everything You Need to Know: What This Recall Means to You and What Actions You Can Take," *Consumer Reports*, March 2, 2017.

[20] *Safety Sells*, pp. 101, 104.

[21] Byron Bloch, "The Coming Revolution in Airbag Technology," *Auto Safety Design*, 1998, p. 1176.

[22] *Safety Sells*, pp. 157 n.41, 159, 185.

[23] *Safety Sells*, pp. 101, 104.

PART 4   Empire of the Son

[24] Jack Ewing, *Faster, Higher Farther: The Volkswagen Scandal*, New York: Norton, 2017, p. 242.

[25] Craig Trudell, "Sixty Million Car Bombs: Inside Takata's Air Bag Crisis: How the Company's Failures Led to Lethal Products and the Biggest Auto Recall in History," *Bloomberg* (*"Sixty Million Car Bombs"*), June 2, 2016.

[26] "GM Rolls Back Contentious Terms in Purchasing Contract," *Automotive News*, February 11, 2014.

[27] *Sixty Million Car Bombs*, p. 7.

[28] Dechert LLP, "Report of TK Holdings, Inc., Pursuant to Paragraph 33.a of the November 3, 2015, Consent Order," June 30, 2016 (*"Dechert Report"*), p. 20.

[29] Kevin Fitzgerald & David Schumann, *In Your Face: An Insider's Explosive Account of the Takata Airbag Scandal*, Recall Awareness: 2019 (*"Fitzgerald"*), pp. 19, 20, 36, 38-41.

[30] U.S. Congress, House Committee on Energy & Commerce, Subcommittee on Commerce, Manufacturing & Trade, "Takata Airbag Ruptures and Recalls," Testimony by Kevin M. Kennedy (*"Kennedy Testimony"*), June 2, 2015.

[31] *In re: Takata Airbag Product Liability Litigation*, Docket No. MDL 2599, (S.D.Fla.), Plaintiffs' Status Report, February 27, 2017 (*"Plaintiffs Report"*), pp. 3-5.

[32] Hiroko Tabuchi, "A Cheaper Airbag, and Takata's Road to a Deadly Crisis," *New York Times* (*"Cheaper Airbag"*), August 26, 2016.

[33] Craig Trudell, "Takata Whistle-Blower Willing to Testify on Deadly Airbag Flaws," *Crain's Detroit Business*, February 5, 2015.

[34] TK Holdings, Inc., "Technical Report on the Current Status of the Takata Root Cause Evaluation Effort," July 22, 2016, p. 20.

[35] *Kennedy Testimony*, p. 2.

[36] *Cheaper Airbag*.

[37] *U.S. v. Tanaka*, Federal Criminal Indictment, December 7, 2016, p. 8.
[38] *Dechert Report*, p. 15.
[39] *Cheaper Airbag*.
[40] *Dechert Report*, pp. 14-15.
[41] Mike Spector & Mike Colias, "Takata Pleads Guilty to Criminal Wrongdoing, Agrees to Pay $1 Billion in Penalties," *Wall Street Journal*, February 28, 2017.
[42] Mike Spector, "Takata U.S. Employees Saw Problems in Airbag Tests," *Wall Street Journal*, November 24, 2015.
[43] *Cheaper Airbag*.
[44] *Sixty Million Car Bombs*, p. 10.
[45] *Ibid*.
[46] *Fitzgerald*, p. 129.
[47] *Ibid*., pp. 76, 78-80.
[48] *Dechert Report*, p. 26.

Part 5   Open Kimono

[49] Hiroko Tabuchi, "Takata Saw & Hid Risk in Airbags in 2004," *New York Times*, November 6, 2014.
[50] *Fitzgerald*, pp.161-62.
[51] Honda Motor Company, Defect Information Report, Recall No. 08V593, filed November 11, 2008.
[52] *Fitzgerald*, pp. 167-68, 182, 184, 222.
[53] *Dechert Report*, p. 25.
[54] Ben Klayman & Yoko Kubota, "Deadly Airbags Backfire on Firm That Crossed 'Dangerous Bridge,'" *Reuters*, January 13, 2014.
[55] National Automobile Dealers Association, *The Impact of Vehicle Recalls on the Automobile Market, Used Car Guide*, 3d Quarter, 2014, p. 16.
[56] Takata Corporation, Annual Report for 2013, "Message from the Chairman."
[57] U.S. Department of Transportation, Office of Inspector General, *NHTSA's Management of Light Passenger Vehicle Recalls Lacks Adequate Processes & Oversight*, Rpt. No. ST2018062, July 18, 2018 ("*OIG Report 2018*"), pp. 16-17.
[58] "Report Casts Harsher Light on Takata, Hints of Cover-Up Going Back a Decade," *Crain's Detroit Business*, November 10, 2014.

59 Craig Trudell, "Air-Bag Maker in Global Crisis Used Unusual Explosive," *Bloomberg*, October 27, 2014.

60 "Takata Chairman Stays Out-of-Sight as Airbag Crisis Imperils Dynasty," *Japan Times*, November 12, 2014.

61 Jeff Green & Jeff Plungis, "Honda Death Probed as Homicide Adds to Air Bag Scrutiny," *Bloomberg*, October 27, 2014.

62 Craig Trudell, "Warning: This Airbag May Contain Shrapnel: Airbag Supplier Takata Faces Legal Problems Amid Driver Deaths and Mounting Recalls," *Bloomberg*, October 30, 2014.

63 Norihiko Shirouzu, "Inside Takata, Tantrums, But Little Sense of Crisis Over Airbags," *Reuters*, November 30, 2014.

64 "Takata Air Bag Defects Far More Severe Than Revealed," *Japan Times*, October 19, 2014.

65 *In re: TK Holdings, Inc.*, Case No. 17-11375 (D.Del.), Declaration of Scott E. Caudill in Support of Debtor's Chapter 11 Petitions and First Day Relief ("*Caudill Declaration*"), ¶ 60, p. 32.

66 Takata Corporation, "Ensuring Quality Across the Board: The Report of the Independent Takata Corporation Quality Assurance Panel," February, 2016, p. 4.

67 Hiroko Tabuchi, "Takata Offers Its Rebuttal to Report of Secret Airbag Tests," *New York Times*, November 12, 2014.

68 *Caudill Declaration*, ¶ 86, p. 44.

69 "Trust in Takata to Solve Crisis is Dissolving," *Crain's Detroit Business*, December 8, 2014.

70 *Fitzgerald*, pp. 225, 228, 267.

71 U.S. Congress, Senate Committee on Commerce, Science & Transportation, "Examining Takata Airbag Defects and the Vehicle Recall Process" ("*Senate Commerce Hearing*"), November 20, 2014, pp. 20, 51.

72 Adrienne Roberts & Mike Spector, "Motorist Deaths Jumped in 2016," *Wall Street Journal*, February 16, 2017.

73 John Stoll & Mike Spector, "Traffic Fatalities Surge," *Wall Street Journal*, October 6, 2016.

74 "Who's Self-Driving Your Car?" *The Economist*, September 5, 2016.

75 National Safety Council, *Motor Vehicle Fatality Estimates*, January 13, 2016.

76 *Senate Commerce Hearing*, pp. 67-68.

77 *Fitzgerald*, pp. 161-62, 255, 263-64.

78 *United States v. General Motors Corp.*, 518 F.2d 420 (D.C. Cir. 1975) (*emphasis supplied*)

Part 6 Asleep at the Wheel

[79] U.S. Department of Transportation, Office of Inspector General, *Review of the Office of Defects Investigation, National Highway Traffic Safety Administration*, Rpt. No. MH2002071, January 3, 2002 ("*OIG Report 2002*"), pp. 17, 19.

[80] U.S. Department of Transportation, Office of Inspector General, *Additional Efforts are Needed to Ensure NHTSA's Full Implementation of OIG's 2011 Recommendations*, Rpt. No. ST2016021, February 24, 2016 ("*OIG Report 2016*").

[81] Transportation Recall Enhancement Accountability and Documentation Act, Pub. L. No. 106-414, 114 Stat. 1800 (2000).

[82] *OIG Report 2002*, Memorandum from Jeffrey W. Runge, M.D., Administrator, NHTSA, to DOT IG, December 4, 2001, p. 39.

[83] U.S. Department of Transportation, Office of Inspector General, *Follow-up Audit on NHTSA's Office of Defects Investigation*, Rpt. No. MH2004088, September 23, 2004 ("*OIG Report 2004*"), p. 14.

[84] U.S. Congress, Senate Committee on Commerce, Science & Transportation, "NHTSA's Efforts to Identify Safety-Related Vehicle Defects," Testimony of Calvin L. Scovel, III, Inspector General, U.S. Department of Transportation, June 23, 2015, p. 11.

[85] *Ibid.*, p. 16

[86] U.S. Department of Transportation, Office of Inspector General, *Inadequate Data & Analysis Undermine NHTSA's Efforts to Identify & Investigate Vehicle Safety Concerns*, Rpt. No. ST2015063, June 18, 2015 ("*OIG Report 2015*"), p. 8.

[87] *Ibid.*

[88] Clifford Atiyeh, "Why NHTSA is More Defective Than the Defects It Investigates," *Car & Driver*, June 30, 2015.

[89] *Plaintiffs Report*, pp. 1-2.

[90] Lance Cooper, *Cobalt Cover-Up: The Inside Story of a Deadly Conspiracy at the Largest Car Manufacturer in the World*, Grand Rapids: Zondervan, 2020, pp. 197-205.

[91] *Sixty Million Car Bombs*, p. 19.

[92] *Caudill Declaration*, ¶ 57, p. 31.

[93] Karen Freifeld, "Takata Retains Prominent Lawyer Levander in Air Bag Scandal," *Reuters*, November 18, 2014.

[94] *Kennedy Testimony*, June 2, 2015.

[95] *Fitzgerald*, p. 211.

[96] NHTSA News Release, May 4, 2016.

[97] *Dechert Report*, pp. 1-2, 14.

98 Andrea Fuller & Adrienne Roberts, "Car Makers' Struggles with Recalls Leave More Risky Vehicles on the Road," *Wall Street Journal*, November 1, 2018.

99 *OIG Report 2018*, pp. 1-2.

100 U.S. Department of Transportation, National Highway Traffic Safety Administration, *Vehicle Safety Recall Completion Rates Report*, pp. 3-4, May 2017. *See also ibid., Vehicle Safety Recall Completion Rates Report*, December 2018.

101 David Shepardson, "U.S. Says 2.7 Million Additional Takata Airbag Inflators to be Recalled," *Reuters*, July 11, 2017.

102 U.S. Department of Transportation, Statement of Secretary Anthony Foxx, Nov. 3, 2015.

103 Takata Corp. Annual Report for 2015.

104 *Sixty Million Car Bombs, p. 16.*

105 *Ibid.*

106 David Shepardson and Paul Lienert, "Takata Failed to Report 2003 Air Bag Rupture to U.S. Road Authority," September 24, 2016.

107 *U.S. v. Takata Corporation*, Case No. 16-20810 (E.D.Mich.), Rule 11 Plea Agreement ("*Takata Plea Agreement*"), January 13, 2017, pp. 7, 10-11.

108 *Ibid.*, pp. 14-15.

109 Paul Lienert & David Shepardson, "Takata to Plead Guilty," *Reuters*, January 14, 2017.

110 *Takata Plea Agreement,* Kennedy Declaration, January 10, 2017.

111 *See* www.autoairbagsettlement.com

112 David Shepardson, "Ford Agrees to $299.1 Million U.S. Takata Air Bag Settlement," *Reuters*, July 16, 2018.

113 Takata Corp. Annual Report for 2016, p. 16.

114 David Shepardson, "Takata Whistleblowers to Share $1.7 Million Award," *Reuters*, March 27, 2018.

115 Jie Ma, "How a Billionaire Family Fell from Grace After the Takata Airbag Scandal," *Bloomberg*, June 28, 2017.

116 Sean McLain & Mike Spector, "Troubled Airbag Maker Takata Files for Bankruptcy in the U.S. & Japan," *Wall Street Journal*, June 27, 2017.

117 U.S. Congress, Senate, Committee on Commerce, Science & Transportation, Hearing No. 115-281, June 28, 2017.

118 NERA Economic Consulting, "Takata Individual Restitution Fund: Estimation of Current & Future Liabilities," December 27, 2017, and "Takata Individual Restitution Fund & Takata Airbag Tort Compensation Trust Fund: Estimation of Current & Future Liabilities – 2019 Update," September 13, 2019, p. 4.

119 *Ibid.*

120 *OIG Report 2018*, p. 6.

[121] Adrienne Roberts, "Aging Vehicles in U.S. Give Auto Shops a Lift," *Wall Street Journal*, November 23, 2016.

[122] *OIG Report 2018,* pp. 5, 26.

[123] U.S. Dept. of Transportation, Online Biography of James C. Owens, Acting NHTSA Administrator.

[124] *OIG Report 2018*, p. 38.

[125] David Shepardson, "Audit Faults U.S. Oversight of Auto Safety Recalls, Takata Inflators," *Reuters*, July 18, 2018.

[126] Independent Monitor of Takata and the Coordinated Remedy Program, *The State of the Takata Airbag Recalls,* November 15, 2017 ("*Monitor Report 2017*"), p. 1.

[127] *Ibid.,* p. 69.

[128] Independent Monitor of Takata and the Coordinated Remedy Program, *Update on the State of the Takata Airbag Recalls*, December 21, 2018 ("*Monitor Report 2018*"), p. 2.

[129] Independent Monitor of Takata and the Coordinated Remedy Program, *Update on the State of the Takata Airbag Recalls*, January 23, 2020 ("*Monitor Report 2019*"), p. 1.

[130] *OIG Report 2018*, p. 26.

[131] *Monitor Report 2018,* p. 5 n.4.

[132] U.S. Congress, Senate Committee on Commerce, Science & Transportation, Subcommittee on Consumer Protection, March 20, 2018, Testimony of Rick Schostek, Honda North America.

[133] National Highway Traffic Safety Administration, Statement, April 4, 2011.

[134] U.S. PIRG, *Unsafe Used Cars for Sale: Unrepaired Recalled Vehicles at AutoNation Dealerships*, October, 2019.

[135] *Monitor Report 2018*, p. 42.

[136] Bernie Woodall, "Honda Says Fatal Crash Involved Takata Air Bag Inflator Rupture," *Reuters*, January 30, 2015.

[137] *Monitor Report 2019*, p. 9.

INDEX